Community work
One

Community work

One

edited by

David Jones
Principal, National Institute for Social Work

and

Marjorie Mayo
Lecturer in Community Work, University of Surrey

Routledge & Kegan Paul
London and Boston

First published in 1974
by Routledge & Kegan Paul Ltd
Broadway House, 68–74 Carter Lane,
London EC4V 5EL and
9 Park Street,
Boston, Mass. 02108, USA
Set in 11 pt Imprint
and printed in Great Britain by
The Camelot Press Ltd, Southampton
© Routledge & Kegan Paul Ltd 1974

ISBN 0 7100 7709 2 (c)
ISBN 0 7100 7741 6 (p)

Contents

v

Contributors

The Albany: Sharon Collins was fund-raiser 1971–3 and Acting Director 1973–4; Jenny Harris and John Turner were members of the Brighton Combination 1967–71 and then of 'The Combination at the Albany' 1971–4; Paul Curno was Director of the Albany 1966–73 and is now with the Central Council for Education and Training in Social Work.

Bob Ashcroft read philosophy, politics and economics at Oxford where he later did a B.Phil. in politics. He is now an Action Research Fellow of Working Class Adult Education working from Liverpool University and is attached to the Vauxhall CDP. His current research is into the relationship between social consciousness and education.

Sean Baine has been involved in community action in Notting Hill and in Paddington. Formerly general secretary of Westminster Council of Social Service, he is at present studying for an MA in social administration at Brunel University.

Peter Baldock is a Principal Assistant Social Worker (Community Development) with the Sheffield Social Services Department. He was previously Student Unit Supervisor at the Manchester Council of Voluntary Service (Manchester and Salford Council of Social Service).

John Benington has been Project Director for CDP in Coventry since January 1970. Trained as a social worker, he has worked as a probation officer in Manchester, where he lived in Moss Side for four years and helped to set up a project among immigrant and other local young people. He was also involved in the early stages of the Moss Side People's Association.

Richard Bryant is employed as a fieldwork teacher with a student unit which is based in the Gorbals district of Glasgow. He was formerly a lecturer in the Department of Social Administration and Social Work, Glasgow University.

Philip Bryers is a lecturer in community work at the University of York and Honorary Secretary of the Association of Community Workers. He was formerly Deputy Secretary of the Shropshire Council of Social Service.

John Crook graduated from Birmingham University and worked as a Statistics Officer in Lancashire Children's Department. After obtaining an MSc from LSE he returned to Lancashire where he became an Area Children's Officer, and then Assistant Director of Social Work, Research, Development and Training in Somerset. Now he is Chief Social Services Officer in the Bradford Metropolitan District.

John Dearlove took a D.Phil. at the University of Sussex where he is currently a lecturer in politics. He has undertaken extensive research in Kensington and Chelsea, and is author of *The Politics of Policy in Local Government* (London, 1973).

The East London Claimants' Union has been active for three years. It is based on weekly meetings at Dame Colet House in Stepney Green. The members are pensioners, the sick and disabled, the unemployed, single parents and strikers. It is affiliated to the National Federation of Claimants' Unions. The article was written collectively.

Hywel Griffiths, Professor in Social Administration at the New University of Ulster, Coleraine, was Director of the Northern Ireland Community Relations Commission. Previously he lectured on community development at the University of Manchester, and acted as consultant on that subject to a wide range of statutory and voluntary organisations. He has extensive experience of working in community development overseas.

Michael Harloe is a Senior Research Officer at the Centre for Environmental Studies. He has worked with Swindon Corporation planning the social aspects of a major town expansion scheme, and has also completed a study of the operation of the Town Development Act in Swindon. Recently he has been doing research on organisations in the

London housing market and on housing aid and advice centres. He teaches sociology to town planning students at University College, London.

Meryl Horrocks is a lecturer in applied social science at the University of Nottingham. In 1968–9 she was Scientific Officer at the Building Research Station and in 1969–72 Research Associate at the University of Birmingham Centre for Urban and Regional Studies, where she worked on an SSRC-funded study of social planning in new communities. (The data on social development work in new towns used in chapter 9 were collected in the course of this project.)

Keith Jackson was appointed tutor-organiser for the Workers' Education Association in South Wales and North Staffordshire in 1962, where he worked with shop stewards, trade unionists and groups carrying out community studies, as well as political and social studies generally. In 1967–70 he was lecturer in social science, Liverpool University Extra-mural Department, with responsibility for work with community groups, and for education and in-service training courses. Since then he has been Assistant Director and Head of Social Studies Division, Institute of Extension Studies, Liverpool University, responsible in particular for setting up and engaging in the project on which his paper is based.

David Jones has been on the staff of the National Institute for Social Work Training since 1962. Previously he was National Secretary of Family Service Units from its inception. He was at the Graduate School for Advanced Studies in Social Welfare, Brandeis University, 1965–7, and at the Center for the Study of Welfare Policy, University of Chicago, in the summer of 1971. Joint author with Robert Perlman of *Neighbourhood Service Centers*. First Chairman of the Association of Community Workers.

Jennifer Joslin has been an area team leader in Islington Social Services Department since April 1971. In addition, she supervises a Family Advice Centre in her area, one of the National Children's Bureau projects on youth work in a community setting.

Adah Kay, after graduating in social anthropology, has done research jobs which have included working in the GLC Thamesmead Design Team and studying ways of facilitating public participation in planning for the London borough of Southwark. Since then, she has taken a postgraduate diploma in Town Planning. She is currently teaching in the Planning Department of the Architectural Association, and in the General Studies Department at the Royal College of Art.

Aryeh Leissner has worked with street gangs and in community work and action research in New York. After directing an action research project on street club work in Tel Aviv, he became Senior Research Officer of Family Advice Services Study (1966–70) and of Action Research Study on Community-Based Services for Children and Youth in FAS Settings at the National Children's Bureau. He is the author of *Family Advice Services* and *Street Club Work in Tel Aviv and New York* and is co-author of *Advice, Guidance and Assistance* with Angela Herdman and Elizabeth Davies.

Harry Liddell is a former Convenor of the Hutchesontown Tenants' Association, Gorbals, Glasgow. He has for many years been active as a trade unionist and shop steward in the engineering industry.

Peter Marris works at the Centre for Environmental Studies, and is the author, with Martin Rein, of *Dilemmas of Social Reform*, a study of American community action programmes between 1960 and 1970. He has written a number of articles on the American experience of experimental social planning and its relevance to Britain. His other work includes books and papers on aspects of development in Africa, as well as studies in Britain of higher education and of bereavement.

Marjorie Mayo has been a research fellow in the Southampton University team of the Community Development Project. Before this, she taught in the Social Administration Department at the London School of Economics. She has also worked on a community development project in Nigeria. She has recently been appointed to a teaching post at Surrey University.

George and Teresa Smith, after teaching abroad separately in India and Thailand for two years and spending a further two years on postgraduate social science courses at Oxford, worked in South Yorkshire on the West Riding EPA project, responsible for research and the development of preschool work. Teresa is now a lecturer in community work in the Department of Social and Administrative Studies, University of Oxford, and George, a research fellow at Nuffield, is involved

in the University of Oxford Social Evaluation Unit's research programme for the Liverpool and Birmingham Community Development
Projects.

Pamela Warren started her working life on *Punch*. She subsequently
spent five years as Training and Personnel Secretary of the YWCA.
After a spell in the USA she has spent the last six years as General
Secretary of the Camden Council of Social Service.

Foreword

The Association of Community Workers which initiated this book is currently reviewing the relevance of the concept of professionalism to community work. If professional status separates a practitioner from his client, if professional training encapsulates an unchangeable body of expertise, if professional qualifications are used to exclude those with fresh knowledge from unconventional backgrounds, community workers in general want none of it. But if one of the hallmarks of a profession is its ability to capture the lessons of practice in the written word, then community work might be said to have come of age with this volume.

From the start, the publication of essays on current thinking and new directions was seen not merely as a literary venture but as an action project in its own right. Our object throughout has been to encourage those with experience and knowledge of the field to commit themselves to writing as part of a strategy to achieve change and growth. Though many of the contributions record work done, we hope that they will also provide the inspiration for work yet to be started.

The project has drawn on the resources of the Association of Community Workers at a number of levels. Many members have contributed articles and ideas. The Council provided overall guidance and nominated the editorial board. The board itself has discussed the evolution of the volume and sometimes of individual contributions and has succeeded in establishing the sort of close teamwork which is vital to a venture of this sort. A group of readers agreed to act as advisers to the editors and although for this volume only some had in fact to be consulted the willingness of all of them to be called upon when necessary has been a valuable support and encouragement.

The major responsibility inevitably has fallen on our joint editors, David Jones and Marjorie Mayo, to whose skill, experience and solid hard work the Association of Community Workers, and we hope our readers, will feel deeply grateful.

John Ward
Chairman, Association of Community Workers

Jef Smith
Chairman, Editorial Board

Introduction

David Jones and Marjorie Mayo

The impetus for launching this collection of essays came originally from within the Association of Community Workers. It was felt that there was a shortage of adequate and up-to-date critical written material on community work theory and practice in Britain and likewise a shortage of outlets for such material through existing academic and professional periodicals, the journals of related disciplines having neither sufficient space nor enough interest. On the other hand it was widely believed that the material did exist in embryo in the minds of numerous practitioners, community activists, teachers, researchers and other professionals. If the outlet could be organised the potential contributors could then be stimulated or goaded into writing.

In practice, this has proved to be the case. With only a little stimulus and very little goading, the contributions began to appear, both from academics already relatively used to writing, but also from hard-pressed practitioners with very limited time at their disposal. It would almost have been possible to produce another volume just from promised contributions which failed to materialise before the dead-line for this volume. This bears out ACW's confidence in the vitality of the field and underlines the importance of creating a forum such as this, where theory can be developed in relation to practice. The intention is to publish further collections annually.

This relative wealth of material can be explained by the state of community work in Britain; a new and rapidly growing activity in its own right, with perhaps the fastest growing job market of any of the 'helping' professions. Community work has also become one of the most fashionable ingredients in boosters for more established professions, like the Civil Service, medicine, law and teaching. Some criticisms of this boom in community work projects is offered in some of the chapters, particularly in the section on strategies for change. New ideas and approaches are being generated – and old ones rediscovered –

very fast, much faster than the rate at which they are being written down, digested and analysed. The trends of thinking and action which have contributed to the assumptions, purposes and practices of community work can be traced back a long way and to a variety of sources. Despite this, contemporary community work as a deliberate and systematic activity is a new phenomenon. Many of the more intractable and contentious issues discussed in these essays have only come to the fore in this country within the last five years or so and new approaches are still at an exploratory stage so that any final assessment of their potential is premature. The contradictions and frustrations evident from the practice discussed in this volume must be seen within this context and time perspective.

Understandably practice has outrun critical assessment. Even where many of the newer programmes, such as CDP and YVFF, attempt to build in evaluation, this is by no means a complete solution; outlets are still required for public discussion of their interim reports before publication of the final version, maybe five or seven years hence; and for projects without such built-in evaluation there is all the more need for other means of achieving the same goal. It is evident from their contributions that several of the practitioners themselves have been aware of this need. Where contributors have been insufficiently rigorous and self-critical, it is hoped that others will be stimulated to raise the issues and take them further in future volumes.

In selecting material, the Editorial Board has deliberately opted for inclusiveness rather than exclusiveness. We have wanted to mirror the wide-ranging nature of the field of community work, both as an activity in its own right and as a newer element in other older professions. We have also attempted to include some critique of the development of community work as a profession and some discussion of alternatives; for example, the role of professionals as no more than that of technical aides to local and autonomous disadvantaged groups, which are organised by indigenous leadership to fight their own issues for themselves. Variations on this theme are discussed by the East London Claimants' Union, Sean Baine, Bob Ashcroft and Keith Jackson, Harry Liddell, Richard Bryant and John Benington among others.

Inevitably, inclusiveness has resulted in a variety of forms and levels of presentation. Academics, researchers, professionals, practitioners and activists express themselves in differing styles and idioms and with different objectives in mind. Some of the contributions have lengthy bibliographies while, at the other extreme, a consumer is represented via the transcript of a tape-recorded interview. The content rather than the form must provide the justification for such stylistic promiscuity: and the belief in the necessity for greater communication and inter-change between these varied participants.

In fact, the tape-recorded interview is presented as the first of a series of experiments, which we believe to be potentially of great significance in this respect. The purpose of attempting such a form is to reach new sources of material beyond the traditional means of publication; to assist the fieldworker and in particular the community group in communicating valuable experiences which would otherwise fail to reach beyond an orally transmitted and typically localised culture. The second experiment in form is the collective statement from an organisation of the consumers of the social and community work services – in this case, the Claimants' Union. Clearly the style and presentation of such a collective statement must, of necessity, present a striking contrast, particularly with the more academic chapters, starting as they must with different premises and different intentions. The collective statement has its own particular function and must be judged in its own context. However jarring the tone or critical and contentious the conclusions may seem, these direct expressions of feeling and opinion from those at the receiving end of services can hardly be ignored by community work.

The heterogeneity of content might be defended simply as being representative of the real state of the field of community work. We have already argued that this is actually the case. But the Editorial decision in favour of inclusiveness represents more than a passive recognition of reality. It also stems from a positive position on the necessity for developing this series as a forum where these different debates can be taken forward at their different levels.

In relation to practice, no one strategy or method is likely to be appropriate in all circumstances or for all purposes. Situations, ob-jectives and resources are various and a range of approaches is therefore legitimate and desirable. Simplistic formulations may offer workers a seductive security but are liable to be insufficiently tailored to meet people's needs in specific situations. Policies and practices have to be judged in terms of their consequences for those affected.

We also take the view that in relation to professionalism community work should not aspire to be a profession in a narrow and traditional sense. By its very nature it has an inter-disciplinary, inter-professional, inter-organisational emphasis. Although a form of practice in its own right, it can and should be developed in a variety of settings and organisations. At the same time it should be an essential component in the practice of a wide range of existing professions, including education, planning, administration, social work, medicine and the law.

Another source of variety is that of the contributor's theoretical, ideological and political position. There are contributions amongst others from liberal, reformist and Marxist perspectives. This reflects the real differences of approach to be found in the field. A collection of this kind could not otherwise perform the essential forum function. For these reasons, there has been no attempt to hammer out a party line either amongst the contributors, or amongst the Editorial Board. This publication is intended to provide a forum for these many different interests so that the debate can begin in earnest.

The chapters might perhaps have been organised in sections based on these differences of perspective; but this would have been difficult, in practice, since not all of them make their theoretical position sufficiently explicit or demonstrate consistent and distinctive practice implications. In any event, whichever form of categorisation we used we found that some chapters cut across several boundaries. Thus, for example, Pam Warren's contribution is as relevant to the grass-roots approach as it is to the role of voluntary bodies. Ashcroft and Jackson's chapter could be considered as a contribution on the role of the professions and on strategies for change. Public participation in planning also cuts across these boundaries. The categories are intended then to be no more than an initial guide to themes within the book; and if they are interpreted as more definitive than that, they will have defeated their own purpose, by becoming restrictive, whereas they are meant rather to launch the reader into his own comparisons and contrasts. Our own cross-references, in the introduction to each section, attempt to take the reader further in this process.

In the future we hope to include contributions on a number of major topics omitted or only touched on in this collection. For example, community work in race relations and health services. Doubtless we shall be made aware of further gaps, not just via criticisms, but through contributions for further volumes.

We are grateful to the National Council for Social Service for permission to quote from Aryeh Leissner's article in *Social Service Quarterly*, summer 1973.

The Editorial Board would particularly like to express thanks to Priscilla Foley and to Maureen Webley of the National Institute for Social Work for much secretarial and reference work in the preparation of this volume.

Part I Change, Conflict and the Grass Roots

Marjorie Mayo

In this section, we want to take the reader beyond some of the current rhetoric about conflict in community work literature. This has tended to cluster around a crude dichotomy between conflict and consensus as models of community work practice, assuming that the worker or the group in question has a free choice between either as a tactic.

> The conflict model of community action is subscribed to by those who believe that the interests of the poor can only be safeguarded by confronting the power structure in direct action, and this may take the form of rent strikes, obstructing main roads, squatting, demonstrations and boycotts.
>   The consensus model of community action, on the other hand, assumes that the best interests of the poor are served by expanding access to the power structure rather than confronting it.[1]

Alinsky[2] has been taken as the extreme – and eminently quotable – advocate of conflict as a tactic in opposition to the more consensus orientation of community development as it evolved in less developed countries up to and including the first Community Development Project papers[3] in this country.

Hywel Griffiths's contribution on community work in Northern Ireland deals with another dimension to this question: conflict, not as a strategy or tactic, but as the key factor in the economic, political and social structure of the situation in which the community worker is attempting to operate. In this case study, the conflict situation defined as sectarian, religious or ethnic conflict, is analysed as a negative and reactionary form of social cleavage. Elsewhere in this book, the economic, political and social structure is also defined in terms of fundamental conflicts of interest, but as conflicts between social strata or classes (e.g. the chapters by East London Claimants' Union, Sean Baine, Bob Ashcroft and Keith Jackson and Adah Kay). These conflicts are

I

analysed as inherent in the structure of each specific situation, setting the limits to what can realistically be attempted or achieved by the community work process or community action, regardless of the actual strategies or tactics pursued. Whether these are, or should be, more, or less, consensual is a separate question, depending upon the particular circumstances and objectives. Although the boundaries of what can be achieved may be shifted by community action over a period of time, the underlying conflicts of interest will not, themselves, have been resolved in this way, alone.

On the level of strategy and tactics, John Dearlove's essay examines some of the negative features of conflict. His discussion of the ways in which institutions can force groups into conflict tactics, only to incorporate them, by dividing them or deflecting them from their original goals (or simply by holding out until they become disheartened and fall apart) raises important and until now inadequately considered issues for the grass-roots activists. So far, resistance to these processes of neutralisation has taken place more at the level of practice than of theory (e.g. the Claimants' refusal to 'participate', without real power or influence, in their own poverty).

On the other hand, without reference to some other chapters, this contribution could leave the reader with an extensively negative view of the possibilities for any meaningful change at all as far as the most exploited strata of society are concerned. The examples are primarily drawn from an area where the institutions are excessively rigid, leaving local groups almost no room for manœuvre. Although ultimately the institutional response may not be too dissimilar in other areas, the crisis point may be reached later in the process, thus allowing community groups some prior chance to develop their organisational skills and strength as part of a longer-term social and political development for change. Peter Marris's chapter illustrates the possibility of such a development, with reference to the growth and strengthening of black organisations in the ghettoes in the USA.

Future contributions might usefully develop these themes, using experience from other areas and situations. They might also begin to examine the possibilities for resisting co-optation and promoting more substantial change through the development of alliances between community groups and trade unions, and political organisations with greater power in their own right.

As it is, some of the chapters on grass-roots organising do begin at least to consider this question of their power base. The Notting Hill chapter and the Claimants emphasise that the first necessity for the grass roots is to wake up; and through building their organisations, to feel their collective strength. It is argued that no reliance upon the goodwill and efforts of others can ultimately substitute for this collective involvement of their own. This is relatively obvious when central or local government officials or party politicians offer support for reasons of their own self-interest or expediency; it is less obvious but still important when support comes from other neighbourhood organisations. The aspiration for active collective involvement and the upsurge of grass-roots political energy recurs throughout this section, as the starting-point. Beyond this general message the contributions diverge. The East London Claimants' Union regard the avoidance of bureaucratisation as so crucial that they admit only the loosest of federations with other unions or groups of the disadvantaged (a position not shared by all the claimants, some of whom are closer to a more orthodox, democratic centralist perspective). The Notting Hill Workshop on the other hand emphasises the mutual support between a network of different groups, all operating within a neighbourhood. By contrast, some of the other workshops and the contributions from Ashcroft and Jackson, Liddell and Bryant, and from Adah Kay, start from a class analysis and thus conceptualise the problem of gaining power in terms of building up a specifically working-class movement. They stress the development of links both between the most disadvantaged and the less acutely deprived strata of the working class (see chapter 3), and also between workplace and home-based organisations. The Liddell and Bryant chapter discusses the latter theme on the level of the practical experience and insight of a trade union leader who has also become deeply involved in the tenants' movement. But it remains to develop these themes theoretically, in terms of longer-term strategies. This has already been indicated as a key subject for future contributions.

References

1 Cyril S. Smith and Bryce Anderson, 'Participation through community action', in Geraint Parry (ed.), *Participation in Politics*, Manchester University Press, 1972.
2 S. Alinsky, *Reveille for Radicals*, Chicago University Press, 1945; *Rules for Radicals*, Random House, 1971.
3 Community Development Project, 'Objectives and strategy', internal paper, revised September 1970.

1 Carrying on in the middle of violent conflict: some observations of experience in Northern Ireland

Hywel Griffiths

So I told him, Mr Griffiths, I told him. I told him what was wrong. And I said to him, 'You mark my words, Mr R., the grass roots in this country have woken up and they are never ever going to go to sleep again' – *Protestant working-class member of a tenants' association, speaking of an encounter with the Chairman of a statutory Board, September 1972*

Frank is alright really! He has put on quite a bit of weight, mind you, and is generally a bit depressed. But one thing which keeps him going and which he is really quite pleased with are the community development classes which he holds regularly for some of the internees. He has borrowed some books to use and he even has a college lecturer attending his class – he is very pleased about that – *Catholic visitor to Long Kesh, speaking about an internee, June 1972*

Introduction

It is somewhat of a luxury nowadays to think back to those academic debates during the early sixties concerning appropriate strategies for producing social change. There were those students who came from the developing countries and who were impatient for progress and for results. They had witnessed the effect of revolutions in Cuba and China and were intolerantly aware of the corruption and the controlling interests of reactionary groups in their own society. They were young, well informed and intelligent, and they were very sincere. People like the group of young economists at the University of Nigeria who, to

5

give practical expression to their theories of rural development, would have enrolled all the rural peasantry in a vast agricultural army: once they had got the power of course. Or like the international group of students at Swansea University who with shock realised that they had just concluded that the only way to obtain necessary social reform in many of their countries was by shooting those who were in power.

Then there were those who had been brought up in a liberal European tradition but who still found it difficult to accept consensus strategies as the ideal. In those years much of American literature in a number of professional fields was heavily infected with consensus values and it was not until after civil rights, after Alinsky, that conflict became recognised as a respectable strategy. Not that the literature provided an accurate reflection of reality then or any other time; there being a flow of fashion in issue interest and in conceptualising as much as in other matters. But the acceptance of conflict as a legitimate strategy for social change by those who were at heart conservative and primarily interested in evolutionary processes of change left the door open for those who took the classical conflict view of society to expand their views and to give support to conflict strategies in every situation as preferred strategies.

In trying to decide where one stands on this matter, the main difficulty is in obtaining an agreed understanding of the term 'conflict'. Most people would accept the idea of social change as axiomatic, and consequently that this change is produced by the competition of different interest groups who differ as to means or ends or both. Many, perhaps, would be prepared to go further and regard conflict of a sort as an essential ingredient of group or individual relationships, having a cohesive rather than a divisive effect. The division seems to lie between conflict which at the end is judged, albeit subjectively, to be functional, and that conflict which on examination appears to be dysfunctional. Consensus-oriented people would see all conflict as dysfunctional and in a conflict situation would be clear in their strategy of seeking some equilibrium. Conversely, conflict-oriented observers would presumably see all form of conflict as essentially functional and would be less concerned about alleged social cost or moral erosion. For the rest of us, unhappily, there is no easy formula and to be involved in a conflict situation is to live in a state of continual ambivalence.

This is the daily problem of anyone trying to work in a situation of violent conflict. The question one has to answer daily is not whether one goes along with conflict as an accepted strategy for obtaining social change, but how much conflict can one accept? At what point and at what level do the conflict strategies of violence become unacceptable in terms of personal principles and in terms of what one feels society cannot tolerate? Every day a personal balance has to be struck in which an attempt is made to adapt the legal concept of reasonable force to a situation in which force escalates and reasonableness evaporates.

In Northern Ireland after three years of bitter conflict and innumerable acts of violence it is possible to point towards social gains which indicate that the conflict has been to some degree functional. But it is also possible to point towards heavy losses (not least of all those who have died and the manner of their death) in terms of tremendous social and moral erosion which, in the absence of any indications of resolution at this time, provides weighted evidence of its dysfunctionality.

To illustrate the dilemma for community development, I propose in this paper, as far as space permits, to give some indication of what a community development programme in Northern Ireland consisted of, what it tried to do and what it achieved, and then to describe some of the effects of the conflict on the programme, on the personnel, on various agencies in the community and upon the community itself.

The community development programme

The programme I describe was established as part of the policy of the Northern Ireland Community Relations Commission. The Community Development Officers (CDOs) which it employed were by no means the only professionals engaged in community development in Northern Ireland. A number of local authorities, for example, began to appoint officers with this designation, as did the Northern Ireland Council for Social Service. But it was the only discrete programme and it had one or two unique features. Much emphasis was placed on the team concept while allowing maximum opportunity for individual experimentation and area group initiative. Decisions were made after fullest consultation, and the responsibility for decision-making itself was delegated as far as possible. Initiatives taken in the field were backed up by initiatives taken at inter-agency and governmental levels. Also it was a programme which in the first year included a heavy component of in-service training in which all participated; thus contributing again to the development of the team concept. Later on, this concept was to prove invaluable as the pressures within the community on individual CDOs became too great for one person to handle in isolation.

The Team was originally established in September 1970. At the beginning it consisted of ten people only. Within the two years which followed it grew to seventeen. To appreciate properly the way in which it worked, some account has to be taken of the events which accompanied the various phases of its operation.

The beginning of the field-work programme coincided with the beginning of the IRA bombing campaign. From January 1971 until the end of July, as staff were establishing themselves in the areas of their work and building up relationships, the IRA were building up their campaign of terrorist activities. By July, when the community development programme was beginning to take shape and there was beginning to appear some reward for effort, the bombing had increased to a crescendo. This was the first phase.

The second phase began on 9 August 1971 with the introduction of internment. This had both a short- and a long-term effect. In the short term the newly developed field programme had to be abandoned completely in order to convert the organisation into an emergency relief agency. This lasted for about a month and a half and was totally disruptive. In the long term, the reaction to internment on the part of the Catholic community led to various forms of withdrawal and an increased polarisation which had lasting and serious effects on the work.

The third phase was almost one of beginning again in many areas. It was one of carrying on despite all the disadvantages and of seeking new ways of work. It was also a phase during which much effort was diverted to dealing with individual problems.

The fourth phase extended from January 1972 until the summer. During this period, conflict of another kind with the government over support and resources for the programme came to a head, resulting in the resignation of the Chairman of the Commission, the Director and later three CDOs from key positions. During this period Stormont was prorogued – Mr Whitelaw became in effect the third Prime Minister in the two-year period and Lord Windlesham the fourth successive Minister with responsibility for Community Relations.

It is necessary to note these facts here if only to underline the strain to which this limited programme was exposed and the rapidity of changing events in the context of the community in which it operated. Seen in this light, the reports from the field at the end of the first full year of operation that active support was being given to 394 community organisations, including tenants' and community associations, voluntary youth organisations, redevelopment area associations and small development action groups, can be regarded as a considerable achievement. Indeed, giving support to community organisations and groups in one way or another has formed the greater part of the work of the community development team.

At the beginning of 1971, in anticipation of the creation of the Northern Ireland Housing Executive, an attempt was made to foster some kind of provincial federation of tenants' and community association on the lines of the National Federation of Community Associations in Britain. The need for such an organisation which could negotiate standard regulations for such things as charitable status, grant-aid, and representation on housing management was widely felt and provided a strong stimulus for this work. Unfortunately, despite having achieved two province-wide meetings of delegates and broad agreement on the final draft of a constitution, the fact that some tenants' representatives were Republican in their sympathies and others were staunch Unionists meant that the embryonic organisation was not able to weather the storm of August 1971. The subsequent employment of the rent and rate strike as a political weapon by leaders of the minority community provided the final coup de grâce.

But small local associations serving the needs of individual estates or of various established communities in urban areas and small villages in the rural areas have continued to flourish and to grow. Many of these are inevitably sectarian in membership inasmuch as they serve small areas which are homogeneously either Protestant or Catholic. But an encouragingly significant number are not sectarian in outlook and are prepared to work together when the need arises. Some have been created in areas of mixed residence and have been forced to work hard to withstand the threat of approaching violence and the outbreak of sectarian discord. That many have been successful in this is a tribute to the hard work and dedication of their leadership and the commitment to a common identity and sense of humanity of their members.

Some very successful associations emerged during 1971 as a result of the local response to the need for defence in areas of tension and fear. In quite a number of areas of Belfast, for example, when the anticipated threat of some kind of invasion did not materialise, vigilante groups, without losing sight of their original purpose, began to look for some other constructive outlets for their energies and so formed themselves into community action groups. What was encouraging about these groups was the fact that they were motivated towards 'action' and so began vigorously to tackle problems which hitherto they had, perhaps, tolerated apathetically.

It is, presumably, one of the risks taken in attempting to develop skills, knowledge, and confidence amongst community leaders that they may later employ them towards ends with which the CDO, or whoever the interventionist may be, may not approve. But is this really a problem? If the community action group which has been helped is really of the community, then the problems which it identifies are real problems for that community. If the community development process which has been encouraged is soundly based then, even if mistakes are made, lessons will be learned from them. If real strength has been created in the community and a real sense of sound responsibility created, in time it will achieve its own balance.

Evidence of how this can occur even within a conflict situation is afforded by the following extract from an evaluation of their work by the CDOs who at the time were working in an area of which a large part professed to be disaffected.

> We can point to 23 groups which we are servicing regularly with ideas on action, and which approach us on issues such as the preparation of a constitution or the carrying out of a community survey, or other things about which they had a lack of confidence.
>
> We can point to 7 groups which through our help have received some grant-aid which has increased their ability to solve some local problems and furthered their activities in the local community. We can point to 15 departments and external agencies with whom we have established regular contact and which, during our time here, we have encouraged to meet needs which otherwise they might not have known about.
>
> We can point to 8 projects all of which have resulted in some growth in the local community which was not there before.
>
> We also admit that there are a number of groups which, for one reason or another, have not sought our help, and we can cite a number of ideas and proposals which have just not materialised. But so what? To what end? Have we really contributed to any significant change in our area? Or have we merely reinforced the status quo of a troubled society?
>
> We feel that we have contributed something to the development of the local community. In the areas in which we are working a basic honesty has emerged from many local groups which profess little or no experience of community involvement. Rather than do things for them we have encouraged, and even insisted, that they do things for themselves. The result of this is we now find that some positive and forward-looking groups are taking a real lead in their local community. The evidence of

this is where we find people making constructive statements and going off to discuss their problems with government officials in a rational and realistic fashion. Prior to this involvement with these groups the people concerned would have depended on others, even expecting us, to do these fundamental things for them.

The lesson to be learned from this honest appraisal is that even at times of great conflict over, as in this case, a political issue, people continue to use other strategies to pursue the satisfaction of other needs which continue despite the conflict. Indeed it is this continuation of normal life and social interaction, albeit attenuated in certain directions, within the dominating constraints of the central conflict which is most impressive.

What was implicit in the quoted evaluation above, but which was made explicit in the aims of the community development programme, is the task of creating relationships.

Community centres

One of the very first needs of any community group or association is to have a place where they can meet and hold functions. In Northern Ireland this is not always easy for a number of reasons. Traditionally, the provision of amenities of this kind has been left in the hands of sectarian groups. Thus many churches have halls attached to their places of worship, some of them elaborately equipped; the counter-balance of the Catholic parochial hall has been in most areas the Orange Hall. Many of these sectarian organisations profess an openness and willingness for others to use their premises (although some do not), but the offer is rarely taken up because potential users feel uncomfortable entering premises situated, as it were, on the territory of others and perhaps bearing the symbols of an alien ideology. Another factor which creates difficulty is that in the past, perhaps because of the proliferation of sectarian or denominational establishments, local authorities in Northern Ireland have neither provided, nor been encouraged to provide, amenities of this kind to the extent that they have been provided for example in Britain since 1945.

As a result of this, many CDOs in the field reported case after case of newly formed community organisations concerned with all sorts of problems from development to provision for youth who experienced difficulty in finding suitable premises. There appeared to be a wide-spread demand for low-cost community buildings which could be erected both with and without voluntary participation in construction.

This problem was taken to the Department of Architecture at The Queen's University, Belfast, where it was enthusiastically received by both staff and students as a real-life design problem capable of being included in the course as a project. A meeting was arranged between the architects and representatives of community organisations from all over the province in which the latter talked about their needs and the sort of practical problems which they faced. In the following weeks the architects set out competitively to produce a number of designs and followed up the first meeting with visits to groups and potential sites. Finally the designs were presented by the architects to the re-assembled group of community representatives who discussed critically the advantages and disadvantages of the ideas presented.

What was achieved? New ideas were generated about how the problem might be tackled and diffused widely. Academic study at Queen's was related to a contemporary problem. Ordinary people had the opportunity of making relationships with developing architects and planners. Information on practical difficulties, design factors, the possibilities of new materials, and costings was widely exchanged on a group and individual basis. For many it was a new and rewarding experience.

And from it other relationships were created. The students became involved with the local authority, finding out what was possible. The representatives of the community organisations began to approach contractors and suppliers and to discuss their problems with local planning authorities. Finally the ideas which were generated were published in simple handbook form and circulated widely not only to potential users but also to potential grant-providers with the intention of both informing and motivating them.

A second example of creating relationships concerns a community project which arose as a spontaneous response to a widely felt and urgent need in a particular community in Belfast.

Protecting the community

A grave and pressing problem facing people living in areas with a mixture of Catholic and Protestant neighbourhoods has been the continuous pressure throughout the two years towards segregation. Many fled during the summer of 1971 because they simply lost confidence and felt that they were exposed to danger. (And many others have fled since and continue to do so.) But there were many more who fled because of engineered intimidation and the importation of violence from the more obvious flash-point areas. People who had been neighbours for years, living in constant harmony, were torn apart by the malign intrusion of others seeking to maximise feelings of hatred and fear.

In one such area hitherto untouched by sectarian discord, the first violent incident provoked a small wave of intimidation which sent shock-waves through the whole community. It also dispatched armies of rumour, much more erosive of social relationships than the actual events they purported to refer to. The problem was, how could rumour be stifled? How could correct information be relayed so as to dispel fears? Another question was, how could you believe what you were told?

To tackle these problems, a few representatives of the main political groupings in the area, all politically opposed to one another but united in their desire to defend their community, met together. From the very beginning the CDO who had encouraged the action group to form gave as much support as possible to the initiatives of this group. First, they found that they had to go out to create relationships with other leaders in the community. From this a couple of local conferences were held: a local communication system was established to provide swift and accurate means of communication if and whenever trouble should occur. In the end this group found itself going beyond the borders of its own community to discuss its problems with representatives of the various administrative and political structures whose actions were affecting not only their community but others as well. In this process there was not only an exchange of new information but, moreover, relationships were created.

Professional problems

When two sections of a community are locked in conflict perceived in simplistic win-lose terms, every concession to one party in the conflict is seen as a loss or defeat to the other. The establishment even of a Community Relations Commission was perceived generally as a liberal gesture of concession towards Catholics. With the tendency which parties in conflict have towards externalising their problems, this meant a general expectation on the part of the Protestants that the work of the

Commission was nothing to do with them and the Catholics felt that it was nothing more than meaningless window-dressing.

But the practical effect of all this has been that CDOs have for the most part found themselves working in Protestant and Catholic areas separately. Sometimes an individual CDO has found it possible to work only in areas and with groups of one sectarian identification.

Because most of the community leaders with whom they deal command a base of sectarian influences, another professional problem is created. When a group come forward to take action in respect of some community problem it is sometimes difficult to distinguish the motivation of the leaders. Are they coming forward simply with a genuine concern for the problem? Are they leaders who wear two hats? Do they perform both a militant sectarian role forced upon them by the situation and a genuine community leadership role? Or are they simply leaders in the conflict who are using a genuine community problem to extend their base of influence for political purposes and who have no interest in the welfare of the community as such? This is by no means a problem which occurs only in situations of conflict, but when the conflict is so severe and when its consequences are so appalling, this throws an additional strain on the professional in calculating the correct response.

A third problem for the professional which again is not unique but which is magnified in a conflict situation is that of being compelled to accept different and contradictory roles. The community development role, although political, is the antithesis of political action as such in that it seeks to create political consciousness without creating dependency and without seeking allegiance. But in the realm of this conflict CDOs have found themselves engaged in many tasks which have obliged them to adopt other roles, albeit temporarily. These have included on occasions a straightforward political role, engineering relationships between different political groupings; a welfare role in which individual cases have had to be accepted and helped; and a trouble-shooting role where sectarian-based dispute has broken out on the shop-floor or the building site and they have found themselves involved in delicate industrial relations work.

Organisational problems

Just as professional staff had problems with role-changes in response to the situation so, too, did the organisation and the programme as a whole. For example, and it has already been referred to, in the summer of 1971 the whole programme was put on the shelf and the organisation converted into an emergency relief agency. The dimension of this conversion will be understood when it is realised that in the space of a month over 2,000 cases of individuals in need were dealt with; the staff was temporarily quadrupled and an appropriate new structure formed, 115 families were physically moved to new homes, over 3,000 people were ferried to different destinations in the city, between 70 and 100 damaged houses were repaired to habitable condition and a research project, which was established to monitor the movement of people who fled from their homes, produced the first reliable report on the subject the following month (see *Flight*, Northern Ireland Community Relations Commission, occasional paper).

Nor did the organisation of the programme escape the direct consequences of the prevalent violence. The block in which the head office was situated was bombed in September 1971. The Londonderry office was damaged five times by explosions in the street and in adjacent buildings until in the end the staff were forced to move to new premises; but not, unfortunately, to escape further bomb damage. Other offices were damaged by blasts; cars used by staff were destroyed; one had his car hi-jacked and placed on a barricade, and everyday work was continued through the constraints of bomb-scares and constant security checks which in the end everyone accepted as normal. What were more difficult to accept were the risks attached to going out at night to meetings which involved crossing different areas, of Belfast in particular.

All this, of course, created tremendous problems with regard to staff morale. Without the team relationship (which at times had almost an incestuous quality about it, but which continued to return again and again to outward going thinking), it is doubtful if individual members of staff could have withstood the pressures under which they worked. Added to the daily frustration of trying to do something constructive when so many others were bent on destruction, the inadequate resources available to the programme carried the obvious implications that no one really expected the programme to achieve any worth-while results.

Again, it has to be observed that this problem of staff morale and the obvious suspicions of their purposes by established authority is by no means peculiar to Northern Ireland. But in a situation like this of great conflict, the consequences of these predicaments are more compelling and are productive of greater strain upon the programme. Indeed the programme itself, instead of being contributory to the ultimate resolution of the conflict, becomes in turn a victim of the conflict.

The effect on the community

Walking through one of the inner-city areas in Belfast past the boarded-up shop-windows, the barbed wire military emplacement, the burned outhouse, the gap in the buildings where a bomb or redevelopment has left its mark, one is struck by the apparent normality of everyday life despite the environment. The bustle of urban life and the normality and easy friendliness of the people is difficult to relate to the scenes of violence portrayed by the mass media.

Working in the community, the CDO knows the constant tension which permeates the lives of many: the loss, the heartbreak and the hatred which exists and the erosion of normal social controls which has taken place.

Areas of endemic violence produce in the inhabitants a kind of exhaustion which allows one to think only by the day; where there has been an attack of some kind – a shooting incident or a bomb – the very air becomes charged with the build-up of emotional tension seeking release. There is no point then of expecting a group of people collected together to discuss an issue of common interest either to think rationally or to be prepared to project their thinking into the future. Another opportunity for getting something done has gone, and one has to wait for a more opportune time.

One result which can be claimed for the conflict is that the community map in many areas of Belfast has had to be re-drawn. Attacked, intimidated or simply frightened, many families who once lived in areas predominantly inhabited by people of the opposite sectarian identification have fled for security to live 'amongst their own kind'. To facilitate this movement, local branches of extremist Protestant and Catholic organisations have usurped the function of housing management from the Housing Executive and control the allocation of houses from the public stock in their areas. But they are not the only ones to move into the vacuum created by the departure of the politician and by the loss of faith in traditional political processes. There has been a general mushrooming of small do-it-yourself organisations who, as they acquire strength in this time of crisis, will have to be reckoned with in the future. In this respect not all the effects have been losses, even if the price paid makes it not much of a bargain.

The effect on agencies of the state

One of the hidden costs of conflict are all those things that might have been done if the conflict itself did not prevent them, or if the various governmental agencies responsible for doing them were not using up all their energies and much of their resources in coping with the results of the conflict. Many people outside Northern Ireland are familiar with the scenes of destruction in the bombed-out centre of Londonderry and will be aware of the enormous loss which they represent. Not so obvious are all the jobs which did not come to Derry or the development plans which have had to be put back. Of course, even in the midst of conflict, the Administration endeavours to pursue development targets and to continue with the normal processes of public service. But the strain of continuing to do so against a background of continuous conflict and repeated emergencies in the end takes its toll. In the end it produces a kind of siege mentality in which one can either try to forget that the enemy are at the gate or steel oneself to carry on somehow in the hope that sooner or later life will return to normal.

In the everyday management of local affairs it means the constant switching of resources to deal with new and increasing demands for services. It means having to do something about staff who may refuse to perform the duties they are paid to do in areas where they fear, rightly or wrongly, that their lives are at risk. It means an increase in costs and a lowering of productivity. It means that the whole programme for the reform of local government and the design of the new system which has cost so much, not least of all in sheer hard work, is placed in jeopardy by the likelihood of serious delays.

One particular public service which has been seriously affected by the conflict is that of the police. It is the policeman's unfortunate lot to reflect both the avowed and unspoken values of his society. When the Unionist administration controlled Stormont, the police were regarded by many of the Catholic minority as enforcers of the rule of that regime. As the conflict spread, the police were always in the front line and antagonism towards them grew. When it was the turn of the Protestant gangs to take to the streets, the police found themselves at once the target of hatred from both majority and minority communities. It seemed that to attempt to enforce the law against 'our community', when they were expected instead to be enforcing the law against the other community, could only be construed as an act of hostility and betrayal.

Bcw

To work in an area which hardly ever sees a policeman on beat patrol or to drive through town where the only policemen to be seen are standing armed on guard duty outside the police station or manning barricades is to realise the loss to the community of an essential service normally taken for granted. But this absence of the police and their loss of support in the community generally is symptomatic of a wider condition. It is the weakening of all forms of social control to the point that in some areas only convention and the habits of everyday life prevent the incipient anarchy from becoming chaos.

The consequences

I have tried to show how, in various ways, the conflict has affected the community development programme, both directly in its effect upon the staff and the organisation and indirectly in its effect upon the community and the public services. With regard to the latter, four major effects have been observed: the discrediting of political leadership; through the prorogation of Stormont and the reorganisation of local government, the loss of any effective form of democratically elected government; the erosion of confidence and will in the public services and in the administration; and the sometimes obvious, sometimes subtle, erosion of most forms of social control. All this suggests a huge vacuum in the functioning of the society and this would be the case were it not for the intervention of another party to the conflict, the army.

The employment of violence as a method of direct action for social change and the unscrupulous use of force produced, inevitably, the counterreaction. The army was brought into the situation in 1969 to stand between the parties engaged in violent conflict in order, it was intended, to allow normal political processes time to resolve the conflict. The longer the army was retained in the situation, the short-term gains which it achieved were replaced by longer-term losses. Gradually it was drawn into the conflict in many different ways with results which have been widely recorded and are generally well known.

What is perhaps not so widely recognised is the way in which the role of the army has inevitably widened from the simple application of force in support of the civil power to a general permeation of the processes and institutions which order the society. The influence of the army on political decision-making is a matter for speculation, but the very force of its numbers, its vast system of intelligence and its deployment throughout wide sections of the community must make it considerable. There is additionally abundant evidence also of its intervention at all levels in the community, from the street to the town hall, in both the political and civic life of the community. In many cases this intervention may be motivated by the army's own needs for obtaining information, in others it is the simple product of seeing a particular need in the community and wanting to get something done.

There is nothing sinister in this intervention of the army: there is no conspiracy to subvert the normal processes of community life. And yet it must be said that the increasing involvement of the army in the life of the community, its massive resources, the force which it represents, its particular hierarchical concept of authority, and its discipline, constitute a serious obstacle to the resolution of the conflict and the restoration of normal civic life. Its very existence as an all-powerful agency in the community is the antithesis of community development. Inadequate and ill equipped as any local community may be to deal with its problems, it gains nothing from having them dealt with in an arbitrary manner by an external agency over which it has no control. If that community is inadequate and ill equipped, that is where the community development process begins.

It was the serious and violent nature of the conflict which brought the army into the situation in the first place. Getting the army out is going to be enormously difficult and a seemingly impossible task at the moment. But for the good of the community and for the good of the army itself, this must be the objective which is given first priority.

Conclusion

This paper has been concerned with presenting in a descriptive way some aspects of community development experience in a situation of violence. In consequence of this, the source material from which many of the examples and observations are drawn derives mainly from Belfast and, to a somewhat lesser extent, Londonderry. These have been the two places where the conflict has been most intense and in which the level of violence has remained continuously high. They are not typical of Northern Ireland as a whole, but their combined populations represent probably nearly half the population of the province as a whole.

They are also the two places where the effects of the violence and the conflict are the greatest, particularly upon ordinary working-class people. The two quotations with which this paper began were from

Belfast men, for example. In the past, the long exercise of power by one political party with no effective opposition encouraged a style of government which at best was benignly paternalistic and at worst arrogant. It was a system well insulated from open criticism on all major issues. It was also a system which could be influenced by the middle classes through a network of personal relationships, even though they were largely inactive politically. But it was also a system which was unreachable and unshakeable by a large proportion of the community who continued fatalistically in their everyday life, believing either that the government was looking after them or was prejudiced against them, depending upon their political and religious allegiance.

All this has now changed. These very same people have become politicised; they have learned to do things for themselves; they have learned that they can organise and that, in the absence of any external agency upon which they feel they can depend, they can depend upon themselves and upon the talent and ability which lies within their own communities. They feel that all the institutions of society in which they placed their trust have let them down and there is a well-developed determination that this will not happen again.

Recognition will have to be given to this important development in a number of ways. Traditional institutions, if they mean to survive, will have to re-create their relationships with those people upon whom they depend for support and allegiance. New institutions which are, or will be, created will only flourish if they can capture the support of the many community action groups and associations which have formed. This support in turn will only be available if it is actively sought by consultation and by the creation of opportunities for participation in the making of the new arrangements. With regard to some issues, such as the role of a civilian police force, this involvement will probably be the determining factor and thus central to the whole affair.

The best way to gain support and to involve the various community organisations is by giving them recognition and by giving them support. They in turn need help: they need opportunities for training and education, they need consultant assistance from time to time, and also on occasions they need financial assistance. But over and above all else, if they are going to support any new arrangements, they need to feel that they are party to the enterprise. In the recent government Green Paper, *The Future of Northern Ireland*, in which the various options facing the province were set out clearly for the purpose of discussion, it was observed (p. 83):

There is not least the great need to rid Northern Ireland of the presence and threat of violence. Both political theory and practical experience show that no scheme of government, however carefully drawn, can do more than present an opportunity for progress. It is in the hearts and minds of the people of Northern Ireland and not just in the aims of Government or the words of Acts of Parliament that the capacity for working and living together must flourish.

There is a vast constituency awaiting the government which is prepared to adopt as a strategy for social change those methods and techniques which will give the people the opportunity to respond and participate; it will also expose for ever that violence is a strategy of ignorance, despair and deception.

References

Community Development Forum, *Social Needs and Social Needs Legislation*, Belfast, 1972.

Hayes, M., *Community Relations and the Role of the Community Relations Commission in Northern Ireland*, London, Runnymede Trust, 1972.

Jackson, H., *The Two Irelands*, Minority Rights Group, Report no. 2, London, 1971.

New Ulster Movement, *Violence and Northern Ireland*, Belfast, 1972.

Northern Ireland, Community Relations Commission, *The Emergency Operation*, Belfast, 1971.

—— *Flight*, Belfast, 1971.

—— *Cheaper Community Centres*, Belfast, 1972.

—— *Community Self Survey*, by R. S. P. Weiner, Belfast, 1972.

—— *The Future of Local Government*, by H. Griffiths, Belfast, 1972.

—— *Housing in Northern Ireland*, Belfast, 1972.

Northern Ireland Government, *Review of Economic and Social Developments*, Belfast, HMSO, 1971.

—— *Violence and Civil Disturbances in Northern Ireland in 1969*, Belfast, HMSO, 1972.

Northern Ireland Office, *The Future of Northern Ireland*, London, HMSO, 1972.

Rose, Richard, *Governing without Consensus*, London, Faber, 1971.

Sunday Times Insight Team, *Ulster*, Penguin Special, 1972.

2 The control of change and the regulation of community action

John Dearlove

For many, the comfortable myth of the affluent society has been exploded, and there has been an increasing recognition that poverty and deprivation affect millions. The scale of the rediscovery has led a smaller number of people to express unease about the utility of established solutions. The effectiveness of consensual styles of social change has been questioned; the Labour Party is seen as having failed;[1] and the predominant[2] casework approach in social work is regarded as 'positively harmful',[3] as it serves 'to reconcile the poor to their station . . . [and] to plaster up the sores of an unjust society'.[4] At the same time there is an awareness that the poor are not active in securing their rights within the law, still less do they organise to press for change which might bring them a more equitable share of the national cake. In the face of these difficulties and deficiencies, it is argued that conflict must be the major generating force to secure change;[5] community action is needed; and the social work profession must be radicalised so that social workers serve as advocates of the poor and deprived, as 'mercenaries in their service'.[6] Arguments of this kind have not gone unnoticed by the more authoritative voices in our society.[7]

Now, I do not doubt the inadequacy of the casework approach, but because there is a developing literature which points to the difficulties which are likely to beset the successful introduction and establishment of an alternative radical social work,[8] I will not consider these problems here. In this paper I wish to dwell on community action[9] – on groups of poor which are urging demands on government for substantial innovation or change in the pattern of governmental commitments which, if taken up, would necessitate an extension of the scope of government into the private sector and some redistribution of income and resources between social classes. I will suggest that there are problems and tensions inherent in community action groups; I will argue that the authorities are able to control and regulate these groups

22

and resist their demands for change and innovation; I will further suggest that this resistance affects the development of community action groups – for if they are to survive, then they are usually forced to change the pattern of their activities in such a way that they cease to pose any substantial challenge to government, and may even come to assist government in the maintenance of the established order. However, before I consider the control and regulation of these *groups* of poor, I will briefly identify some of the rules regulating the claims which the *individual* poor make upon the resources of the state, and I will note the principles which underlie this control. If these latter tasks are undertaken, we are in a better position to appreciate the necessity for the control and regulation of group claims, be they from community action groups, or from radical social workers.

The regulation of the individual poor

There are a number of rules which regulate the individual claimant's access to welfare benefits. First, 'the wage stop rule is designed to ensure that the net income of an unemployed person is no greater when receiving supplementary benefit than it would be if he were following his normal full-time occupation'.[10] Second, 'since the middle of 1968 the Supplementary Benefits Commission has operated the four-week rule in regions where it "feels" there is an adequate supply of unfilled vacancies. If claimants are single, fit, unskilled and under 45 years, they are told that their entitlement to benefit will be limited to four weeks. Skilled and married men with children may have the four-week rule applied after they have drawn benefit for three months.'[11] Third, if it is thought that a person has left a job 'voluntarily' without 'just cause', part of his benefit is disallowed for a period of six weeks. Fourth, the Supplementary Benefits Commission will only meet a claimant's rent in full if it is thought to be reasonable both for the accommodation and for a person of claimant status. Finally, the cohabitation rule disqualifies a woman from benefit in her own right if she is thought to be living as a common law wife.

The rules may be harsh, but the application and the effect are still harsher. Customers are kept as clients;[12] their aggregation is discouraged;[13] and rights of representation and appeal are inhibited by the rules and procedures that surround them.[14] If claimants are not actually denied their rights, they are certainly often in ignorance of them, an ignorance which is hardly countered by the limited and scant provision of information by the authorities.[15] The claimant is kept humble and deferential, and this humility is further encouraged by the knowledge that much depends upon the discretion of the official at the counter.[16] Applications for welfare benefits are 'degradation ceremonies'[17] and it is hardly surprising that the poor 'do not apply for their "rights" because it places them in positions where they are judged, evaluated, tested for eligibility; and where their honesty and character are cast in doubt.'[18]

Rules and regulations do not float free of the economic and social structure, and the system of welfare benefits enforces and polices the work system. The wage stop rule ensures that those receiving benefit are always worse off than when employed. Similarly the four-week, 'work-shy', rule clearly has the effect of forcing people into the labour market, just as the voluntary unemployment rule is designed to hold people to their work situation. A pool of low-paid labour is encouraged, and low-paid work is enforced. A work ethic is propagated by these rules, and still more by the culture of humility which greets claimants. The stress is on self-support, family support, and individual solutions in a free market. The effect is to keep individuals off the state and in the private sector, and in this the state is helped by the social work profession.[19]

The regulation of community action

Since the rules regulating individual claimants' access to public resources serve to keep many in need in the private sector, we should not be surprised to find that the state keeps groups of poor in a similar position. By and large those in government are concerned to ensure that collectivities remain their supporters and subjects. Ideally, however, they are keen for groups to assume a role which actually helps *them* in the provision of services for which there is an established demand, but failing this then they are happy if groups assume a self-help role so that they provide for themselves without any recourse to public assistance. The state desires subjects, clients, supporters and helpers, not masters, customers, demanders and disrupters.

This concern to keep voluntary groups on the output side of government is institutionalised in a Charity Law which prohibits charitable groups from attempting to change the law,[20] and also finds embodiment in the views of politician and social worker alike. Although at one time there was the feeling that the rise of the Welfare State would render voluntary social service unnecessary, this view has been short-lived and there is an increasing recognition that groups of this kind have a crucial role to play. The influential Aves Committee was 'left with the conviction that the social services as we know them, and as they are developing, give almost unlimited scope for voluntary effort.'[21] The authoritative voices in our society articulate what Broady has called a 'typical administrator's view of voluntary organisation', and he cites as an example of this view the remarks made by the Joint Parliamentary Secretary to the Ministry of Health at a conference on community services for health and welfare: 'it is for the local authorities to establish what the gaps are that need to be filled and to say what services they expect from voluntary effort. . . . It is for voluntary organisations in their turn to mobilise the resources to fill these gaps.'[22] In a similar vein, the Seebohm Committee urged the desirability of encouraging community development by arguing that it was a 'process whereby local groups are assisted to clarify and express their needs and objectives and to take collective action to attempt to meet them. It emphasises the involvement of people themselves in determining and meeting their own needs.'[23] A senior councillor from the Royal Borough of Kensington and Chelsea similarly considered that groups should remain on the output side of government, when he stated: 'It is our policy to cooperate with groups . . . Where voluntary bodies are willing to do things, and can do things as well as a local authority, the only difference being that the ratepayers are saved money, then I'm all for it.'

The covert control of community action

Numerous groups and individuals accept and absorb this ideology,[24] or else they are aware of the difficulty of moving government and so assume a non-demanding role right from the start. This highlights the fact that what is most noticeable when we consider the control and regulation of community action is the apparent absence of, and indeed the lack of necessity for, any overt control. Contrary to the hopes of the left and the fears of the right, there is but limited dissent and disorder from the poor. By and large these people remain the subjects of government; they exercise no mastery, but are passive and unthinking supporters of an institution which affects their very existence. I have already pointed out that the poor are not active in claiming their rights within the law, and it is this category of the population which generally participates least in the political process. There is the paradox that those who have most need of succour and help from the public sector are also those who are least active in directing demands in that direction.

It is precisely this that I had in mind when I argued that, on the surface, there is an apparent lack of necessity for any control. However, if we go on to consider *why* the poor are politically inactive, we are led to conclude that control is more subtle, for potential disorder and disruption is killed at source before the poor ever move to the stage of articulation and aggregation.

Traditionally, political participation is explained in terms of utilitarian models and thus it is frequently argued that non-participation is indicative of satisfaction with the way the affairs of government are being conducted. This is an optimistic and pleasant explanation, but it is utterly inadequate, and in my view the search for a more convincing account of the non-participation of the poor demands a consideration of the inhibiting and policing effect of the ruling ideas in capitalist society – ideas which suggest that 'the economic system is open, and economic success is a matter of individual merit.'[25] This is the self-help doctrine; people '*know* that if you work hard and take advantage of all the opportunities available, you *can* climb out of poverty and reach the top – well, perhaps not *the* top, but certainly a comfortable level of living.'[26] It's the familiar 'rags to riches' story. If Jack's not alright, then he could be and he should be, and if he's not then it's because he's bad and lazy, for the presumption that every able-bodied person has the 'ability to work and succeed if they only tried hard enough [has] led to the inevitable conclusion that those who have left off trying are bad'.[27] Myths of affluence and never having had it so good may have been exploded in certain circles, but they still dominate the popular consensus. There is a stress on the desirability of private consumption and the evil of public expenditure and therefore there is a search for 'private solutions to public evils'.[28] It is not surprising that we hear much about the abuse of supplementary benefit, and only little about widespread tax evasion, since knowledge and ignorance of these matters serves to reinforce the dominant self-help ideology. Anne Allen, a journalist, has noted that[29]

> one of the myths of our age is that there are 1,000s of able-bodied men sitting about keeping their families on supplementary benefit, and somehow managing to buy cars and take foreign holidays on what the kindly (lunatic) state gives them unquestioningly. In one form or another this is the criticism I receive every time I write on poverty or any section of the community with special needs. 'I managed without asking for help, so why shouldn't they?,' they ask.

This self-help ideology with the related view that the poor are morally or personally defective carries with it the explicit assumption that, although the poor may be given assistance, they should in no sense demand it, or regard it as a right. They should be thankful for any crumbs which they receive: 'policy challenges from the very people who are the recipients of help, and who are therefore expected to be grateful, call forth a shock reaction'.[30]

This ideology eats into the poor's view of themselves, and is reinforced by their contact with the local social security offices. It accounts for the failure of people to claim their rights, for 'one way to evade the unpleasantness of being dependent is to avoid getting help at all in a dependent situation.'[31] The poor and the deprived are forced to see their situation as *their* fault. Poverty is a 'humiliating condition which most people are ashamed to acknowledge',[32] and the feelings of guilt and shame which they experience mean that they do not *want* to act, still less to organise, for to do so implies a public admission of *personal* failure. As Coates and Silburn point out, 'the poor do not necessarily see themselves as a group at all and are not necessarily aware that their own immediate and personal difficulties are elements of a public problem.'[33] Of course there is apathy, alienation, defeatism and cynicism, together with a vicious circle of reinforcing factors which tend to hold people to their position of poverty,[34] but more important in terms of political activity there is a strange acceptance of the position of poverty. There is a fat-city complex, where people consider that 'there must be people worse off than I am, so please don't trouble',[35] and this is reinforced by 'knowledge' that the rich are not happy.

Given the widespread acceptance, propagation and reinforcement of these sorts of beliefs which have a clear controlling and policing function, perhaps the amazing thing is not that the poor are politically inert, but that some of the poor manage to become politically active for some of the time. However, if the poor do move to the stage of collective organisation, they face problems and tensions which can limit their effectiveness before they ever move to encounter and challenge government.

The problems of organisation and leadership

The essence of poverty and deprivation is the absence of slack resources and the absence of power. The only substantial resource available to the poor is the solidarity of their numbers and this is pretty effectively broken up by the prevalence of the self-help ideology. If the poor do seek to move to activity, then they lack information, confidence and a knowledge of just how to go about things. There are particular problems of mobilising the 'poor-poor', but at the same time 'in redevelopment areas . . . community projects suffer from the likelihood that the most able and articulate people will be trying to move out.'[36] Notwithstanding this, efforts at involvement usually only get to grips with the 'rich-poor', and at the same time the conflicts within these areas often get played out in the internal politics of the group, so limiting the political effectiveness of community action:[37]

> The disruption within a community group arising from the apparent conflict between different interest groups within the population (e.g. tenants/owner-occupiers; established residents/ newcomers; indigenous/immigrant) only serves to make the task of organisation more hazardous, and restrict the choice of issues which are of political relevance to all members of the community.

The problems of organisation and leadership springing forth from amongst the poor are keenly recognised – indeed they lie at the base of arguments which point to the necessity for radical social work, community organisation and community development. In practice, many efforts at community action have at their centre a middle-class radical who sees himself as servicing the aims and objectives of a wider group of poor, which he seeks to build up and mobilise. However, there is the problem of the leader relating both to the group and to the local authority which he seeks to influence. On the one hand, supporters of the poor feel that they know the council, and they consider that visible public-protest styles of communication should be used to press their demands and win success. On the other, the middle-class leader is likely to want to try an initial private and reasoned approach, for he is aware that protest tactics could well antagonise a council which may just be prepared to bend if approached in the proper manner. The difficulty for the leader lies in the fact that the people he is representing are 'accustomed to being ignored or even exploited by vested interests [and] suspicions of a "sell-out" are easily aroused by co-operation between their leaders and established organisations.'[38] These beliefs may separate the leader from the group, leaving him stranded between the local authority and a group which is rapidly folding. In addition to this problem there is invariably a tension between getting things done and involving the poor.[39] The middle-class activist may seek to assume a non-directive approach but he rapidly moves to assume a more positive and dominant role, and once this occurs there is the danger of his imposing middle-class values and aspirations upon the group, and of the group being reluctant to follow. Community action may be killed from within if it succeeds in getting off the ground in the first place, but if a group holds together, it is likely to face considerable problems in its dealings with government.

The limits of a consensus strategy, but the problems of conflict

There are a variety of modes by which groups may choose to intervene in the policy process,[40] and all too frequently we hear the authorities pointing out that groups, in adopting a conflict style of demand presentation, go about things the wrong way. A distinct impression is created which suggests that if only the groups were moderate and reasonable and prepared to raise demands through the 'proper channels', then success would greet their claim. What is the reality of this view, and what is the possibility of using a consensual mode of social change?

In fact, I have already suggested that such a style of intervention may be ruled out by the poor people involved in community action, and it is not impossible that the rhetoric of participatory politics and the concern with mobilisation may serve to inhibit the middle-class leader from assuming a mediating and reasoning role. However, it is important to realise that the problems which lie in the way of the consensual style of demand presentation are more fundamental than these observations imply, for the *authorities* themselves and the established interest groups are mainly responsible for frustrating and disrupting the success of this approach. Those who argue that groups should use the proper channels perpetuate a myth that the only obstacle to policy change and a favourable governmental response lies in a communication blockage between governors and governed: if the policy-makers are given information, they will respond favourably to a demand grounded in a genuine social need. It is true that the forces which encourage the selective use of information are likely to mean that political decision-makers are ignorant of many problems and needs,[41] but the suggestion that communication is *the* problem ignores the existence of interests and the forces for maintenance, and assumes a reasonableness and a possibility for give-and-take which is quite often lacking. Democractic rhetoric encourages the public to believe that reasonableness and consensus are possible, but in reality a 'low-keyed' strategy is just not available to bring success to groups of 'newcomers', who 'must rely on high pressure tactics'.[42] In most cases, groups which are not sympathetically regarded by the authorities, and which urge change and innovation in the pattern of established public policies, do make a first attempt to gain access for their demands by quiet, more acceptable, methods, but their invariable failure to gain effective access by a strategy which is completely controlled by the authorities forces them into a more aggressive style of demand presentation. Protest is further encouraged by the fact that the authorities always fail to consult the interests affected before they make a decision. In addition, the prestigious 'established' groups, which could possibly win success for the claims of radical community action groups by using a proper channels approach, are aware that they have a good ongoing relationship with the local authority and are reluctant to put that relationship in jeopardy by associating with community action groups. The secretary of a leading housing trust in Notting Hill pointed to the importance of this when explaining why the trust was reluctant to support the Notting Hill Summer Project. 'We tried to help the Notting Hill Summer Project, but we realised we were in deep water and so we got out. We could have given a veneer of respectability to the organisation, but it would not have helped us or the people in the area.'

The consensual approach will get no more than the authorities want to give. In many cases it has failed,[43] and in my view the cause of this failure lies more in the intransigence of the authorities and the established groups than in the excesses of community action. There is only any point in groups continuing discussions as long as they evoke a well-intentioned and serious response from the government, and all too often the concern of government is to talk out demands, knowing full well that delay and procrastination affect the continued viability of community action. Many community action groups never even get to the stage of a fair hearing at the hands of government, but those which do are almost forced to break off talks in order to retain their integrity and their supporters. However, in doing this, and in moving to conflict tactics, they put themselves into a position of extreme vulnerability. Lip-service is paid to the right to protest, but it lacks legitimacy, and at the local level powerful myths sustain the view that there should be no politics, no controversy and no conflict, but only ordered and reasonable debate between people who agree on fundamentals. Groups which challenge this consensus and which seek to move into the area of non-decisions,[44] opening up a politics which has been reduced to administration, inevitably challenge a councillor's right to govern and the assumption that government is the sole repository of knowledge and initiative.[45] In doing this, groups confront the myths which centre on the link between governors and governed supposedly forged in the heat of free elections, and thus expose themselves to a range of powerful and destructive rhetoric. In other words, protest can easily play into the hands of government,[46] for it can allow the government to conveniently ignore the demand, and instead concentrate its considerable energy upon publicly challenging the legitimacy of the tactics, the credibility and responsibility of the pressuring group. Radford has pointed to the use of this tactic against those campaigning for more humane conditions in the hostel for the homeless at King Hill: 'Throughout this struggle, those of us who were not ourselves homeless, were accused by the council of being trouble-makers, who were manipulating the homeless for political ends.'[47] Similarly, a councillor from Southwark explained why it was necessary, *and* how it was possible, to reject the demands of squatters: 'The thought in Southwark is, if we come to the same agreement as in Lewisham, it would mean that we have been pushed into it by the militants. This is just not on. I abhor militancy'.[48]

Governments, like the authorities in universities, have a siege mentality: if only they can hold out long enough, they can hope that the pressuring groups will disappear or change. Supporters of community action do not have a mortgage mentality, they demand success and they demand it quickly, for organisers 'know that the process of committing residents to the project and of developing the projects role as a local movement of opposition is only possible through the continuing attempt to force that limited, difficult-to-achieve change.'[49]

Forcing community action to adopt a conflict strategy and then attacking that strategy and the group is only one of a number of techniques which authorities use to resist and suppress demanding groups, for they are equipped with an arsenal of 'exclusion devices'[50] which enable them to defend their established policies, their right to govern and the legitimacy of their resistance to dissenting residents and activists. Clark and Hopkins discuss the tactics of suppression adopted by the authorities to deal with Community Action Programs in America;[51] Davies has argued that planners 'have taken on the mantle of . . . "the evangelistic bureaucrat" in order to immunise themselves to the persistent criticism made of them as they exercise their trade';[52] and the claims made by authorities that they are sources of expertise, knowledge and professionalism[53] are all tactics designed to reduce customers to clients and to reduce masters to subjects, and as such they serve as slogans which can be used to resist demands for change or innovation.

In the face of these governmental pressures, community action groups, concerned to urge change and innovation on the authorities, experience considerable difficulty in surviving *and* in maintaining their radical direction. There are a number of developments and responses which are possible.

The development of community action

No one familiar with the poor and deprived areas of our cities can fail to be struck by the way in which groups urging change and innovation rise and fall with amazing rapidity, and this highlights the fact that perhaps the most common response to the difficulties faced by groups of radical poor is their tendency to *fail and fold up*.[54]

This is not the only development which is possible, but survival has its costs, and the price that is paid is that the group change, and shift away from raising any substantial challenge to the established policies and authorities.

I have already mentioned that the supporters of community action demand success in return for their continued allegiance, and I have suggested that difficulties lie in the way of these groups ever achieving the sort of objectives and changes which they see as desirable, so we should not be surprised to find that *groups down-scale the demands which they make*. In the context of British politics, demands for improvement in the housing situation have usually been suppressed and, in their stead, groups have turned their attention to the less costly, less funda- mental and less controversial matters of nursery and play facilities. The successes which many groups have achieved in pressing demands of this kind have allowed the authorities to claim that they are responsive in catering to need, and so they perpetuate an illusion about the reality of the forces which influence the development of major public policies. In many cases, groups are aware of the obstacles which lie in the way of gaining the substantial changes they consider necessary and, because of this, never even attempt to raise them, but concentrate instead on the attainment of limited and partial objectives. Marris and Rein point out that the American Community Action Programs 'were under pressure to produce results, and reluctant at the outset to run too great a risk of failure: so they accomplished first the programme which came easiest . . . rather than those which mattered most.'[55]

The self-help ideology is a powerful one, and it encourages the search for individual solutions, or at least for collective solutions which do not involve the authorities. Many groups start off as self-help groups but, where this is not so, the frustration and rejection of demands, coupled with the obligation which activists may feel to the poor who have been involved, may lead to *self-help solutions*. For example, the Angell Ward Neighbourhood Council, in documenting the history of its uneasy relationship with the London borough of Lambeth, draws a number of lessons from the experience of delay and opposition, one of which is that 'the Neighbourhood Council must continually seek ways of financing, establishing and running projects independently of the Lambeth Borough Council.'[56] In other words, community action groups may come to provide for themselves what they originally considered to be a need which should be seen as a right to be met fully and adequately by the state. Groups which develop in this way may receive limited financial aid from the authorities, but where this occurs there is usually the unspoken assumption that the group will do nothing to embarrass the authority. There is no doubt that this transformation is welcomed and encouraged by government, for the authorities often define community action as self-help, considering that this is the proper sphere of activity for group concern. In effect, what emerges is a form of community socio-therapy which transforms activism into compliance, reduces community disorganisation and integrates marginal groups into the established order.

Ideally, the authorities like groups which do more than help themselves; they like groups which actually *come to help government by assisting in the provision of a service* for which there is an established and recognised demand. Many social welfare groups in deprived areas which are assuming the latter role and operating on the output side of government had their origins in radical campaigns to force changes in public priorities and provision. It was only when they failed in this attempt that they became active in the provision of a service. Frequently they were goaded into this role by an authority which taunted them to show that they really cared and were responsible, and were not just out to cause trouble for political reasons. The bait has often been taken, and radical energy is controlled, for groups in this position may be dependent on local authority finance, and even where this is not the case then the sheer scale of their task will leave them with little time (and still less energy) to protest about inadequate public provision.

In Kensington and Chelsea the two major housing trusts, the Kensington Housing Trust and the Notting Hill Housing Trust, both had their origins in campaigns which were concerned to urge on the council the necessity for a more extensive public housing programme. The Kensington Housing Trust was formed in 1927, but had its roots in the Housing Sub-committee of the Kensington Council of Social Service which was set up in 1920 to refute the claim of a local councillor that there were no slums in the Royal Borough. For the next six years the Committee was exclusively concerned with extensive propaganda activity, but they failed to persuade the council to extend its housing programme. The move to form a housing trust came in 1926 when[57]

> a deputation from the Kensington Housing Association led by Lord Balfour of Burleigh called on the Great Western Railway to protest against the conditions of a street of houses called Wornington Road . . . which was in their freehold; the railway representatives retaliated and suggested that, if they felt so strongly about this, the Kensington Housing Association should buy the freeholds which were falling in, and manage the properties themselves. The Kensington Housing Association accepted the challenge and set up the Kensington Housing Trust for the purpose. The Trust bought these forty-eight houses and the work began.

In the next forty-six years the Trust acquired some 900 tenancies, and has come to work increasingly closely with the local authority.

The Notting Hill Housing Trust was formed in 1963, but its background lay in a petition organised by the Notting Hill Social Council which urged the local authority to acquire more property in the borough. The Borough Council responded by offering every assistance to help form a new housing trust. Although relations between the local authority and the Trust were initially rather tense, these have eased considerably in the last few years. Now, the Trust is centrally involved in working with the local authority in preparing a study on the possible redevelopment of the Colville area of the borough, and a major role is envisaged for the talents of the Trust and private enterprise.

This transformation from pressure group to service provision has been noted with respect to the American Community Action Programs for, 'when conflicts have occurred, the consequences have not been beneficial to the poor. The resolution of such conflicts seems invariably to be in the direction of the dilution of effective social action and a regression toward less abrasive community organisation, particularly toward a substitution of social services for community action.'[58] Similarly, in the case of the London borough of Camden, Mrs Wistrich noted that 'many of the voluntary organisations with which the Council worked began as pressure groups designed to secure improvements in services. In several instances, the organisations came to work closely with the Council and to provide services with the Council's cooperation and support.' She goes on to note that 'where the Council financed the greater part of an organisation's activities there was always the danger that they would lose their distinctive character and the possibility of vigorous and independent representation.'[59]

Sunley has pointed to the difficulties which lie in the way of social workers moving out of an individual casework approach. Indeed, he notes that where there have been attempts at change then 'perhaps as a result of interagency snafus and frustrating experiences in dealing with governmental bureaucracies, many caseworkers have tended to fall back into the "adjustment" solution for environmental problems', for even though they recognise that there are better solutions and approaches, these are just not available to them.[60] I think similar problems beset community action groups, in that the difficulties they have experienced in attempting to change public policies so that better provision is made for whole categories and groups of the population have encouraged these organisations to shift away from this in favour of their *providing a service which aims to get individuals their rights within the established law*, and which acquaints them with the possibilities for individual improvement. In a word, one has seen the growth of unofficial information services which are frequently giving advice and help on a quite staggering scale. For example, the Housing Action Centre (which grew out of the Notting Hill Summer Project and the Notting Hill Housing Service) claims to have helped some 4,000 families in the eight months since its formation in October 1971. As well as providing general advice and problem-solving, the Centre has a Welfare Fund which can be used in emergencies to prevent homelessness and family break-ups, and it also aims to use the Register of Housing Needs as a means of seeking more long-term and fundamental solutions, though one must wonder how much energy is left to deal with the latter objective, given the continual pressure of casework and enquiries.

Work of this kind has not gone unnoticed, or unrewarded, by the authorities, and in Kensington and Chelsea plans are afoot for the Centre to move into the official Aid and Information Centre in 1974. The first annual report of the Centre considers 'it will be a key decision since there is much to be said for retaining independence and our present voluntary status', but goes on to note that 'it is already well-established that considerable gains have already been made by co-ordinating our work more closely with the Borough Council and the services which it provides'.

Another comparatively recent development has been the concern to make the full services of the legal profession available, without charge, to the people of a deprived area. The first fully staffed law centre, the North Kensington Neighbourhood Law Centre, handled some 2,000 cases in its first eighteen months of operation. The lawyers at the Centre are mindful of the charge that they are perpetuating and under-writing a system of rules which may itself be inadequate and unjust, but they claim that 'the experience of the Centre offers a unique opportunity to analyse the practical effects of the law upon the lives of the underprivileged. . . . Where the law provides a remedy, we should publicise the fact so that others can take advantage of it; where it does not, we should equally publicise the fact so that reforms can be brought about.'[61] The Centre is short of staff and short of money, and each lawyer has a huge caseload. One can understand and sympathise with the difficulty which they must experience in ever being able to find the slack resources to push for the changes in the law which their experience tells them are urgently needed. Bringing quality legal services to the poor is a tremendous advance and gain to those who can make use of a Centre which has a catchment area of some 100,000. Marris and Rein consider that the development of this service 'could perpetuate the dependence of the poor upon their professional advocates'.[62] At any event, services which offer advice and aid to the poor can only fit those individuals into a slightly more comfortable niche within an established order which shows little sympathy to their collective plight. Moreover, they may serve to deflect attention from the causes of social ills, for their considerable success in servicing a large clientele may convince the authorities that information and the granting of rights within the established legal and economic framework constitute *the* solution to the problems of poverty and deprivation.

If community action groups urging demands for change and innova-tion on local authorities do not fold up, I suggest that their survival is maintained as a result of down-scaling their demands, turning to self-help activities, developing a social welfare role or involving themselves in assisting the individual to fit into, and gain rights within, the estab-lished order. Groups which originally sought to challenge established authorities and policies frequently finish up providing services which are welcomed by the authorities because they ease the pressure on them.

Now although these developments represent the usual tendencies, what happens if radical community action *survives and sustains* itself through the period of authoritative siege? How then do the authorities control the challenge?

I suggest that an answer to this lies in the enthusiasm which is now being expressed for co-operation and 'maximum participation'. [63] *'Professionals have sought to preserve their institutional power and autonomy by co-opting their challengers.'* [64] Authorities might claim that their preparedness to co-operate with radical community action groups shows their concern to be responsive and meet social needs. I suggest that this claim cannot be seriously countenanced, as co-operation will be extended *only* to those groups which survive and so pose a challenge and a problem to *government*. [65] In effect, where groups are not suppressed or changed, then the concern is to buy them off, [66] to 'muffle them' [67] and to restrict their independence, and one very effective way of doing this is to extend a measure of participation and involvement. Participation of this kind may even lead to changes in public policy, but the changes are rarely such as to effect a substantive redistribution of resources; they represent instead a symbolic or token response [68] designed to indicate that something is being done about problems without the necessity of needing to move beyond that indication; the gesture reduces dissent and criticism and controls political disturbance. [69]

It is one thing to argue that the absence of political participation and influence by the poor is deplorable, [70] but it is quite another to say that participation is *the* solution to the problem of poverty. In a sense, negotiation and co-operation with the authorities is the end towards which community action must work, for 'to assume that such bodies can be by-passed is blithely optimistic'. [71] However, it is important to be aware that government can control this participation and use it to its own advantage in such a way that there may be only slim gains for those categories of the population supposedly represented through the process of co-operation and participation. Participation channels dissent into a system of established rules and offsets the spontaneous, but disruptive, participation of local protest groups; [72] it enables the authorities to 'monitor' and get detailed information on the people in the areas to be redeveloped; [73] it can force, or educate, the participants to gain an awareness of governmental problems and policies and this will not only inhibit the public from pressing for solutions to their own problems, but will also enable the authorities to legitimise their decisions with the stamp of public approval; and finally it can serve as a vehicle to fit groups of people into the established economic arrangements by involving them in social matters which aid community integration. To some extent, participation can mean 'extra work and inconvenience', [74] and can make 'life more difficult for the officials' [75] but, by and large, 'for the bureaucracy, participation has often served to ensure that its programs will function smoothly and meet with minimal resistance' [76] and so it tends to 'become another vehicle for the extension of bureau-cratic control'.[77]

Theoretically, there are potential advantages for the clients of government if they are able to participate in the formulation of public policies,[78] but in practice the experience of participation has rarely been a vehicle for this sort of involvement. For example, in Newcastle-upon-Tyne, an Advisory Committee consisting of councillors, officials and citizens was set up in 1966 to discuss the plans for the Rye Hill area, but a citizen said of his involvement and effectiveness: 'It's like going home and your wife says, "Would you like bacon and eggs for tea?" and you say, "No, I'd like steak and chips", and you end up with bacon and eggs – she listens to what you have to say, but it's still bacon and eggs.'[79] Even if participants are allowed to do more than react to established proposals, there is still the problem that the 'poor-poor' are unlikely to be involved.[80] Indeed, one might almost say that participation is only likely to be more than the channelling of participant activity to the preordained goals of the higher authorities if the participants are con-fident, articulate and therefore middle class; where this is the case, the hopes of the poor are in the hands of self-appointed advocates who are beyond the recall of those whom they claim to represent.

In America, moves to involve the poor and extend participation have a rather longer history, and their experience suggests that participation has been a failure:[81] 'a sentimental gesture, or another cynical exploita-tion of the poor'.[82] In hard reality, 'elites tend to resist yielding the power to propose solutions to problems to non-elites. And . . . non-elites eventually tire of this stalemate, and citizen participation comes to mean little more than the presence of a few "citizen advisers" attached to a service agency that serves as a buffer between the poor and the affluent society.'[83] It is small wonder that some commentators have argued that 'the *rejection* of the ideology [of citizen participation] may be causing *greater* returns and advantages to the target groups than had they accepted it' but, even so, 'the target group appears to be in a difficult position when the bureaucracy offers them the "citizen participation" ideology. They lose if they participate, and they some-times lose if they don't participate.'[84] Participation is a panacea[85] fostering an illusion that the apathy of the poor is the prime cause of poverty and deprivation; it may be a non-event; and if the poor are at all involved, then their involvement is invariably gained by holding up and building up false expectations and unrealisable aspirations.[86] Apathy and defeatism are rational responses to a situation of powerlessness, and to move out of this stance is to get bruised and further disillusioned.

Conclusion

In pointing to the control of change and the regulation of community action, I do not wish to suggest that community action has had no successes, and neither do I wish to claim that winning reforms will somehow hold back more radical changes. However, it is important to be aware that government has a capacity to resist demands for change and innovation and this has an effect on the development of community action and serves to reduce dissent and disturbance and to channel radical energy towards activities which are more supportive of the state and the established order. Moreover, community action tends to occur in areas that are already on the move and, to the extent that they are successful, they accelerate the process of change in those areas and so squeeze the problems of poverty elsewhere. There are no local solutions[87] to inequality, and a redistribution of resources is not likely to be occasioned until the deprived gain effective power and pose a threat to the established order. That threat may be contained and controlled for a very long while.

References

1 See, for example, Anne Lapping (ed.), *Community Action*, Fabian Tract no. 400, London, Fabian Society, 1970, p. 2.
2 P. Halmos, *The Faith of the Counsellors*, London, Constable, 1965; see also Ray Lees, 'Social work, 1925–50: the case for a reappraisal', *British Journal of Social Work*, 1 (4), 1971, pp. 371–9.
3 R. Silburn, 'The potential and limitations of community action', in D. Bull (ed.), *Family Poverty*, London, Duckworth, 1971, pp. 134–44, see also S. Briar, 'The casework predicament', *Social Work*, 13 (2), 1968, pp. 5–11; R. A. Cloward and I. Epstein, 'Private social welfare's disengagement from the poor: the case of family adjustment agencies', in M. N. Zald (ed.), *Social Welfare Institutions*, New York, Wiley, 1965, pp. 623–44; H. J. Meyer, E. F. Borgatta and W. C. Jones, *Girls at Vocational High: An Experiment in Social Work Intervention*, New York, Russell Sage Foundation, 1965.
4 D. V. Donnison, review of B. Wootton, *Social Science and Social Pathology*, *Almoner*, 12, 1959, p. 172.
5 See, for example, W. Bloomberg and H. Schmadt (eds), *Power, Poverty and Urban Policy*, Beverly Hills, Sage, 1968, vol. 2, p. 252; R. Holman, 'The wrong poverty programme', *New Society*, 20 March 1969, pp. 444–5; G. Brager and H. Specht, 'Mobilising the poor for social action', in R. M. Kramer and H. Specht (eds), *Readings in Community Organisation Practice*, Englewood Cliffs, Prentice-Hall, 1969, pp. 223–32.

6 H. Miller, 'Value dilemmas in social case-work', *Social Work*, 13 (1), 1968, pp. 2–33; Ad Hoc Committee on Advocacy, 'The social worker as advocate: champion of social victims', *Social Work*, 14 (2), 1969, pp. 16–22; J. Morrish, 'The relevance to agency-based workers of community work and social action', *Social Work Today*, 1 (2), May 1970, pp. 22–5; N. Bond, 'The case for radical casework', *Social Work Today*, 2 (9), July 1972, pp. 21–3; M. Mahaffey, 'Lobbying and social work', *Social Work*, 17 (1), 1972, pp. 3–11; D. Thursz, 'Social action as a professional responsibility', *Social Work*, 11 (3), 1966, pp. 12–21; M. Rein, 'Social work in search of a radical profession', *Social Work*, 15 (2), 1970, pp. 13–28.

7 Committee on Public Participation in Planning, *People and Planning* (Skeffington Report), London, HMSO, 1960; Committee on Local Authority and Allied Personal Social Services, *Report* (Seebohm Report), Cmnd 3703, London, HMSO, 1968; Calouste Gulbenkian Foundation, *Community Work and Social Change*, London, Longman, 1968.

8 R. Sunley, 'Family advocacy: from case to cause', *Social Casework*, 51, 1970, pp. 347–57; D. Carter and J. Barter, 'Climbing off the fence', *Social Work Today*, 3 (10), August 1972, pp. 4–6; Ad Hoc Committee on Advocacy, 'The social worker as advocate'.

9 For a definition of community action see R. Holman, *Power for the Powerless*, London, Community and Race Relations Unit, British Council of Churches, 1972.

10 R. Lister, *The Administration of the Wage Stop*, Poverty pamphlet no. 11, London, CPAG, 1972, p. 1.

11 Child Poverty Action Group (CPAG), *Poverty – Facts and Figures*, London, CPAG, 1971, p. 7.

12 A. Keefe, 'Is the customer never right?', *Social Work Today*, 1 (11), February 1971, pp. 23–8; M. Lefton and W. R. Rosengren, 'Organisations and clients: lateral and longitudinal dimensions', *American Sociological Review*, 31, 1966, pp. 802–10; J. G. Davies, *The Evangelistic Bureaucrat*, London, Tavistock, 1972, esp. p. 220; F. P. Piven and R. A. Cloward, *Regulating the Poor*, London, Tavistock, 1972; B. B. Schaffer, *Easiness of Access: A Concept of Queues*, University of Sussex, Institute of Development Studies, Communication no. 104, 1972.

13 See, for example, a report of the way members of the Claimants' Union were handled by officials; *People's News*, 4 (20), 10 July 1972.

14 CPAG, 'A policy to establish the legal rights of low income families', *Poverty*, 1, 1969.

15 See, for example, CPAG, *Newsletter*, 6, spring 1972.

16 H. Rose, *Rights, Participation and Conflict*, Poverty pamphlet no. 5, London, CPAG, 1970.

17 Davies, *The Evangelistic Bureaucrat*, p. 79.

18 Holman, *Power for the Powerless*, p. 9.

19 Social workers are substantially concerned to fit people into the established order. They are carriers of a self-help ideology which aims to find private solutions to public problems. They confirm a person's position of inadequacy and need for help, and thus help to perpetuate an ideology

of inequality. The predominant casework approach serves as a major impediment to the collectivisation of the poor.

20 Charities Act 1960. See also *Report* of the Charity Commissioners for England and Wales for the year 1969, London, HMSO, 1970, esp. pp. 5–7.

21 Report of a joint committee of the NCSS and the National Institute for Social Work Training, *The Voluntary Worker in the Social Services*, London, Bedford Square Press and Allen & Unwin, 1969, p. 92.

22 M. Broady, *Planning for People*, London, Bedford Square Press, 1968, p. 39.

23 Seebohm Report, para. 480.

24 This is especially so in the American context; see R. P. Wolff, 'Beyond tolerance', in R. P. Wolff, B. Moore and H. Marcuse, *A Critique of Pure Tolerance*, Boston, Beacon Press, 1965, pp. 3–52, p. 9. In the British context, see Bob Holman, 'Handsworth adventure playground', in A. Lapping (ed.), *Community Action*, Fabian Society, 1970, pp. 37–40.

25 Piven and Cloward, *Regulating the Poor*, p. 148.

26 E. Graham, 'The politics of poverty', in J. L. Roach and J. K. Roach, *Poverty*, Penguin, 1971, pp. 300–14, p. 304 – original emphasis.

27 W. C. Haggstrom, 'The power of the poor', in F. Reissman, J. Cohen and A. Pearl (eds), *Mental Health of the Poor*, Chicago, Free Press, 1964, pp. 205–23, p. 211.

28 E. P. Thompson, 'At the point of decay', in E. P. Thompson (ed.), *Out of Apathy*, London, Stevens, 1960, pp. 3–15, p. 6.

29 Anne Allen, 'The feel of poverty', *Poverty* (CPAG), 6, spring 1968, pp. 3–5.

30 Brager and Specht, 'Mobilising the poor for social action', p. 227.

31 Haggstrom, 'The power of the poor', p. 211.

32 P. Marris and M. Rein, *Dilemmas of Social Reform*, London, Routledge & Kegan Paul, 1967, p. 185.

33 K. Coates and R. Silburn, *Poverty: The Forgotten Englishman*, Penguin, 1970, p. 56.

34 M. Harrington, *The Other America*, New York, Macmillan, 1962; Oscar Lewis, 'The culture of poverty', *Scientific American*, October 1966, pp. 19–25; R. Blauner, *Alienation and Freedom*, University of Chicago Press, 1964; E. Litt, 'Political cynicism and political futility', *Journal of Politics*, 25, 1963, pp. 312–23; M. Rosenburg, 'Some determinants of political apathy', *Public Opinion Quarterly*, 18, 1954–5, pp. 349–66.

35 Anne Allen, 'The feel of poverty'.

36 Anne Lapping, 'Social action', *New Society*, 2 January 1969, pp. 5–7; see also V. Bottomley, 'Families with low income in London', *Poverty*, no. 8, 1972.

37 C. S. Smith and B. Anderson, 'Political participation through community action', in G. Parry (ed.), *Participation in Politics*, Manchester University Press, 1972, pp. 303–18, pp. 317–18.

38 Brager and Specht, 'Mobilising the poor for social action', p. 231.

39 On this tension see especially R. Mitton and E. Morrison, *A Community Project in Notting Dale*, London, Allen Lane, 1972.

40 For an outline of four modes of intervention see H. Specht, 'Disruptive tactics', *Social Work*, 14 (2), 1969, pp. 5–15.

41 For an illustration of the importance of this in the Royal Borough of Kensington and Chelsea, see J. Dearlove, *The Politics of Policy in Local Government*, Cambridge University Press, 1973, chapter 9.

42 A. J. Bornfiend, 'Political parties and pressure groups', in R. H. Connery and D. Caraley, 'Governing the city: challenges and options for New York', *Proceedings of the Academy of Political Science*, 29 (4), 1969, p. 65; see also D. Hill, *Participating in Local Affairs*, Penguin, 1970; J. Ferris, *Participation in Urban Planning: The Barnsbury Case*, London, Bell, 1972.

43 For a general comment on the failure of this strategy see Bloomberg and Schmadt, *Power, Poverty and Urban Policy*. For specific illustrations of the failure in the British context see Lapping (ed.), *Community Action*, esp. pp. 37, 42, 43.

44 See the work of P. Bachrach and M. S. Baratz, especially 'Decisions and non-decisions: an analytic framework', *American Political Science Review*, 57, 1963, pp. 632–42.

45 D. Ball, 'Council and community', *New Society*, 7 January 1971, pp. 18–19; Hill, *Participating in Local Affairs*, esp. pp. 62, 50; Broady, *Planning for People*, esp. pp. 44–5.

46 See Marris and Rein, *Dilemmas of Social Reform*; K. B. Clark and J. Hopkins, *A Relevant War Against Poverty*, New York, Harper & Row, 1969; T. Smith, 'Protest and democracy', in R. Benewick and T. Smith (eds), *Direct Action and Democratic Politics*, London, Allen & Unwin, 1972, pp. 305–14, esp. p. 312.

47 Radford, in Lapping (ed.), *Community Action*, p. 42.

48 Cited in Ball, 'Council and community'.

49 N. Fruchter and R. Kramer, 'An approach to community organising projects', *Studies on the Left*, 6 (2), 1966, pp. 31–61, p. 36.

50 See Dearlove, *The Politics of Policy in Local Government*, chapter 9.

51 Clark and Hopkins, *A Relevant War Against Poverty*, esp. pp. 241ff.

52 Davies, *The Evangelistic Bureaucrat*, p. 3.

53 M. R. Haug and M. B. Sussman, 'Professional autonomy and the revolt of the client', *Social Problems*, 17 (2), 1969, pp. 153–61.

54 Holman, *Power for the Powerless*; Anne Holmes, 'Urban action', *Time Out*, 116, 5–11 May 1972.

55 Marris and Rein, *Dilemmas of Social Reform*, p. 34.

56 Angell Ward Neighbourhood Council, *October 1971–May 1973*, p. 69.

57 Kensington Housing Trust, *Annual Report*, 1963.

58 Clark and Hopkins, *A Relevant War Against Poverty*, pp. 242–3; see also H. Wolman, 'Organisation theory and community action agencies', *Public Administration Review*, 32, 1972, pp. 33–42.

59 E. Wistrich, *Local Government Reorganisation: The First Years of Camden*, London Borough of Camden, 1972, p. 253.

60 Sunley, 'Family advocacy: from case to cause', p. 349.

61 North Kensington Neighbourhood Law Centre, *Annual Report*, 1972, p. 4.

62 Marris and Rein, *Dilemmas of Social Reform*, p. 188.

63 Seebohm Report, para. 491; see also Skeffington Report.

64 Haug and Sussman, 'Professional autonomy and the revolt of the client', p. 2.

65 For an important development of this theme in the context of relief-giving in the USA, see Piven and Cloward, *Regulating the Poor*, esp. p. 69.

66 T. J. Lowi, *The Politics of Disorder*, New York, Basic Books, 1971, esp. p. 59; Piven and Cloward, *Regulating the Poor*, esp. p. 68.

67 Lapping, *Community Action*, p. 2.

68 M. Edelman, *The Symbolic Uses of Politics*, Urbana, University of Illinois Press, 1964.

69 J. Maniha and C. Perrow, 'The reluctant organisation and the aggressive environment', *Administrative Science Quarterly*, 10, 1965–6, pp. 238–57; P. Selznick, *The Organisational Weapon*, New York, McGraw-Hill, 1952.

70 For examples of the absence of their participation, see D. M. Muchnick, *Urban Renewal in Liverpool*, London, Bell, 1970; Davies, *The Evangelistic Bureaucrat*; N. Dennis, *People and Planning*, London, Faber & Faber, 1970.

71 Silburn, 'The potential and limitations of community action', p. 143.

72 R. A. Cloward and F. P. Piven, 'The professional bureaucracies: benefit systems as influence systems', in Kramer and Specht (eds), *Readings in Community Organisation Practice*, pp. 367–8.

73 Dennis, *People and Planning*.

74 Davies, *The Evangelistic Bureaucrat*, p. 164.

75 C. Duke, *Colour and Rehousing: A Study of Redevelopment in Leeds*, London, Institute of Race Relations, 1970, p. 76.

76 L. B. Rubin, 'Maximum feasible participation: the origins, implications, and present status', *Annals of the American Academy of Political and Social Science*, 1969, pp. 14–29, p. 29.

77 Cloward and Piven, 'The professional bureaucracies: benefit systems as influence systems', p. 359; see also Lowi, *The Politics of Disorder*, pp. 65ff.

78 Deputation to Sir Keith Joseph, 'Involving the client in policy-making', *Social Work Today*, 2 (3), 6 May 1971, pp. 22–3.

79 Davies, *The Evangelistic Bureaucrat*, p. 162.

80 S. J. Brody, 'Maximum participation of the poor: another holy grail?', *Social Work*, 15 (1), 1970, pp. 68–75; Ben Whitaker, *Participation and Poverty*, Fabian Research Series, no. 272, London, Fabian Society, 1968.

81 Although for a more optimistic view, see S. Kravitz and F. K. Kolodner, 'Community action: where has it been? where will it go?', *Annals of the American Academy of Political and Social Science*, 1969, pp. 30–40.

82 Clark and Hopkins, *A Relevant War Against Poverty*, p. 248.

83 J. van Til and S. B. van Til, 'Citizen participation in social policy: the end of the cycle?', *Social Problems*, 17 (3), 1970, pp. 313–23, p. 321.

84 E. A. Krause, 'Functions of a bureaucratic ideology: "citizen participation"', *Social Problems*, 16, 1968–9, pp. 129–43 (p. 140) (my emphasis).

85 Brody, 'Maximum participation of the poor: another holy grail?'.

86 S. Aronowitz, 'Poverty, politics and community organisation', *Studies on the Left*, 4 (3), 1964, pp. 102–5; Whitaker, *Participation and Poverty*; Fruchter and Kramer, 'An approach to community organising projects'.

87 R. Aronson, 'The movement and its critics', *Studies on the Left*, 6 (1), 1966, pp. 3–19; Silburn, 'The potential and limitations of community action'; Marris and Rein, *Dilemmas of Social Reform*.

3 Adult education and social action

Bob Ashcroft and Keith Jackson

Introduction

Working-class adult education, community development, and the relationship of theory and research to both, are lush pastures for ambivalence, uncertainty and contradiction. Muddling through, getting things done, however confusedly, are elevated to the state of major operation principles; the development of substantive theoretical frameworks, incorporating explicit value systems and strategies, is denigrated as a time-wasting luxury. Such a view is common among community development entrepreneurs and professionals and by the more naive among non-professional political activists. The opposite position is argued here: that not only does theory not hinder practice; it informs practice and makes success more likely. Indeed the very notion of 'success' (or failure) in social action only has meaning if it is related to a theoretical perspective of intention. Too much of the descriptive work on community development, and experimental education, is merely a post-hoc eulogy of whatever happened to happen.

It is true that much academic research and theory has not proved helpful to those engaged in social action. A great deal of social scientific methodology is useless if not positively harmful. But then again perfectly sound babies are regularly thrown out with the bath-water, and the arid quality of much contemporary Anglo-American social science and political theory hardly warrants a retreat into irrationality. It must be added that the need for a theory is not the same as a demand for dogmatic rigidity. The need for sensitive creativity in both thought and action is paramount, and some hypotheses are bound to be abandoned as inadequate explanations of reality, and therefore as inadequate bases for social action. However, it is still necessary to be aware that this is what one is doing. Imaginative adaptation is one thing, 'ad hoc doing' is quite another.

This article is an attempt to sketch a theory of social action in adult education in a working-class inner-ring area of Liverpool; to indicate how relevant (or irrelevant) the theory has been as a guide to action by looking closely at some practical applications; and finally to indicate some likely future developments. It is worth mentioning that although this programme is set in the Liverpool University Institute of Extension Studies, there is no intention of perceiving it as part of the normal provision of a University extra-mural department. The greater flexibility which is reflected by the department's recent change of name (from Department of Adult Education and Extra-mural Studies) and the explicitly experimental nature of the Home Office Community Development Project have led us to take seriously the idea of action research and experiment in the field of adult education. This requires letting theory determine practice to a much greater degree than would be allowed by accepting institutional norms as they apply to regular provision. We would argue strongly that such an approach is incumbent on anyone talking seriously about research and experiment in any field.

Community Action and Poverty

The very existence of this collection of essays is testimony to the growing importance attached to the concept of 'community' and its relevance for social action. Additionally, our own work is closely associated with, and partly financed by, the Home Office Community Development Project. It is therefore necessary to analyse the implications of the use of the notion 'community' for social action in general and adult education in particular. Before doing this it is necessary to consider an attendant notion in community development projects, that of poverty.

'Community development' in the Home Office projects is concerned to resolve problems of poverty and the correlative failure to take advantage of social services which could alleviate the consequences of low income and other forms of social stress. If this definition were accepted, the problem would be to develop strategies for assisting the poor to break out of the poverty cycle; or alternatively to assist professional workers in being more efficient helpers than they have been in the past because of attitudinal rigidity, or organisational malfunctioning in social-service delivery. What is important in this perspective is the primacy which is given to the existence of poverty. It is not difficult to see why the theories which are most seductive to those who wish to explain the continuing manifestations of squalor in an otherwise affluent society, are those which either explain the poor in terms of their own sub-cultural disabilities or the concomitant failure of the social service professionals to understand these disabilities. Why is this so?

First, although these theories necessarily contain an explicit commitment to 'positive discrimination', they raise no problems about the fundamental question of the way in which resources and access to power are distributed in advanced industrial societies. Indeed it is now part of the conventional wisdom to question the mere re-allocation of resources to the poor. (The poor are often delineated metaphorically as a 'bottomless pit' into which one can continuously shovel resources with no apparent effect. But empirical evidence for the 'bottomless pit' hypothesis has hardly been overwhelming.)

Second, to see poverty itself as the primary problem and to seek solutions, however marginal, allow one to escape charges either of 'actionless thought' or more extreme charges of politically motivated callousness towards the suffering of the needy in order to promote disaffection from the regime.[1] But there is also nothing new about marginal intervention to alleviate poverty; and even if CDPS can claim special insights, expertise, and a jargon with which to deal with deprived neighbourhoods, what they are doing in substance is little different from that of a long line of political reformers and social workers. Arguably, the central question for those engaged in community action is no longer 'what sorts of positive discrimination may assist in resolving the relatively intractable problem of poverty?' but is now in fact 'what is it about our kind of society which makes any realistic move towards positive discrimination impossible?'[2]

For the reasons given above it is necessary to argue that poverty is a function of a central web of socio-economic relationships and that its abolition depends upon changing these relationships. The poor in any society are those who suffer most extremely from a system of exploitation of many by a few. The position of the poor worker, like everybody else in our society, is determined by his position in the market. Quantitatively it is indisputable that the affluent section of the working class have more control over resources than the poor, but qualitatively their respective positions are the same, they are both controlled by market forces in a way in which those who control the market are not.[3] In short, the problems confronted by the poor are only soluble in a wider political context which resolves the problems confronted by the working class as a whole.

This immediately, and problematically, raises the issue of the relevance of the concept of community as a guide to political action.

In some contexts the use of 'community' is simply a useful catch-all way of analysing those aspects of the lives of people living in areas with a wide range of social problems other than those which they confront when at work: as *residents* they are concerned with education, housing, vandalism, etc., but not wages and conditions. The utility of resident action is not disputed; on the contrary it could, with much sense, be argued that the working class have defined access to resources too narrowly and have concentrated over much on achieving better wages and conditions in the work-place, while virtually ignoring the extent to which they are exploited as consumers of social welfare (broadly defined to include education, housing, recreation, etc.). However, the wheel has now come full circle. The notion of community has taken on a positive significance.[4] When community workers and activists grope uncertainly after 'community control' of social welfare, what might this mean in operational terms? To be absolutely specific, what would happen if the Vauxhall (CDP) area of Liverpool was given its share of the local authority and central budget for the residents to handle democratically in their own areas? The consequences, it is suspected, would not be nearly as exciting as the proponents of 'community control' would wish to argue. First, this would be so because limited and negatively discriminatory budgets remain just as limited whoever controls them. Second, if the work situation of the residents, much the most significant determinant of their life-chances, were omitted from the formula of control, it would be rather like controlling the fleas in a circus and allowing the elephants to roam free. For both these reasons it is argued that 'community control' would simply lead residents to realise that their problems had their origin in society and not in their local community. If that is the aim it should not be questioned, but as an end in itself it is not at all satisfactory.

Educational relevance and neighbourhood

Considering education in the light of the above remarks raises problems about the type of strategies which could be relevant in the lives of the exploited. In Educational Priority Areas, for example, it is argued that education in working-class neighbourhoods must be made more 'relevant' to the lives of the people who live there. Much of the traditional curricula of the state system is condemned as having little meaning for those living in EPAs. Curricula and styles of presentation in teaching should be determined by the locality in which people live.

Dr Midwinter has advocated 'a close and unremitting investigation of their own environment in all its aspects' for EPA children. For the moment let us consider the three crucial concepts of 'relevance', 'investigation' and 'environment'.

'Relevance' has been explicitly equated with familiarity and immediate instrumental value, and certainly unfamiliarity with objects and concepts discussed in conventional learning situations has created obstacles for those wishing to learn. But it hardly follows from this that one should take for granted 'the familiar' and use it as a datum for an educational philosophy. The argument could in fact be reversed. It could be argued that working-class children ought to be taken right outside their neighbourhood through the application of positive discrimination so that the unfamiliar, and therefore irrelevant, become both familiar and relevant. Any satisfactory interpretation of education requires the combination of challenge to experience as well as confirmation. It is a truism that everyone lives somewhere, and that local problems and situations are the first to impinge on the consciousness of a resident, but we should distinguish between what is peculiar to an area and what is true of many areas in general, because of their place in the economy, and the housing and social service market. For reasons already given the educationist must make available tools of analysis not obviously arising from immediate perceptions of local reality. Pure economic analysis and political theory are relevant to the 'key issues' which local advocates of change must identify.[5] Extending beyond political and economic theory, the best in existing culture, not merely local culture, must be available to those who want to break out of their culturally constrained and exploited position 'deprived of the means of translating what they know into thoughts that they can think'.[6]

'Investigation' raises even more problems. In fact it is the critical concept in pedagogy. A bunch of bananas can be investigated arithmetically, artistically, geometrically, topologically, geographically, historically and in many other ways; so can the immediate environment of children. More important, the latter can be investigated quietistically or critically. Critical investigation could range from a Marxist approach to a petit-bourgeois advocacy of thrift, to escape from the realities of inner-city Liverpool when looking at drinking and gambling!

Finally, what is called the 'environment' is essentially determined by the meaning which one has given to the words 'relevance' and 'investigation'. If the neighbourhood or the community is seen as a small geographical area surrounding the school then investigating it will do nobody much good. If the neighbourhood is seen as a consequence of a total social system, then it is difficult to discuss it without questioning the validity of the distribution of power, status and income within that system. In short, much of community education philosophy could reinforce the constraints on awareness and personal development which leads to some areas being designated EPA in the first instance – an educational form of Catch 22. Indeed this does appear to be the case, since while it is argued in the EPAs that children educated in this way would grow up with an attitude of 'constructive discontent' and that this would in turn lead to social change, the common definition of social change can hardly be considered radical, as when Dr Midwinter claims that: 'For valid reasons, society insists on a differential system of status, income and circumstances which critically affects educational performance.'[7]

A strategy for working-class adult education

To make explicit what has so far only been implicit in analysing the negative consequences of community education strategies, the alternative strategy being advocated here is one of interpreting the needs of people living in a central Liverpool area as arising not from their living in a poor community, or even from their being poor people in a 'warm and living community', but as arising from their membership of the working class. Class is in turn an effect of the worker's relationship to the ownership and control of the means of production in our society; it is not, it must be emphasised, a product of kinship ties or affective community relationships. In a 'welfare state' society the 'notion of class must be widened not only to focus on property and the market, but to include control of and access to public services'.[8] For the study of housing policy, the notion of housing classes has proved useful,[9] and recent studies of tenants' associations have shown that they can realistically be considered to reflect forms of 'consumer proletarianism' and concomitant exploitation of the worker as resident.[10] For educationists working alongside working-class adults a class analysis allows them, in terms both of intervention and of action: (a) to see the problems of inequality and resource allocation not as an oversight of well-meaning officials and politicians, but the *raison d'être* and the dynamic of the economic system; and (b) to relate education to social action in such a way that the social and cultural values which education might embody aim to help workers increase their consciousness of their class position and its consequences.

Ccw

Resources and relevance

A class perspective, while being inherently pessimistic about significant re-allocation taking place without fundamental social change, at least allows one honestly to recognise the allocation of resources as being a major problem. In educational terms, for example, a recent study by Byrne and Williamson[11] emphasises lack of resources in working-class areas as the principal variable in educational 'failure', rather than the more fashionable, and arguably escapist, linguistic and cultural factors. Residents in central Liverpool suffer from a cumulative lack of resources over their whole lives, and this fact should guide central features of an educational strategy and also the interpretation of success and failure of such strategies. The interpretation of the adult education programme attached to EPA in Liverpool is couched entirely in cultural terms. How does one communicate with the working class? How can they be enabled to communicate with each other? The fact that activities within the programme were attended *free* within an adult education system that is otherwise universally based on fee-paying for courses is given no mention. It could be that the most important feature of that experiment was this piece of specific positive discrimination and yet it was ignored because of the initial theoretical perspective.

Theoretically, at least, it may be possible to do a cost-benefit analysis of adults from different social classes and their correlative willingness or unwillingness to attend conventional education courses after school-leaving age. 'Cost' could be extended to include factors other than the payment of fees (although in the case of the low-paid and the unemployed this alone may be decisive). First, few classes are held in working-class areas, and high transport costs may be important.[12] Second, attending educational classes demands the use of scarce physical and mental energy. The worker who has spent a day on an assembly-line or building site is unlikely to want to spend his residual energy in a class unless the benefits are considerable. Third, workers work longer hours and more days per annum than do the middle class, consequently the time available to the worker for any leisure pursuit is more limited. Fourth, workers are much more likely than others to work shift-systems, and continuous attendance on any course is difficult if not impossible. For women there are additional factors associated with large families, etc.[13] A quantitative analysis of these factors, without introducing any cultural variables at all, may indicate that a realistic policy of positive discrimination in conventional continuing education would involve paying[14] a substantial number of working-class men and women to attend classes if the marginal cost of attending such classes were to equal the marginal utility derived from them. At the least, positive discrimination should be genuine. In a project such as ours in Vauxhall educational services must be made available to adults at zero cost[15] and should be available in the area itself.

The whole resource question raises the issue of relevance in a completely different light. It is both a key issue for the area, and a highly relevant one for study in an educational programme. 'Locally relevant education' should be about the availability of resources in the neighbourhood. Residents are entitled to know what are the relative per capita expenditures by public authorities among different areas of the city, and the country at large, along with the resources available through the market system in wages, salaries, and profits. Unfortunately much of this information is not readily available. Community Development workers, like educational theorists, tend to see the real issue as being a cultural or an organisational issue. Doubtless research will proliferate on attitudes and attitudinal change in the local authority, as will research on organisational reform to deliver 'the goods' more effectively. One suspects that at the termination of most CDPs exactly how many 'goods' are available to distribute in the inner-ring (in contrast to the middle-class suburbs) will still be unknown, and will still be the same. Adult education should enable local people to see this situation and its implications quite clearly.

Social action and education

We have already indicated that working-class adult education must be directly related to social action, action which aims to tackle the problems which arise from their social position. One way of interpreting this in terms of educational theory is to recognise that learning requires more than receiving information and ideas. 'Learning by doing' is in many ways a valid educational principle. We shall argue shortly that a more important way of interpreting the relationship between action and education is to recognise the elements of working-class culture with which education must be imbued. To tackle action implies an increase in the awareness that people have of their position; this is just as important as the greater completeness in learning skills and applying knowledge which comes from practice and application. But what sort of action should we have in mind?

While it is not contested that working-class adult education should be associated with action, there are two reasons for being sceptical about interpreting action-orientated education in terms of highly localised concerns. First, as has been argued at length in this paper, local issues are essentially manifestations of societal problems, and action leading to social change will emerge from an awareness that this is so. An almost precise analogy can be drawn with conflict in industry; the economism characteristic of British trade unionism has by and large resulted in some sections of the working class benefiting, in terms of improved wages and conditions, at the expense of other sections of the working class. Economism has not resulted in a significant re-allocation of income, status and power in favour of workers as a group and against the interests of the owners and controllers of the means of production. Similarly, highly localised community action which is not related to a much broader class movement is more likely to benefit active working-class areas at the expense of the apathetic working class, and not at the expense of existing elites. This, of course, does not mean that local groups should be any less militant in pursuit of power and resources; it does mean, however, that the way in which local activists pursue these goals will be quite different. Alliances among community groups, at city and hopefully at national level, will be made central to strategy and not be seen either as peripheral icing on the cake or as irrelevant. Parochial militancy has unanticipated consequences for other people. Certainly militant groups can prevent motorways being driven through *their*, area but other areas then bear the costs. The motorway is still built somewhere.[16]

The second reason for scepticism about the notion of education for localised political action is a quite conventional belief that workers, like everybody else, define education much more broadly than as being an 'unremitting investigation of their own environment', and they are right to do so. There is no necessary connection between being middle class and enjoying Elizabethan drama, classical music, foreign languages or mathematics. In fact the processes of the British educational system have made traditionally important disciplines relevant for the majority of students only for the purpose of acquiring dubiously valuable job tickets. Arguably the worker, if he wishes to study a traditional discipline, is less likely to conform to the alienated norm; he is more likely to see subjects as being valuable for their own sake. Not of course that most academic subjects are merely of intrinsic value (and here the circle can be squared): people can be politicised just as easily, and radically, by reading Sartre's *Roads to Freedom*, looking at Picasso's

'Guernica', seeing Brecht's *Days of the Commune*[17] as they can by looking carefully at local traffic routes, super-markets and slum housing, or even reading Marx's *Capital*. The relationship between learning and social action is far more complex than most contemporary educational theorists, even on the political left, are willing to concede.

Culture and education

This line of argument leads straight to heresy. We have already questioned the fashionable concern with curricula and cultural disadvantage, and have argued instead that a substantial part of the answer to poor school performance lies in providing adequate resources for working-class children. Let us now go further. Conventional educational wisdom invites one to ask the question, 'Why don't children want to learn traditional disciplines (the three R's, etc.)?' Let us instead ask, 'What is it that prevents children who do want to learn the traditional disciplines from learning them?' (It is important to bear in mind that poor educational attainment alone would make either question legitimate.) In Britain, the argument that it is not the curricula which are irrelevant to working-class children but, on the contrary, that it is the school which is irrelevant to the proper teaching of reading, writing, numeracy, etc., has hardly been explored[18] in theoretical or practical terms, as it affects the working class!

There is more evidence that in our society this is the major failure within the educational system, certainly for workers and their children who have ability, than that the form and content of curricula are irrelevant. Incongruences between the values and the interests expressed in education and those of the class into which they were born cause strain and inconsistencies for working-class students. The most interesting evidence in this context has focused on the problem as it applies to successful working-class children and students. There is clear evidence of disjunctions and incongruences between value-systems as workers' children are encouraged to reject the values of the working class for those of the middle class. This applies to working-class students at grammar school,[19] but also in higher education, where it has been concluded in one study by Marris that the indifference to political issues characteristically displayed by working-class students 'helps to exclude the social differences that elsewhere constrain relationships, and releases intellectual enquiry from a concern with immediate limitations on its practicality.'[20] For those who do not succeed or, in conventional terms cannot succeed, these ambivalences and incongruences, it may be argued, are even less worth trying to resolve. 'Education is not for us.' It is not relevant in a much more fundamental sense than is normally implied by progressive educationists concerned with subcultural differences. An ability to cut this Gordian knot characterises the most successful workers' education elsewhere, as, for example, in the literacy programme of Paulo Freire in South America. For conventional educational success the worker must disguise or desist from his efforts to become aware and conscious of class values and interests, and must mute and tone down his endeavours to promote them. As Paulo Freire argues for the third world, education is one means of trying to socialise the 'dominated classes' into reproducing the 'dominators' style of life . . . because the dominators live "within the dominated".'[21]

For the opposite to be the case, education must be relevant not merely to the immediate experience of workers living in central Liverpool but to their future well-being and development; not merely to them as individuals (which may be sufficient for some to 'climb out of their position') but to the class of which they are members.

Educational success, that is learning new skills and breaking out of local and social constraints on intellectual and social awareness, need not imply a rejection of those in the same class position. On the contrary, it is more likely to result from a commitment to promote and extend the values and interests of the class as a whole. This is not self-evident, but it is a central proposition of our strategy.

It is proposed, therefore, that an adult education strategy for a working-class area should include the elements which will enable workers to become conscious of their social position, and to determine for themselves the shape and form which education should take accordingly. The situations which this could help to clarify are manifold but closely interrelated. Differences between what a student becomes and what he has been do not involve guilty or morbid rejection of the past or of those who have not learned new ideas and gained new perspectives. Success need not be climbing out of the condition of his peers but part of a process of changing that condition. Solidarity and fraternity are positive values within this framework which should infuse relations between all those engaged in the various activities chosen by those who wish to learn. What is more, values of this kind seem far more helpful in establishing satisfactory relations between teachers or educational organisers and 'students' than any of those associated with social or community work. The uncertain ethics of the helping profession, and so-called non-directiveness, can be replaced by something far firmer and more dignified for all concerned. If we can break away from the conventional mode of educational success educationists are not in central Liverpool to *rescue* workers, or merely to *help* them, but to establish a position of *solidarity* with them. The difference between 'them' and 'us' is not broken down by 'learning to speak the language of the natives' but by becoming one of 'us', not in romantic terms, but on issues that really matter.

This is of course no more than a programme, a means of determining and interpreting possible lines of action. Success or failure will be as difficult to measure as in any other programme. Recent events illustrate at least some possibilities in terms of political action and political education.

The strategy applied

During the late summer of 1972 a 'key issue' did arise in central Liverpool and it is therefore useful to illustrate how the general strategy outlined above might guide specific activities. The future standard of life, and relations with the housing market of people in the area, were directly and crucially affected by the Housing Finance Act. A community development strategy seemed to define this as irrelevant, external and 'political'. Our educational strategy indicated that it was a highly relevant issue in dealing with which local residents were entitled to educational resources.

A proposed day conference

We began, in conventional adult education terms, to consider the possibility of holding a day conference on the Act. This would be a means of 'making educational resources available to residents' groups'. The usual form would be to invite a speaker or speakers to give a neutral account of the Act. Such speakers might include an academic, whose field was contemporary politics or social administration. The conventions would also allow, however, a statement from official (e.g. local authority) and non-official (e.g. Child Poverty Action Group) sources giving the pros and cons of the 'neutral' area of the Act, that is, the question of benefits and rebates, and the effect on local people now that the Act was passed. Just possible would also be a debate on the Act in political terms with speakers in favour and against. For all these areas to be covered effectively a great deal of talk would be necessary and a compromise would almost certainly be required to fit the time available. However, it was soon apparent that decisions about the nature of such an educational programme were not required. This led directly from our original theoretical position which argued that we should set up the programme on the lines local people required. Consequently a meeting was called for all residents interested in knowing about the Act to discuss the possibility of a 'day conference'.

It was immediately apparent at the meeting that local residents were puzzled, almost angrily so, by the proposal. There was even some concern that the means of consultation had been to call a meeting about a meeting when there were numerous less time-consuming ways, within the whole network of contacts already evolved by the more general community action programme in the area, of discussing and debating an appropriate way of dealing with the issue. There was certainly reason to ask why this had not been done, within a project concerned with the needs of the area, when the Act and its consequences had been discussed nationally for a very long time.

More substantively, the residents rejected the traditional approach which was put to them for discussion. Their reasons were partly associated with the immediacy of the problem. Rent increases were due in three weeks' time. If any action was to take place, it would have to be formulated very quickly (again, this might be considered an implicit if not deliberate criticism of all of us who had been engaged on the community project). Much more generally, they were confused by the idea of a day conference. They wanted a 'mass meeting' called to consider action, not just the Act itself, and they did not see the need for politicians and local authority officials to help them understand it. If the 'facts' (about rebates, etc.) were facts, then an informed speaker was sufficient. In a sense they were not asking for the passive neutrality we had conventionally considered, they were asking for an informed critique. We decided that this was a greater challenge to our position as educationists than inviting speakers. A member of the team would 'teach' in this context, turning, in another, equally conventional, academic tradition, to the original text of the Act and the debate around it, aiming to produce a full and reasoned statement about its purpose, nature and content, and being in a position to answer questions or direct people to the answer in any situation that might arise out of the original discussion.

The meeting was called as 'a public discussion on the "Fair Rents Act" ', indicating that any action which might take place would also be discussed. It may be worth recording that no mention was made in the leaflet of either of the two educational institutions concerned with this exercise, one of whom actually produced the leaflet. This was quite deliberate. We are not a political organisation. Furthermore in relation to this experiment we are not trying to extend formal university extra-mural provision. The theoretical framework we have adopted requires a definite rejection of 'educational imperialism' in favour of an attempt to create working-class control of the operation. We should prefer to be considered as educational advisers and consultants and for people locally not to feel obliged to adopt our institutional forms.

Approximately 250 people attended. They listened to a detailed paper which took between 40 minutes and one hour to present, and the following discussion before action was finally considered took a further 20 minutes or so. During this period there were sections of what was a large gathering in a rather poor meeting-place which occasionally broke into rather disruptive chatter, usually an outcry over immediate and personal implications of the Act. But in general there was remarkable order and attentiveness. It was interesting to see this result when making no concessions to a 'popular' approach in presenting the material. To our knowledge there has certainly not been such a sub-stantial account of the legislation in any popular newspaper or on tele-vision. One reason for the mixture of genuine concentration and patience was undoubtedly that the Act was presented in social class terms. The local residents were explicitly accepted as working class and the basic critique was from a working-class standpoint.

The discussion paper

The nature of this critique needs to be explained further to illustrate how, although presented to a mass meeting, we would claim that its style was pedagogic not demagogic, in contrast to the presentations of most politicians of both major parties addressing meetings at this time. It carefully set the Act in its overall political context, indicated its likely effects in the housing economy, illustrated the basic principles of its rebate system, and laid out some details of the actual rebates available.

In talking of the aims of the Act, the paper stated:

> You may have heard the term 'property-owning democracy' being used by members of the Conservative Government. In general the Act is seen by this Government as the first step to achieving this. A property-owning democracy means a society where as many people as possible own their own house or flat.

At the moment all council tenants are subsidised out of taxation and the rates, so that your rents are lower than they would be if you paid an economic rent. The Government feels that by making those who can afford it pay a 'fair' rent, that is a rent without subsidies, then more people will be encouraged to buy their own home. This in turn will free council property for those who really need it, that is the poor and the homeless.

It was then pointed out that there had been no unfair advantage held by council tenants over those buying their houses, because tax relief on mortgage payments produced broadly the same effects for the house-buyer as direct subsidies. But

the new Act discriminates against tenants of private and council property. The owner-occupier is still subsidised. It should also be remembered that, on the whole, council tenants are much less well off than people buying their own houses. Those who are particularly badly off will certainly be subsidised, but mainly out of rents and rates not general taxation.

In other words, the relatively well off council tenant would subsidise the relatively poor council tenant, and indirectly, of course, the owner-occupier generally whose tax relief would not be removed.

The analysis of the Act's effects on council tenants as a class was sharpened: 'Remember that the purpose of the Act is to reduce council tenants' subsidies by about £30,000,000 a year. In other words, council tenants *as a whole* will be about £30 million a year *worse* off than now.' Further, the Act might divide tenants among themselves not only by producing disparities between rents but also by tending to discriminate over a period between the better off and the worse off through housing allocation intended to balance the housing account. The poorer tenants would find themselves in 'sub-standard accommodation where rents and therefore rebates will be low'.

A full description was provided of the actual mechanics of fixing 'fair rents' and the subsidies which could be claimed, including specimen calculations of the latter. Calculations indicating how such subsidies also reduce the benefits of wage increases by decreasing an income rise were also presented. Furthermore, 'Although we've talked a lot about rebates, these will only matter if they are claimed. All the evidence from other means-tested benefits suggests that they will not be. Take-up of Family Income Supplement to subsidise the low paid worker has been less than ⅓ of those entitled to it. More than a million pensioners do not claim supplementary benefit to which they are entitled.'

In conclusion, the paper returned to the Act's basic consequences for the housing market and the position of social classes in relation to that market, taking into account the way in which, without further demand being engineered, prices were rising exorbitantly already. 'The Act is broadly speaking an attack on the living standards of council tenants. Only the poorest will benefit directly, at the expense of the poor. Indirectly, however, the greatest beneficiaries under the Act will be "the wealthy, those who own property and land".' Indeed, the paper made quite clear its sympathy with a working-class response to the Act, but if that response was to be militant it should not be mindlessly militant. There was no attempt to distort the intentions of those politicians who promoted the Act; on the contrary their position was presented in their own terms. The question posed was: what were the consequences of a society based on the values of a 'property-owning democracy' for workers living in central Liverpool?

The paper ran to five foolscap sides and duplicated versions were available to be taken away from the meeting to read at home or discuss in smaller groups. A telephone number was offered at the end for anyone who wished to pursue questions raised. Fifteen took advantage of the offer. Some asked about rebates, others about rent increases, most wanted speakers to present the paper to other meetings. Finally, seven residents' groups in the area were addressed on the Housing Finance Act in this manner. We estimated that the total number of people attending meetings was about 700 in an area where the adult population is approximately 6,000. An earlier survey had indicated that less than 1 per cent of adults had attended a non-vocational educational class before.

Were these meetings classes? We shall return again to the question of how far the mass meetings were educational, but they were certainly far more deliberately structured as such than much of what is presented as 'educative' on the mass media, and indeed in much 'progressive' education. Certainly, although we should not wish to take this evidence too far, one member of the editorial board of the neighbourhood newspaper, the *Scottie Press*, which printed the following Talking Point, has no doubt that here was an educational exercise.

A team of men from the Education section of the Vauxhall Project staged what amounted to a teach-in on the new Housing Bill. As factually and as impartially as possible Bob Ashcroft and Dave Godman went through the Bill and explained its more relevant clauses to an audience of over two hundred people.

Many people in the Vauxhall Area now have a clearer understanding of the Housing Bill and are free to make up their own minds on the basis of their own interpretation of this Bill.

Is this a breakthrough? I think it is. For the first time, education has come to the adult working classs in an informal setting and in a way that is relevant to their lives. As a frequenter of formal education classes – which I am not knocking – one could not fail to be aware that most working class people are just not interested. These classes are seen as an extension of their school lives and have little relevance to life as it is lived in the Scotland Road Area.

Residents' action

'Critical consciousness is brought about not through an intellectual effort but (through praxis) – through the authentic union of action and reflection.'[22] We have seen that the residents were as conscious as Paulo Freire of the necessary link between action and reflection. We had made sure that our educational intervention had not incorporated a decision to act 'imposed' on local people. However, when they decided to form a Rent Action Committee we felt it entirely appropriate to accept the invitation to act as technical advisers on the legal implications of rent strikes and on matters of organisation.

Perhaps the clearest example of the overlap between education and action was provided by a small neighbourhood within the area. Here 150 people attended the Housing Finance Act meeting and there resulted one of the more powerful tenants' associations in the area where previously the residents' group had been almost defunct. Here too a member of the team has become organisational adviser.

Continuing educational consequences

Mass meetings alone are not enough. So far as the dissemination of detailed knowledge about rebates under the Housing Finance Act is concerned, large meetings are most inappropriate occasions. The treatment of particular cases is essential. In the Vauxhall area there is a locally staffed neighbourhood Information Centre for housing and welfare advice operating from a former public house, initiated, recruited and supported from an early stage of the Home Office Community Development project. Its staff asked the member of the team responsible for the Rent Act paper to give advice on the means of calculating rebates.

Thus, although the stance taken on the Act had been that of a general critique, it was possible to spend four substantial sessions with those local residents who would be called upon to make the Act work for families wishing to claim rebates. The aim was to make these sessions as rigorous and detailed as possible so that any advice to claimants given by the locally resident staff would match that which could be received from official sources.

Nor was this the only direction in which more rigorous and systematic study arose from the 'Fair Rent Act' meetings. While the first example is relatively common in community projects, the second was more directly the outcome of the educational strategy outlined here. The mass meetings, the paper and various discussions surrounding both generated an interest in the structured investigation of social problems. A group has therefore become an organised class in social theory and social problems. With a regular attendance of ten, this class is the hard core of a rather larger group which will also be provided with regular opportunities for study. The level at which the material is presented has been set deliberately high. Some members of the group want to take GCE 'A' levels, others to discuss issues on the basis of reading and writing. No one wants loose informal discussions. This has made it possible to put the informal pub discussion element of 'experimental' working-class education in its rightful place, despite the tendency for the Press to highlight it as exotic. Certainly this class promotes pub discussion at great length, on the basis of previous careful analysis, and usually stimulated by members of the class rather than the tutor himself. But nobody has any doubts as to where the central educational contribution is being made, that is in a more structured context than chatty discussion over a pint.

General interpretations

There were some substantial failures in this operation. The Rent Act should have been tackled earlier, although it is possible that feeling would not have been so high before rent increases were actually imminent. The educational team has not been large enough or sufficiently well organised during the intensive demands of the period in question to capitalise fully on the general interest in education which has arisen. However, in some ways the operation was successful and the basic theoretical position does seem to have increased the likelihood that it would be so. Furthermore an interpretation of the events for future use becomes clearer in the light of that theory.

Most community development, including that which makes use of educational resources, becomes the prisoner of its own strategy of working with small groups. The classical tendency of social and political movements described by Michel's 'iron law of oligarchy' is accelerated and reinforced by systematic effort. Control of information and ideas in the hands of a few is actually promoted rather than being allowed to happen on its own. Mass meetings, treated not as crowds to be manipulated, but addressed on the same terms as any so-called elite group, provide a continual opportunity to widen the scope of knowledge, understanding and awareness. Availability of written material for all emphasises this and enables the circle to be widened further, still at a level far beyond manipulative and stereotyped slogans. Greater use of a local Press alongside this framework would have added to its effectiveness (perhaps, but not certainly, other media may have been relevant too).

Mass meetings are part of the central working-class tradition and culture. As Raymond Williams has succinctly expressed it: 'We may now see what is properly meant by "working-class culture". It is not proletarian art, or council houses, or a particular use of language, it is rather, the basic collective idea, and the institutions, manners, habits of thought, and intentions which proceed from this.'[23] Mass meetings enable an educational exercise to be conducted in a context which emphasises solidarity and social consciousness. We must continually seek other similar opportunities. On the other hand, it would seem that such meetings do not reduce the enthusiasm of those who wish to make a detailed study which goes beyond the immediate need for action, enabling further reflection and analysis on which future action might be based. Apparently such enthusiasm is not diminished, either, by a 'curriculum' which goes beyond the locality in its scope. The creation of dissatisfaction which cannot be met by the more efficient functioning of neighbouring groups in providing local services and activities was not a source of disillusionment and increased apathy, as is sometimes claimed in the community development literature. Education based on a working-class interpretation of political reality was not rejected. We can tentatively assume that it was a substantial element in generating interest and enthusiasm both for action and for further study.

There have been many indications in the factual account above that there is no room for self-congratulation, as though this were a success story. We have still to find the means by which a broad-based educational exercise can be dovetailed with social action. We have gone beyond the stage of discussing only dustbins and rats in the light of such action. Social theory classes indicate the possibilities. But we have not found a means of providing opportunities for people to learn the sorts of subjects we know they wish to learn, within the same action context. Nor, in terms of an interpretation of educational theory, are we satisfied with the notion that a mass meeting is an adequate setting. As in the mass media the concepts 'educative' and 'educational' need to be considered more carefully, and the relations between the two explored in practice. There are other activities in which we have engaged which are even more problematic.

A personal conclusion

It must be emphasised that this article is not intended as an attempt to describe an overwhelmingly important theory, or massively significant actions arising from that theory. Adult education, like community development generally, is a marginal activity. There is no doubt that we will leave Scotland Road in Liverpool much as we found it; a massive monument to an exploitative society; a squalid and oppressive slum which nobody ought to tolerate. The best that we can hope for is that more people who live there will recognise this too, and that their frustration will lead to anger and an informed determination to change it.

Notes

1 The politically sophisticated reader hardly needs to be reminded that, in Britain at least, the most militant demands for change have come from relatively affluent sections of the working class and not from the poor.
2 It is common for politicians to avoid this issue by implying that positive discrimination does not lead to a withdrawal of resources from other sections of the population than those for which such a policy would be advantageous.
3 There is not space to expand this crude statement in this article. For a recent challenge to prevailing views on this issue see J. H. Westergaard, 'Sociology: the myth of classlessness', in R. Blackburn (ed.), *Ideology in Social Science*, Fontana, 1972.
4 It is tempting to argue that neighbourhoods with high levels of poverty are characterised by community-mindedness, rather than the reverse, and that consequently such areas need less rather than more 'community'. This point will not be pursued here but, if it were, one suspects it would highlight many of the paradoxes inherent in 'community development'.
5 P. Bachrach and Martin S. Baratz, *Power and Poverty – Theory and Practice*, OUP, 1970, pp. 47-8: 'A key issue is one that involves a genuine challenge to the resources of power or authority of those who currently

dominate the process by which policy outputs in the system are determined. . . . A key issue is one that involves a demand for enduring transformation in both the manner in which values are allocated in the policy in question and the value-allocation itself.'

6 J. Berger, *A Fortunate Man*, Penguin, 1969, pp. 98–9.
7 Eric Midwinter, *Educational Priority Areas: The Philosophic Question*, Liverpool EPA Project, Occasional Paper no. 1, 1969.
8 S. M. Miller and P. Roby, *The Future of Inequality*, New York, Basic Books, 1970, p. 10.
9 J. Rex and R. Moore, *Race, Community and Conflict: A study of housing policy in Birmingham*, OUP, 1967.
10 P. A. Baldock, 'Tenants' voice: A study of council tenants' organisations with particular reference to those in the City of Sheffield 1961–1971', Ph.D. thesis, University of Sheffield, 1971.
11 D. S. Byrne and W. Williamson, *The Myth of the Restricted Code*, University of Durham Department of Sociology and Social Administration, Working Papers in Sociology, no. 1, 1971.
12 We recognise that the geographical location of classes causes expense to middle-class students too, but that does not affect this point.
13 A survey on post-school education in the Vauxhall area of Liverpool (the area of this project) showed all these to be real factors in residents' non-attendance at adult education in classes. In fact less than 1 per cent had ever attended such classes.
14 We are exploring the possibility of doing this in the framework of various kinds of schemes for tackling the heavy unemployment on Merseyside, e.g. the NAYC Community Industry schemes.
15 This would be in no sense revolutionary. The Danish government has in the recent past made substantial sections of further education free. Preliminary reports of the results of re-introducing fees suggest that the effects on working-class student participation has been much greater than for other sections of the population.
16 It is interesting to note that the (largely middle-class) campaign to prevent the building of the third London Airport in Berkshire is often cited as a model of successful community action. The airport's re-siting at Foulness will, one suspects (data have not been published), transfer the social cost of building to largely working-class areas of north London, through the construction of new roads.
17 All these examples are of the experiences of working-class men and women in Liverpool. Even in the case of the 'hard disciplines' like mathematics, the analysis has validity. A worker in Liverpool described an EPA-type CSE syllabus in maths (maths in the supermarket, counting traffic flow, etc.) as an insult to the intelligence of the children of the area. Moreover, he added that if somebody succeeded in obtaining a job as a draughtsman on the strength of this certificate they would be laughed off the drawing-board within a week. Clearly too much should not be argued from this case but it is not enough to dismiss such a view as further evidence of the way in which workers do not stand in the vanguard of progress, in this case progressive education.

18 The Free School movement here and in the USA is obviously relevant, but there is a need to examine the various elements in that movement carefully. It is worth noting that Ivan Illich and the Deschoolers attack progressive schooling as much as they do traditional schooling partly because of its turning away from traditional disciplines and teaching methods. There is not the space to take this argument further in the present article.

19 B. Jackson and D. Marsden, *Education and the Working Class*, Pelican, 1966.

20 P. Marris, *The Experience of Higher Education*, Routledge & Kegan Paul, 1964, p. 153.

21 P. Freire, *Cultural Action for Freedom*, Penguin, 1972, p. 35.

22 Ibid.

23 R. Williams, *Culture and Society*, Pelican, p. 313.

4　**The political community**

Sean Baine

Introduction

Over the last three years a series of conferences were held for community groups in many parts of the country. These 'neighbourhood agitators' discussed common problems and strategies for change and also attempted to look at underlying philosophy. Arising out of the last conference, a first issue of 'Agitators' Notes'[1] was produced and circulated to a wide audience. The groups attending all had a broad political approach to the community work they were doing, their politics being of the left, whatever actual label is used – socialist, Marxist, etc. The aim of this article is to identify the common ground among these groups and to distinguish their ideas and work from other forms of community work. We feel this identification to be vitally important, particularly when there are moves to professionalise the work and to give it status within social work and government circles.

We wish to talk about not minor distinctions, dealing with tactics or even strategy, but major ones relating to definitions of problems, their causes, and the way in which change might come about. We shall, therefore, look first at establishment views of community work before moving on, at somewhat greater length, to distinguish and discuss what we may call the political neighbourhood organiser's viewpoint.

The establishment view

Two main emphases can be distinguished in the establishment view. The first, and earlier, is the social work view. Community work is seen as constituting one of the three methods of social work. Where casework deals with the malfunctioning individual and group work with the malfunctioning group, community work takes on the malfunctioning community. The breakdown in a community is seen as a breakdown of small group life. Sometimes this breakdown is attributed to urbanisation, sometimes to the increased rate of technological change and

66

sometimes to outside interventions, such as redevelopment schemes. Whatever the cause it is assumed to be self-evident that modern urban man is lonely, lost and alienated – in short, he no longer has a sense of community. In contrast to the present hard times we are presented with an idealised, romanticised notion of a golden age of community when everyone knew his neighbour or had Mum round the corner ready to rush in at the first sign of a crisis. The job of the community worker today is, therefore, to re-create a sense of community; in practice this means to create as many small groups as possible to which people can relate and belong.

Community work in this sense is not just useful to the people participating. It is also seen as having a wider role to play as a means of social control on behalf of society as a whole. The first Gulbenkian Report on community work training[2] thought that 'community work may be seen as one of the means by which society induces individuals and groups to modify their behaviour in the direction of certain cultural norms'. An early publication from the National Council of Social Service made this more specific.[3] 'During the past ten years interesting experimental work has taken place, particularly with children and young people, aimed at directing energies wisely through group activities, often of a quite informal nature. Community organisation must also embrace the removal of sources of temptation to disorder and the provision of tighter controls of public behaviour.'

This sort of social work view seems to be going out of favour, perhaps because psychological views in social work are not now as prominent as they were or it may be that the more physical problems of bad housing, poverty and lack of amenities have shown a marked reluctance to disappear and leave the field clear for people's psychological problems to come to the fore. In place of the social work view we now increasingly come across the 'good administration' arguments for community work.

The underlying belief in these arguments is that resources are being used inefficiently and that ways can be found to use those we have in a more rational way. The problem is one of communication, or rather the lack of it. The distance separating governed and governing means that decisions are taken at too remote a level by politicians and bureaucrats not in touch with the grass roots. In this setting, community work is seen as a means of reducing the gap and opening up communications, a way to get ordinary people to state what they really want and as a basis for better planning. Early literature from the government Community Development Project abounds with references to problems of communication.[4]

> It will be necessary to look behind the more obvious and familiar indications of social ill health, such as delinquency, bad housing, lack of success at school, etc., and to expose the reasons why there is a breakdown in communications, or inadequate contact, between the neighbourhood and the services working within it . . . People living in deprived areas are often more successful in communicating grievances amongst themselves, building them up into symbols of their own social isolation, than in communicating with the service who could help them.

Either of two methods can be used. Attempts can be made to bring together all men of good will in an area to iron out their differences and come to agreement about joint action. Here communication horizontally at a neighbourhood level is seen as important as communication vertically up the government hierarchy. Or the vertical links can be stressed and local people encouraged to express their views direct, as proposed in the Skeffington Report.[5]

Neighbourhood councils are typical of the good administration approach. Michael Young, in proposing their creation, has written:[6] 'some part of the energies which have been exerted in a thousand campaigns against government could be used in and for government if participation were given more of a place inside the framework of administration.' The neighbourhood council is visualised as an ally to the existing councils – but one with its ear nearer to the ground – which would give more weight to local as opposed to central government. The activities suggested for the neighbourhood councils are comparatively small scale, dealing with amenity and welfare matters. The big decisions are still taken elsewhere: basically no one is here talking about radical change.

The political view

What is the neighbourhood organiser's view and how can it be distinguished from the views above? The commitment of those propounding the political view is different. The social worker and administrator claim to be 'neutral' in the views put forward, i.e. they claim to be interested only in neutral processes – of 'promoting community' or 'encouraging participation' – and not in the problems themselves, their causes or their possible solutions. These are matters for the people themselves to decide. The organiser, however, has no such hesitations. To him, partisanship and identification with the concrete problems of the working class and the deprived are essential. He analyses problems and causes and hopes to join with the people who have those problems, to secure improvements. In *Reveille for Radicals*, Alinsky said:[7] 'Liberals charge radicals with passionate partisanship. To this accusation the radical's jaw tightens as he snaps "Guilty!" – we are partisan for the people. Furthermore, we know that all people are partisan. The only nonpartisan people are those who are dead. You too are partisan – if not for the people, then for whom?'

The starting-point is the disadvantaged community with several obvious problems. An early statement from the Notting Hill Community Workshop[8] saw in Notting Hill 'thousands of families who live in decaying multi-occupied houses; too many people paying too much rent for too few rooms. The schools are overcrowded and ill equipped. Children have nowhere to play but the gutter. Traffic is uncontrolled and dangerous. The social amenities are utterly inadequate.' Everywhere, bad living conditions are the starting-point for action. Bad conditions in hostels for homeless families; on the new council estate with few amenities and high rents; in the decaying inner areas of our cities. Bob Holman describes what is happening in Handsworth, Birmingham.[9]

> Mothers anxious to start more playgroups. Joint action has led to a more militant, almost political attitude, expressed in a readiness to assert their rights and to stand up to officials. Some have mooted the need for a tenants association and, hopefully, future developments will concentrate on housing. If the present occupiers of overcrowded, damp, non-repaired dwellings do claim a right to decent accommodation, they cannot expect a ready acceptance by the local authority.

These problems, which can be repeated throughout the country, constitute a start for activity within a community. But the essential differences with establishment views, which obviously recognise these problems as existing, arise over causes. Why are these problems present and why do they persist? The reasons are sought not just at the level of personal or community malfunctioning; they are taken right back to the structure of present-day British society itself. Within this structure, neighbourhood organisers recognise the centrality of conflicting class interests. It is these class antagonisms which result in the concentration of wealth and power in certain areas, and poverty, bad housing, deprived environmental conditions and relative powerlessness in others. So in

Kensington and Chelsea enormous differences occur between the affluent south of the borough and the area of Notting Hill. Factors such as low wages, unemployment, bad housing, inadequate schools and poor health, which are concentrated in inner city areas, are also all interrelated, and reflect ultimately the structure of contemporary capitalist society.

Traditionally, working-class politics have been understandably concerned with the struggle at the workplace, focusing on the immediate issues of pay and conditions (and to a limited extent on the longer-term issues of the structure of the work situation and the demand for workers' control in a socialised economy). Community issues, at least until recently, have had a much smaller place. Trade unions have typically considered their members as workers but they have rarely seen them also as tenants, parents, pensioners or patients. (There are now some signs of change; e.g. trade union support in Liverpool and Glasgow on the rent issue and the TUC action on pensions. This is, partly at least, because their attention has been forced upon these issues by the upsurge of community organising.)

The political parties of the left could have been expected to make effective links between workplace organisations (trade unions) and community groups (tenants, claimants, parent-teacher associations) connected with consumption issues. In practice, however, neighbourhood organisers have not been convinced that the Labour Party has been able to do this effectively – or that it has wanted to. Some still argue for maintaining links with the Labour Party. Coates and Silburn in their book on poverty in Nottingham[10] argue that real change can only come through the existing organs of the left and that 'to assume that such bodies can be by-passed is blithely optimistic; to assume that they would remain impregnable to insistent campaigning on these issues seems unduly pessimistic.' Despite such views, there is now widespread scepticism about whether the Labour Party can be considered a party of the left or a working-class party at all, after the 1964–70 Labour government. The Communist Party and the other left parties have been hampered in developing community organisation in the past by the widespread fears and prejudices of the Cold War period, and at least until the recent upsurge of the extra-parliamentary left, have not had the membership and grass-roots organisational strength to play an effective part in community issues throughout deprived areas in Britain, however effective they may or may not have been in particular areas and issues at particular times. Many of those now involved in community organising have taken part in other extra-parliamentary movements of the late 1950s and 1960s such as CND, the May Day Manifesto group and the ill-fated National Convention of the Left. These collapsed; even their organisation as largely middle-class groups left much to be desired, and a grass-roots approach was preferred by a significant number of participants.

This approach is based on an analysis of power within the community: deprivation is seen as deprivation of power. In all the areas with which activists are concerned, there is an overwhelming sensation of powerlessness, of being caught up in an all-pervading system which operates in favour of certain sections and interests and which effectively excludes others. A famous equation in Notting Hill had it that one titled lady equalled one thousand common people. The community activist sees his job as getting the one thousand together and helping them to make their voice heard.

Notting Hill

Initially, this may mean a breaking down of present structures rather than a coherent formulation of an alternative. Bill Richardson, a past chairman of the People's Association in Notting Hill, saw it as necessary to first look for anti-community.[11]

> It is our job to attack these prevailing patterns if we are ever to advance new ones and that is why I suggest before Community, we must deliberately set about Anti-Community – Disorganisation – don't be alarmed. The circumstances and status quo under which we live do not permit the sort of dignified concern and participation we talk about. Therefore these circumstances and arrangements must be disorganized if they are to be displaced, and changed patterns providing opportunity and means for people brought in . . .

It is only out of such disorganisation that new patterns of organisation can emerge.

In Notting Hill this has developed as 'the spontaneous approach' to revolution rather than the 'pre-planned approach'. No initial blueprints are laid down. The aims of spontaneous revolutionaries are to find in the disorganisation the true springs of collective political action and to maximise the constructive political potential of eruptions of discontent by providing information and support at the right moment. This can build up a resistance movement whose power cannot be predicted. The movement will aim to force the inconsistencies of the system into the open in the belief that revolutionary changes can occur when the existing structure cannot cope with its inconsistencies. What exactly constitutes the revolution is a matter of debate amongst activists. The least extreme position would be to hope for a series of revolutions – not in the bloody or once-for-all sense, but meaning a series of radical changes that taken together would add up to a total transformation of present society.

What does this mean in practice? An early example from Notting Hill illustrates the small concrete situation. Camelford Road was in the middle of a redevelopment scheme. The street was typical of many with all the houses subdivided and containing two or three families, usually with children. The condition of the houses was bad, with damp basements, but landlords refused to do repairs as they knew the houses were scheduled to come down. The Lancaster Neighbourhood Centre – an offshoot of the 1967 Notting Hill Summer Project – was already working in the area and had made a few contacts in the street. It decided to call a meeting in the street itself and five people came forward who became the nucleus of a street committee. Further meetings in the street drew up a list of repairs that needed to be done and, in the campaign that followed, the committee aimed to get repairs done, to get some families rehoused immediately and to make sure as many as possible were rehoused when the street was demolished. Positive results were achieved through both individual casework and direct bargaining with the authorities.

Early in 1969 there was a crisis. The best house in the street, which had been empty for nine months, was being left vacant until the street came down. One of the mothers in the street, who lived in one of the worst basements directly opposite this house, decided to move into the empty house. She asked for and got assistance from the Notting Hill Squatters who had drawn attention to themselves by two token squats in two empty luxury flats in the area. She moved in and was soon joined by another family in the street. At about the same time, the Council announced without explanation a change in the rephasing of the redevelopment, putting Camelford Road back three or four years. The squat immediately became more than just seeking rent-books for the two families. The families issued a statement – 'We see our act as the first step in a fight for better conditions for all the people of Camelford Road and the Lancaster Road (west) Redevelopment area.' The street was behind the squatters and the squatters were behind the street.

It turned out that the house they had squatted in belonged to the GLC and this brought to light for the first time that it was the GLC, and not the local council, which was responsible for rehousing. The squat brought pressure on the GLC to bring forward the rehousing date, and and as a result the GLC agreed to complete the work within a year. By 1970 almost all Camelford Road were rehoused.

The sequence of action here is significant. From a start rooted in casework, the street moved through political pressure on the rephasing, to the support of an illegal activity such as squatting, which was seen to buttress earlier demands. At all times the residents were actively supported by the Neighbourhood Centre, the squatters and others working in the area. This is a vital point to understand. There was within the street a sense of being part of the same struggle, but this also extended to many other groups in the area, and their support helped sustain the squatters till the GLC were forced to capitulate five weeks later.

This idea of groups centred on different issues working with each other is important. In areas such as Notting Hill a network of groups has been built up which identify with each other as being part of the the same fight. An idea of how many such groups might be involved can be seen by looking at the *People's News* Review of the Year for 1971. *People's News* is a weekly news sheet put out by the Notting Hill People's Association, which reports on all current developments affecting people in the area. The Review of the Year contained reports on the activities of all the following groups or individuals: the case of the Mangrove Nine, involving allegations of police harassment of black people; several other cases about police activity in the area; attempts by local black youth to control the Metro Youth Club; the local claimants' union; the Gay Liberation Front; a Women's Liberation Workshop; the free milk campaign; the Notting Hill Theatre Workshop; the work of the Neighbourhood Law Centre; a local community press; much work with kids including summer play-schemes, crêches, playgroups and ideas for a free school; and of course numerous activities round the housing issue – protest at luxury conversions, the position of furnished tenants, numerous squats, and activities at auctions of local property to draw attention to property speculation. None of these groups sees their issue as isolated. Rather they know that advances when they come will be along all fronts at once, rather than in one or two campaigns. And the advances will come through the combined action of all.

Attempts have been made in Notting Hill to give these ideas some formalisation. The first of these came in 1968 with a call for a People's Forum, where such groups could discuss common problems and actions. The letter inviting people to the Forum said:[12]

> It is not an aim to form a new political party, rather to avoid
> this, but simply to explore the possibility of action of
> organizations and people concerned about the misuse of power
> and authority, and who feel they have no means of expressing
> criticism and ideas as things are. A forum for ideas and demands
> to create maximum pressure and embarrassment to those who
> do not represent the people of Notting Hill, and yet occupy
> positions of power at the Town Hall. Another voice is needed –
> a people's voice, independent of the Party machines, strong
> enough to remind officials and politicians alike that they are
> public servants.

This Forum met on two or three stormy occasions but, instead of being
put off by the apparent disagreement, moved to something much more
ambitious.

The idea came forward for a People's Council.[13]

> What it proposes basically is that the party power system is
> reversed, and that people are given the opportunity to vote for
> people they know and trust in their very streets and local
> organisations. It proposes a broad council, consisting of
> representatives from every street in the Borough and from
> every reputable organisation that goes to make the life of the
> Borough.

This Council would then elect an Executive to carry out policy. Two
democratic safeguards were to be written into the constitution. Firstly,
the power by any constituent group to recall its representatives at any
time, and second, the power of the groups to call for the reference back
of all matters of major policy and direction to themselves and the people
everywhere for criticism, consideration and amendment. Given present
circumstances, the People's Council was obviously never meant to be a
fully operating proposition, actually taking over the power of the
traditional council, but it had two objectives. It attempted to be a more
authentic voice for the people in Notting Hill. The contempt for the
'democratic' system is widespread:[14] 'the whole rotten structure of our
society rests upon the non-criticism, non-choice, non-involvement,
non-decision making of the broad base, the millions of working people
who are kicked from every direction and then expected unquestioningly
to vote for candidates they know nothing of.' The People's Council aimed
to represent Notting Hill by keeping its active living parts in touch with
popular opinion and by being willing to act on behalf of the people.
Second, the very putting forward of an alternative way of doing things,

even if this is posed in an idealistic form, starts a questioning of the status quo and leads to the formulation of new ideas. The People's Council itself did not last long but even without it actually being present its spirit lives in the co-operation of groups in the various campaigns. Perhaps one has to look hard for a coherent alternative voice but it is there to be found and is continually manifesting itself. Every time the alternative does manifest itself and influences policy or starts something new it is a victory for the power of local people. It is felt that every piece of power gained for the people is power taken away from 'them'. Where establishment views echo the theme of self-help, the neighbour-hood organisers talk of control, a much more powerful idea. The people must use their power to control what goes on around them. Clearly these are not attempts to take total power locally. To create islands of community power within capitalist society represents Utopian dream-ing. But the locality is always the point of departure, a base of resistance and experimentation.

This is also central to the thinking of those individuals and groups who reject the notion of 'spontaneous revolution'. For example, in a paper to the last conference of neighbourhood organisers, the Camden Community Workshop emphasised that 'the very basis of our strategy depends upon taking "felt needs" in terms of locally experienced problems seriously.'[15] Their style is also intended to be experimental and anti-authoritarian. The group aims to develop 'new ways of relating and communicating with people', so that as individuals, and particularly as members of viable local groups, they develop 'more effective forms of collective action' based on a growing political consciousness of the real nature of their collective problems.

But while endorsing the autonomous locally based group and the local struggle as the point of departure, the Camden paper rejects the view that a series of local victories by themselves can lead to 'spontaneous revolution'. Rather, the local groups must ultimately relate to each other in a wider political framework which must be capable of making both geographical links between community groups in different areas and functional links between different types of organisation at the workplace and in the community. To advance beyond small-scale isolated aims to challenge the very basis of the structure of unequal rewards and benefits in contemporary Britain, they will have eventually to relate to the main-stream of working-class politics via a genuine party or parties of the left.

The Camden group's experience to date reinforces them in this perspective. Despite the existence of some characteristics of a zone of transition in Camden, e.g. a high proportion of furnished tenants and single-person households, the borough is also characterised by the existence of strong working-class organisations in the form of the trades council and unions, a strong left wing of the Labour Party, tenants' organisations with a long history of militancy and a well-developed extra-parliamentary left. In the campaign against the Housing Finance Act the newly formed community groups connected with the Workshop have been working with these working-class organisations both individually and collectively through the Camden Action Committee and the newly formed Camden Federation of Tenants' and Residents' Associations. The Workshop has been energetic in these attempts to build a strongly organised militant working-class movement in Camden. Although based on autonomous people's organisations at street, ward and borough level, the campaign has also been the means of developing wider political alliances. This, from the Camden Workshop's perspective, represents the most significiant method for the long-term development of the Workshop and neighbourhood organisers, if they are to contribute effectively to fundamental social change.

In the meantime, other practical links are also being developed between neighbourhood organisers whether they share the somewhat harder political approach of the Camden Workshop or the idea of spontaneous revolutions as presented by some groups in Notting Hill.

The conferences of 'neighbourhood agitators' mentioned at the beginning of this paper are one example of this. At the last conference the groups present adopted a common statement as a basis for further co-operation, appealing to other groups to join, as follows:

We, as groups involved in neighbourhood organising, are opposed to the capitalist system and the inevitable exploitation this brings.

We organise in the areas where we live, but recognise the need to link up with industrial struggles. The contradictions we seek to bring to the surface are vital, complementary ones, in housing, education, health and social security, play and leisure, and the position of women.

We believe the time is right to intensify our activities in all of these areas, developing collective forms of power, organisation and control and developing the political consciousness of those who are politically powerless.

We seek contacts and co-operation with other similar groups including women, claimants, blacks, and left political parties which share these aims and are directly engaged in similar struggles.

In practical terms, this has meant information-sharing between groups. A register of landlords is being compiled to identify links between different areas, and a Handbook is in preparation which will be a practical guide to neighbourhood organising. Groups, exchange personnel; e.g. workers from Notting Hill have gone to a meeting of private tenants in Camden. The emergence of similar problems brings the formulation of similar demands from different areas, e.g. over improvement policy and 'gentrification' or over the position of furnished tenants.

The different groups probably see different results arising out of such a process. At one end of the spectrum will be those who hope at most to make the poor into an effective interest group on their own behalf, one likely to be more effective than if they left the defence of their interests to others. At the other end there will be those who hope for a total transformation of present society. Both have this in common. They see nothing to be gained by relying solely on those at present in power, of whatever political persuasion. They see their role as being extra-parliamentary, working directly with the working class, the poor and the deprived to help them build up their own power base, independent of present political interests. As *People's News* puts it:

> the working people are being pushed out. More families become homeless each year, others are pressed into smaller space at higher rents. Now is the time to fight back. Go to the local centre of the People's Association. Above all, do not leave it to the Government, or to the Council, do not even leave it to the People's Association; take matters into your own hands. We must all act together Now.

Note

Although this article was written solely by myself, I must acknowledge, as will be obvious from the text, the contributions of many people and groups: in particular I must mention Bill Richardson, Jan O'Malley and Bea Gavin in Notting Hill, and Marge Mayo and John Cowley of the Camden Workshop.

References

1 Available from 60 St Ervans Road, London, W.10.
2 Calouste Gulbenkian Foundation, *Community Work and Social Change*, Longman, 1968, p. 84.
3 National Council of Social Service, *Community Organisation: An Introduction*, NCSS, 1962, p. 58.
4 Objectives and Strategies (Home Office CDP internal paper).
5 Committee on Public Participation in Planning, *People and Planning*, HMSO, 1969.
6 M. Young, 'The Hornsey Plan: A role for Neighbourhood Councils in the new local government', Institute of Community Studies (mimeographed), 1970, p. 1.
7 S. Alinsky, *Reveille for Radicals*, New York, Vintage Paperbacks, 1969.
8 Jan O'Malley, 'Community action in Notting Hill', in A. Lapping (ed.), *Community Action*, Fabian Tract no. 400, Fabian Society, 1970, pp. 28-36.
9 Bob Holman, 'Handsworth adventure playground', in ibid., pp. 37-40.
10 K. Coates and R. Silburn, *Poverty: The Forgotten Englishman*, Penguin, 1970, p. 234.
11 B. Richardson, paper for Notting Hill People's Association (mimeographed), 1968.
12 B. Richardson, letter inviting people to Forum for New Thinking and Community Action (mimeographed), 1968.
13 B. Richardson, paper on People's Council (mimeographed).
14 Ibid.
15 J. Cowley and M. Mayo, manifesto from Camden Community Workshop, 1970.

5 East London Claimants' Union and the concept of self-management

East London Claimants' Union

Welfare state babies

There are many theories to account for the origin and success of the Claimants' Union Movement which started in Birmingham in the winter of 1968. They have included the 'concept of entitlement' theory put forward by Richard Crossman, the 'radicalisation of the campuses' suggested by a social administration lecturer, and the growth of 'graduate unemployment'. Perhaps one possibility which has been most neglected is the fact that the founder members were all in their early twenties. They had been born in National Health Service hospitals, supplied with free orange juice and cod liver oil, examined by health visitors, and their mothers received maternity grants and family allowances. They were brought up in council houses and attended state-run schools where they enjoyed free milk, school meals and medical and dental attention. Their grandparents were all surviving on National Assistance, and from time to time their parents claimed National Insurance.

Being spoon-fed on so much 'state aid' and 'welfare', they represented a new generation. Unlike their parents who had been brought up in the 'depression', seen mass unemployment and survived through one or two world wars, they were not 'grateful' for 'state handouts'. In fact, a new generation had emerged which was only too eager to point out the contradictions in the welfare state and to challenge and criticise its false illusion of grandeur. They saw behind the façade of 'rights' and 'entitlements', and began to point out that the welfare state was never intended to fulfil the function ascribed to it in popular mythology – that of some nationalised Santa Claus. To this new generation, the welfare state was a fraud and a 'con', and a very cheap buy for the ruling class. A modern advanced technology cannot operate with a semi-literate working class. As Churchill said: 'There is no better investment than

79

pumping milk into new-born babies.' Financed as it was initially by American 'aid' (welfare imperialism?), the welfare state prevented a recurrence of the mass militant activity of the 1930s and the political and social dangers inherent in this situation. The welfare state owed little to humanitarian considerations. Social security today operates for the security of the state.

Working-class heroes

During the past thirty years, the organised labour movement in Britain has been beset with problems. The Claimants' Union Movement has tried to learn from mistakes in tackling them in order to avoid similar pitfalls. Both the trade union hierarchy and the Labour Party have time and time again collided with the bosses and been bought off by the government and business interests. They have become incorporated and co-opted into our present economic and political system and out of touch with the realities of working-class life which they are supposed to represent (conned by the establishment). As far back as 1924 the Labour Party colluded with employers against unemployed workers by bringing in the 'not genuinely seeking work' clause and, in 1931, the 'household means test'. Their Social Security Act of 1966 merely bolstered up the means test and elaborated a smoke-screen of paper rights. While it changed the name 'National Assistance' to 'Supplementary Benefits', it had done nothing to reduce the humiliation and degradation experienced by increasing numbers of claimants who have to provide vast amounts of personal evidence and information about their income, expenditure and family circumstances and to be scrutinised and spied on by special investigators and employees of the 'ss' (as it is commonly called). So-called 'socialists' were given places on the Supplementary Benefits Commission—whose chairmen have always been trade union leaders with a reputation for having 'sold out' on the rank and file members. Richard Crossman, Labour's Secretary of State for Social Services, held views on 'scroungers and layabouts' equally as arrogant as those of his successor Keith Joseph. In fact it was probably Crossman who initiated the Fisher Committee of Enquiry into Social Security Abuse. And we should not forget that it was the Labour Party which introduced the vicious 'four-week rule' against the unskilled, unemployed at a time of rising unemployment, and justified and extended the other controls and secret codes used to intimidate claimants today. The trade union leadership frequently fails to reflect the views of its members. The TU movement has a highly centralised rigid and undemocratic structure and bureaucracy. Its 'officials' are in permanent, secure, well-paid posts and thus normally out of touch with the work situation and the difficulties of members. For instance, in recent strikes when workers have been forced to draw supplementary benefits, the 'officials' (who are not in this situation) have frequently failed to appreciate the role of the SS as strike-breakers and the difficulties which strikers have to face in getting benefit. Full-time officials frequently accept the role of arbitrators, mediators and conciliators, and are not unconditionally prepared to back 100 per cent the demands of members.

It is no wonder that many of the 'Left' in Britain became totally frustrated by aspects of the Trade Union Movement and the Wilson government. For this reason, some have become involved in claimants' unions and other local community groups such as squatters' and tenants' organisations.

These small democratically controlled groups can be highly flexible in approach and tactics. They may stand a chance of succeeding where topheavy and rigid bureaucracies have failed. The increasing numbers of battles which they are fighting and frequently winning by direct action of one kind or another are a significant pointer to the most promising kind of militant class and antibureaucratic struggle today.

The National Federation of Claimants' Unions

For the fullest possible involvement and optimum impact, an organisation must find a balance between the strength it gains from being large and the advantages of being small and flexible. The larger a body becomes, the greater its problem of keeping in touch with day-to-day changes at the grass-roots level. In other words, it cannot be sure of getting enough feedback from those it represents to ensure that its response is the most effective possible. Also, in a large organisation, the degree of active involvement and identification with its aims and activities lessens with the growth of numbers and bureaucracy.

The answer to this problem for the Claimants' Union Movement would seem to lie in the idea of a 'network', where individual claimants' unions have the maximum amount of flexibility and autonomy.

We have had to decide whether to preserve at all times a united front nationally, or whether it is not more important that what we say or represent nationally should be based on the free growth and experience of groups which are self governing and therefore learning from their

Dcw

own mistakes. For this reason, we believe that there is little to be afraid of in encouraging maximum freedom and diversity of approach between claimants' unions even at a risk of mistakes and contradictions between one claimants' union's policy and tactics in a certain situation and that of another. It is the feeling that 'This is our Union' which encourages a high degree of activity. Consequently, each claimants' union is self governing and autonomous. That is, the members of each union make their own decisions at a local level. The National Federation of Claimants' Unions is merely the sum total of all those claimants' unions who support the Claimants' Charter:

1 The right to an adequate income without means test for all people.
2 A free welfare state for all with its services controlled by the people who use it.
3 No secrets and the right to full information.
4 No distinction between so-called 'deserving' and 'undeserving'.

In other words, claimants' unions are *not* branches of a national organisation. Each union is a powerful self-managing organisation in its own right, and other unions in the National Federation cannot direct it outside the basic policy charter. Consequently, claimants' unions differ in character and tactics and, in doing so, reflect their individual localities, communities and the personality of their members.

The Claimants' Union Movement has no national headquarters and no national executive, for several reasons. As already mentioned, a great many people in the Movement have experienced and are critical of the bureaucratic and undemocratic structure of the centralist trade union hierarchy. Furthermore, we are probably more conscious of this than other groups in so far as we are constantly fighting the social security system which is one of the biggest centralised bureaucracies of them all. We are opposed to hierarchies since we are fighting for equality. We want a movement in which power really lies at the grass roots. A national headquarters would mean discipline and regulation from the centre. It would mean that the central organisation would be held responsible for the actions of individual claimants' unions. Local unions would then have to consult with it and thus lose their spontaneity and militancy. This could so easily lead to stagnation. We have no central leadership which could easily be bought off by the government or business interests, and fall into the role of mediation, arbitration and conciliation. We have no full-time officials, as we all work full time for the claimants' union. Officials in secure, well-paid posts would become far removed from the harsh realities of claiming.

Thus the National Federation of Claimants' Unions has the limited role of attempting to communicate and co-ordinate activities between bona fide claimants' unions on the basis of a minimum policy charter. It functions mainly by holding quarterly National Federation meetings. Every union is invited to send as many members as it wishes (or can afford) to these meetings, which are held in different parts of the country. Any union may propose a topic for discussion, since there is no standing agenda. A proposed agenda is normally drawn up by the union responsible for arranging the meeting, and amendments may be made to it later. Two people per session are usually elected from the floor to chair the meeting, and two others to take the minutes. Sometimes the meeting divides into smaller seminar groups in which topics can be discussed in greater detail. Voting is not normally necessary, since the Federation tries to reach a consensus of opinion on most matters. Almost everyone is able to speak at these meetings if they wish, and people can discuss matters more fully in the smaller groups and in the evenings. The meeting usually lasts two days. New unions may affiliate if they show themselves to be bona fide and state that they accept the policy charter. Affiliations are usually left to the second day to give newcomers time to understand what they are joining. Although the meetings cannot compel or mandate a union outside the minimum policy charter, a resolution may be agreed regarding some particular aspect of a union's work or policy.

The recent country-wide growth in numbers of claimants' unions has been accompanied by the development of a regional network of communication. The claimants' unions in London have been holding joint monthly meetings for some time. Each union takes a turn at holding and organising these meetings, which have been very successful. They have enabled unions to meet regularly and work collectively on a wide variety of activities, notable among which have been the joint activities at local, regional and national offices of the Department of Health and Social Security. Regional meetings work well because of the personal and regular basis on which they take place. They can act as a close forum for the interchange of ideas and experiences.

Ad hoc meetings are held between quarterly Federation meetings, usually about topics of special or immediate importance such as production of a Guide book or discussion of a national campaign. If a claimants' union wants to call an ad hoc national or regional meeting, then it has the freedom to do so at any time.

Of course, in addition to all this, there is a great amount of informal cross-contact, and numerous channels of communication exist between individual unions and union members. Initiative comes from the claimants' union and does not need ratification from elsewhere.

Local claimants' unions

Most claimants' unions have started by a few claimants and ex-claimants getting together and producing a simple leaflet advertising a regular weekly meeting. These leaflets usually explain to people what a claimants' union is, what it does, and what it stands for. People should not be misled into believing that it is merely an advice bureau or an advocacy service, or some sort of charity or social work organisation. Leaflets are often distributed at local supplementary benefit offices, employment exchanges, insurance offices, social services departments and houses in the locality, etc. The union helps to try to build up membership within walking distance of the meeting place: the right size in geographical area for a union is one you can get around easily, preferably on foot, and not find it difficult to back fellow claimants up at short notice.

People are naturally wary of new groups and organisations. They often suspect that you are a 'front' for some political or social work organisation. Alternatively they might be frightened that they will be victimised in the local social security office if they become identified with a claimants' union and, in fact, this has happened in one or two areas. But one should not despair if only one or two people turn up for every 500 leaflets distributed. Things do not always go well for new unions. Perhaps for many weeks no one will turn up regularly to meetings except the dedicated few. But this can happen to any group. And it often takes a lot of skill and patience on the part of one or two active members to get the claimants' union off the ground and to start members acting and thinking together as a group. Once a union begins winning claims, however, it will attract a steady flow of new and able claimants to the meetings.

Most unions hold weekly meetings since members often cannot wait longer than this if their claims need tackling. Also, policy decisions are taken at these meetings which all members want to be involved in, and new members join, and as many others as possible attend. While many unions only have a handful attending regularly, some have weekly meetings of thirty-five or forty. Above this number, meetings tend to become disorganised and undemocratic since many members are unable to participate fully. When this happens, unions often split into two self-governing ones. Some unions distribute the week's work among members at these meetings so that as many claimants as possible can take part in fighting claims and appeals and the rest of the work. A weekly meeting is much more preferable to offering an 'on call' service, since unions who have tried the latter have found it difficult to get people to meetings and to act as a group. Consequently, these unions have failed to grow, and tend to be seen as some sort of 'emergency social work service'. Similarly, if a home is used as a meeting place, new members may see the union as 'belonging to' the people who live in the house, or as an advice bureau. Some unions operate from offices or centres where they hold their meetings. Others have to borrow or hire a hall for one night a week. Community centres, Co-op Halls, trade union rooms, neighbourhood houses are all possibilities here. A few unions are forced to hire rooms in a local pub, but this is usually inconvenient for most members who cannot afford the beer, and for women with children and people who do not drink.

In some unions it is a rule that claimants should join only at the weekly meetings so that they fully understand what it is they are joining and what the work of the union is. We do not want new members to think we merely want to sort their claim out. The Claimants' Union Movement can grow only if every member becomes active in it. For this reason some unions consider as members only those claimants who pay a subscription regularly, since this method gives a more accurate picture of the live membership and the rate of increase of new members. Some unions have membership forms and cards while others do not.

Some claimants' unions have committees or officers who are regularly elected by the members (e.g. three-monthly). If this happens, it is important that other members have the power of *instant* recall, that officers always stand down before elections and that there are several nominations for each post. Some unions have a formal chairman, others elect a different chairman each week, while others have no formal leadership or chairman. Minutes are kept by most unions, and a few have minute secretaries, while others elect someone each week. Most unions have a treasurer or finance secretary.

It is difficult to avoid a leadership or hierarchy developing in a local claimants' union. Newer members are always less experienced and confident than the original or older members. Nevertheless, it is felt to be important that *all* members should have an equal say in making decisions. Officers or older members should never be able to dictate policy or have more power than other members. No one should be able to make decisions regarding the claimants' union without first discussing this at the weekly meetings. Control must remain at all times with the rank and file. We believe in full involvement by *all* members of the union; there should be no 'experts', no leaders, no 'casework' by specialists, and no indispensable activists. And this is a lot easier than it sounds, for two reasons.

First, the different skills and abilities of individual claimants whether they can read or write, are blind or physically handicapped, have a typewriter or can use a printing press, etc. But everybody can and must contribute something, and the same people should not continually write the leaflets or go on speaking engagements, etc. It is often better for a nervous newcomer to try his or her hand, even if the result is not quite as good as if it had been done by a more experienced member.

Second, the DHSS usually think that by developing a 'relationship' with a few claimants' union members they can smooth down the militant activity of the union and prevent people putting in what they consider 'unreasonable' requests for *new* clothes and furniture, etc. The local SS manager will try to deal with one or two union members and refuse to speak or see any others. He or she will be eager to 'settle' claims quickly, 'discreetly' and in a 'confidential' manner by tempting a few claimants to negotiate over the heads of others. Of course this is the old story of divide and rule, and it soon leads to their trying to encourage unions to make a distinction between the so-called 'deserving' and 'undeserving'. In other words, the SS try to impose their own method of control on the local union by encouraging it to run as a 'casework' organisation, with a few claimants approaching the local office or writing letters or making phone calls 'on behalf of' other claimants.

Social workers

In an attempt to divide the working class, claimants have been labelled 'feckless', and in need of social work help to teach them to budget. Frequently a local supplementary benefit office will contact the local social services department if a claimant asks for more money (to meet a gas bill, for instance). Sometimes claimants are actually told to go to the social services department if they need something like bedding or clothing. Often a claimant who has been refused money by the supplementary benefits will approach a social worker in the hope that he or she will intervene.

Many social workers realise that supplementary benefits are not enough to manage on, and advise people to join their local claimants' union to fight for higher benefits. Some, however, only 'refer' their awkward or militant 'clients' in order to make less work for themselves, and thus keep on good terms with the local ss office. They may use the claimants' union simply as an advice or advocacy service and fail to appreciate its true nature. This can confuse their 'clients' who are sometimes taken aback by the deliberate lack of confidentiality in the union and the fact that it is run by people just like themselves and not by 'experts' or 'professionals'. Some social workers may later be very upset if one of their 'clients' is for instance arrested at the local ss office for taking part in a collective action. In such cases it has even been known for the ss staff to contact and locate a social worker to get her to stop her 'client' from behaving in this way.

A few social workers collude openly with the ss and talk about so-called 'deserving' and 'undeserving' cases with them. They then share 'confidential' information without the claimant's knowledge or permission and come to secret and conspiratorial arrangements about such things as meeting gas or electricity bills 50–50. Occasionally we have even come across examples of social workers who have gone so far as to persuade the ss to stop or reduce payment of benefit when they want to put pressure on an individual or family; for example, when a social worker has wanted to receive a child into care 'voluntarily' from a mother who is opposed to this, or when they have wanted to talk to a man who is never at home about the possibility of him signing a consent paper to his wife's sterilisation.

Many local authority means tests are administered by social workers, such as financial contribution for children in care, home helps, invalid aids. It is no doubt easier for social workers to criticise the Supplementary Benefits Commission than their own employers, and they make it clear that they are not prepared to risk their own job security in order to defend or advance the interests and livelihood of their clients.

Participation versus power

Many members of the 'poverty industry' talk of 'participation' by the 'deprived' or 'disadvantaged' as though this would be a concession forced out of the ss by the power of the Claimants' Union Movement. They fail to appreciate the true nature of power and illustrate a naivety about the functioning of our present society. After all, we could at the most be offered only minority representation on a small number of types of bodies concerned with adjudication or advice.

The local Supplementary Benefit Appeals Tribunals

These are adjudicating bodies which are neither independent nor unbiased, as frequently asserted. In fact, they are an integral part of the Supplementary Benefits Scheme. They can neither increase the basic rates of benefit nor abolish the means test, but are merely concerned with tampering with a few cases where the exercise of discretionary payments or controls is concerned. Unlike the 'sympathetic' trade unionists or social workers who sit powerless on these tribunals, we do not intend to sit in judgment on our fellow claimants, since we support *all* claims unconditionally and we certainly do not want to help the present system to run more smoothly.

Even if we had participation on the Supplementary Benefits Commission itself we would still have no real power to make any fundamental changes. The SBC can merely formulate administrative policy within a legislative framework (laws laid down by Parliament). Like Harold Wilson or Richard Titmuss, we would just become incorporated into the system and be powerless to bring about major changes in it.

Perhaps we should have offered evidence to the Fisher Committee of Enquiry into Social Security Abuse as they did suggest to us. No doubt, if we readily showed ourselves 'co-operative' (i.e. not unco-operative), we might even have been offered a place on this Committee beforehand. But instead, believing that the very establishment of this Committee itself was a calculated political move at a time of high and rising unemployment, vast numbers of strikers claiming SB and a growing realisation of the true nature of the SS system in stemming working-class progress, one would have had to have been exceedingly stupid to have got involved. The people, including social workers, social administrators and trade unionists, who were co-opted into it were as guilty as the trade union bosses who sat on the Donovan Committee which proved to be nothing more than a bolstering up of the Industrial Relations Act. The members of the Fisher Committee failed to see that its prime function was that of stigmatising claimants and reducing their status and self-esteem in the community.

Any of this 'participation' would be a sell-out to the system and an attempt on the part of the establishment to absorb our militancy. To the establishment, participation merely means that a few of us will help 'them' to make decisions about us.

We do not intend participating in our poverty. We intend organising to abolish it. We want the power to destroy the means test system and the values attached to it such as the work ethic, which we deplore. No one is going to 'offer' us the power. We are going to have to take it to run our own lives and have our own say. And when we demand a say in our own lives we do not mean 'participation'. What we say is – a guaranteed income without a means test for all.

Note

Further information (Claimants' Union Guide Book, *Journal of the National Federation of Claimants' Unions*) is available from the East London Claimants' Union, Dame Colet House, Ben Jonson Road, London, E.1.

6 A local view of community work

Harry Liddell and Richard Bryant

As the drive towards professionalisation in community work gathers momentum, there is a very real danger that the work of local activists, the 'natural' community workers of the world, could become increasingly neglected and under-valued. Already there are some signs that community work is tending to become exclusively equated with the activities of the professional workers. For example, much of our current literature deals primarily with the roles, functions, training and employment of professional workers and rarely includes any serious consideration of the contributions which are made, and have been made for many years, by local people who often perform a variety of community work activities without the status, resource backing and salary rewards which most professionals enjoy.[1] While it may be premature to claim, as some critics have,[2] that community work has already acquired conservative 'professional ideology' it is apparent that a process of exclusion is operating at the present time. Because of the conventions of class, education, language and social milieu we – and by 'we' I mean most professional community workers, community work teachers and members of our professional groups who are involved in the promotion of community work – tend to talk among ourselves about the nature and content of community work. The local activist is always somewhere in the back of our minds, often as a symbolic and sometimes romanticised figure, but he rarely appears as a direct contributor to these debates. Criticisms like these form the background to this article, which is an attempt to provide a local activist's perspective on community work and the activities of community workers in one area, the Gorbals, Glasgow. Of course there can never be a single 'local view' and no one person can embody and express the opinions, experiences and expectations of the many thousands of local people who are involved, as part of their everyday lives, in the work of local community organisations. Therefore, the views expressed here represent only one man's experiences and his reflections on these experiences.

Harry Liddell is a former convenor of the Hutchesontown Tenants' Association (HTA), a tenants' organisation which represents the residents of a Scottish Special Housing Association scheme in the Gorbals. The estate contains around 6,000 dwellings, the majority of which are concentrated in high rise flats, and many families from the old Gorbals area have been rehoused there over the last decade. The HTA has been in existence for six years and Harry Liddell's involvement dates from the time, some four and half years ago, when he was rehoused in the area from the old Gorbals. Through his work with the HTA Harry Liddell has encountered and worked with a number of professional community workers, volunteers who are active in the area, and student community workers.

The Gorbals has a long-established history of attracting professional and voluntary resources of various kinds, and among the most recent developments is the setting up of a field-work unit for the training of community workers. This unit, which operates from a shop near to Hutchesontown, appears in the article as the 'social shop'. Apart from his work with the tenants' association, Harry Liddell has had many years of experience as a shop steward in the engineering industry and his industrial and trade union background has naturally influenced his view of the activities of community organisations. Because of this, the relationship between community and industrial action forms a major theme in the article.

The tape-recorded interviews upon which the article is based were conducted in July–August 1972. To minimise artificiality in the presentation of the material, the interviewer's questions and occasional interjections have been included in the text.

RB Why did you first get involved in the tenants' association? Was it because you moved into an area where there were issues about which you felt that something should be done?

HL In a personal sense I feel that everybody should show an interest in the community and this was really the motivating force. There wasn't any particular issue that I felt sore about which drew me in, other than that I felt community-minded enough to be part of it. In the early days I was involved in trade union and political activities which didn't allow me so much time, but as issues developed and things hotted up I became more and more involved. I'm deeply involved now. I was quite happy with the idea that having had some experience in the trade unions and knowing something about ordinary people I could contribute to the development of the tenants' association. From there of course the issues have been so many and so varied that it really became deeply interesting.

RB How much overlap do you see between union organising and tenants' associations?

HL In the most general sense I think there is a rather close link; being involved in the trade union movement you spend tremendous energy along with others and in some cases sacrifice wages, and then suddenly a landlord comes along and takes it off you. This, it seems to me, itself brings the two together. If you're going to fight the boss for a pound it seems logical that you should then resist the landlord trying to take it back off you. Otherwise there's a lot of wasted energy and this isn't only in the field of rents, of course. It goes for many other activities which the tenants' associations can cover but where the trade unions are not involved. Such as trying to improve the area, improve the amenities, landscaping, so that the much-bandied-about terms of 'improving the quality of life' and giving people better places to live in become more than just clichés. We try to make them a reality. I would think that a large number of the people who are involved in tenants' organisations are trade unionists, in the sense of being members of trade unions. But there's more to it than just being trade unionists. Because invariably active trade unionists are probably active trade unionists out of a sort of class consciousness and the same class consciousness can find its expression in tenants' organisations. In Glasgow there is a history and tradition of the link between the shop stewards' committees and the tenants in resisting increased rents. It was this kind of united action which was responsible for the introduction of the 1916 Rent Restriction Act[3] which eventually affected the whole of the country. The scene of the action was on the Clydeside. This gives Glasgow a historical background and tradition. It's not alive all the time. But as certain situations become sharp, as is happening now with the sharpening caused by the approach of the new Rents Bill,[4] everyone is becoming aware of the need to do something. But equally aware that it can best be done through the involvement of both the tenants' organisations and the trade union movement. Because while tenants can become involved in a protracted struggle, as is happening right now in some towns where they are withholding rents, it can become so long drawn out that the tenants might become tired quicker than the authorities. But when the trade unions become involved, they are in a position to sharpen the thing up considerably and help to eliminate this long-drawn-out affair. It will need a sharp confrontation to defeat any government Bill; it won't be defeated where the tenants are dragged before the courts.

RB Tenants' associations tend to be rather impotent bodies when it comes to big issues. They lack the power and sanctions of the trade unions.

HL Why the tenants don't have the same power as the trade unions is because of the difficulty of organising tenants' associations. It's fragmented in the sense that you have so many different landlords – the Glasgow Corporation, the SSHA, the New Town Development authorities, the various housing associations and the private factors – and they're all imposing rent increases at different times according to when their financial year ends. So that everyone isn't confronted with this issue at the same time, and sections are being picked off one by one. It's so easy to do this and so difficult to organise against it. Whereas the trade unions can take action on any one day and everyone is involved, it's also much more difficult to organise in the community. On the shop floor you have two hundred or two thousand people all within four walls and you've got people with authority, shop stewards and the like, who are authorised to call meetings, etc.

In a community it's much more difficult. Amongst the trade unionists who are interested you've got shift work and other activities and, amongst the women, working part-time to contend with. To get everyone together at one meeting at one time is virtually impossible. Just because you don't get the attendance you would like it doesn't mean there is a lack of interest, there is an interest, but there are a whole number of reasons why people can't attend. Women are also tied down by young families and things like that. Of course the joining of a trade union means you're committed to certain policies and if you don't comply with these policies there are certain sanctions which can be taken against you – you can be disciplined – you can't discipline a tenant for not complying with the policies of a tenants' association. It's not that type of organisation. It's vitally important that people should become involved and in many cases it might be for the first time in their lives. This is one of the difficulties about it, because it is often for the first time in their life. Even here there are problems, because the leading committee members take on the responsibility of doing things for them, to the point where the tenants themselves won't be too involved. When it comes to rent strikes, if it comes to that, the local organisation take it upon themselves to collect all the rents, rather than have the poor lady who's never been involved before, have this confrontation with the factor,* even if maybe she'd be afraid and maybe not know how to go about it. This is a bit of a problem too. But the extent that people are prepared to identify themselves with whatever activity is going on,

* Factor is a Scottish term which refers to a manager of property.

they are becoming involved to a degree and this involvement is something that can be developed. If they see an action has been carried out successfully on their behalf by others then they become aware that this is good; it can be done. This is one important thing about it. The difficulty about activities in the political field is that the tenants' associations have not had many successes, despite the fact that we have had stacks of successes in many other fields. It's not any problem to get a new bus shelter, to get a new telephone, to get a piece of waste land landscaped, even to improve bus services or argue about a new community centre and maybe one day get it. This is all encouraging, helping to establish the authority of the organisation, and allowing this to be seen in people's eyes. But only when we start getting some successes in the political field will people be conscious of their ability to *control* political affairs which, at the end of the day, is really what is going to count. I would like to envisage tenants' associations developing to the point where they can establish authority in precisely the same way as the shop stewards' committees have done. The shop stewards didn't come into being overnight. It was a long struggle to identify individual shop stewards and it was a further struggle to identify them as shop stewards' committees, for them to achieve recognition as committees, and it was a further struggle to establish their authority as committees. But now that they have done all this it has strengthened the democracy in unions. There was a period when the more progressive committees, with the utmost support and respect of the workers that they represented from the floor of the shop, in trying to pursue the interests of the members they represented, were, in many ways, obstructed by the higher authorities. Not by intention, I would say, but precisely because the authorities were not at the centre of the issues. They didn't have first-hand knowledge of the issue, and were trying to see it in a sort of academic way – see where it was written under the rule book – rather than seeing how it was affecting people. I would like to see tenants' organisations develop to the point where they have as much authority, in their own locality, as a shop stewards' committee has in its own factory now. Then we would also have to consider the role of people coming from the outside realising that they were not living in the conditions, or living with them, and to that extent not being just aware exactly of what the problems were – in the same way as the higher-up trade union leader, because he's been away from the floor of the shop for ten or twenty years. Everything is in a developing situation; he obviously doesn't have the experience of what is happening on the floor of the shop today as he had of what happened ten or twenty years ago.

It's always a developing situation and the reason the shop stewards' committees have established their authority in the way that they have is because people have been able to devote themselves to this kind of thing and tenants' associations will only establish the same recognition and authority to the same extent that there are people who are devoted to doing it well. The bit that makes it more difficult for the tenants' associations is that the members have, invariably, to do it in their spare time, while a lot of the shop steward's activity can be conducted in the employer's time. This is a much happier situation.

RB   The question of the time available to work for tenants' associations raises the issue of whether full-time workers should not be employed by these organisations. How do you view this suggestion?

HL   Well, I think at the moment it is very necessary, particularly at the Glasgow level. In Glasgow, nearly every tenants' association is affiliated to the Glasgow Council of Tenants and, at a further level, there is the Scottish Council of Tenants which covers a wider area.[5] It has become so big an organisation now that I think there is need for at least one full-time secretary in Glasgow and also for the rest of Scotland. Of course one of the problems here is finance, and how you get the finance. Trade unions get finance by so much a fortnight. There is a limited sum, an annual sum, but the kind of money which is involved in tenants' associations would make it extremely difficult to have full-time organisers. That doesn't mean to say that there are not always some people, probably retired, who don't devote themselves almost full-time to what they're doing anyway and this is one of the good features of our organisations. It would be good to have the kind of money so that we could even have an office. Although there are facilities through the trade unions – particularly the Glasgow Trades Council, whose office we can use – it's not specifically a tenants' office and it would be a good idea if we had one that was.

RB   Would you see an argument for trade unions providing money for full-time organisers of tenants' associations, or would you see other sources of support being more appropriate?

HL   I think this would very much revolve around the level of development of the tenants' organisations themselves and their ability to establish their authority as permanent organisations. Because there is a tendency for them to flourish when there are issues on and then to taper off when things are quiet. There's no lack of support, including financial support, from the trade unions to meet particular issues that the trade unions are prepared to identify with. But when it comes to the trade unions giving out money generally to organisations without knowing what it's for, then they themselves are tied by their own constitutions as who they can give money to and how they can spend it. This is perfectly understandable, because members contribute the money and they've got to have control over how it's spent and who's going to get the money. It could well be a residents' group of owner-occupiers living in suburbia. So the financial support will come in on issues to the extent that the trade unions will support the issues, but I don't envisage more general aid developing at the moment and not even in the fore-seeable future. You see it becomes a bit phoney when some other organisations support an organisation. Each organisation has got to find its own level and its own organisation, and this includes its ability to raise finance. Fund-raising activities do go on, and on the other side of it some tenants' associations always want to do something more social – spend money on social events, such as Christmas presents for old people – which is all very good. In others there might be an emphasis upon spending money on campaigning and more political activities.

RB   You mentioned the need for full-time organisations at the city and national level; what about the need for full-time workers in local areas? Given that some retired people do work in an almost full-time capacity already.

HL   I don't think one should put too much on retired people. There *are* odd ones and they usually are retired trade unionists. In the local organisations, old people are rather restricted, one reason being that, because they are retired, they have physical restrictions placed on them. Others who seek to play a more prominent role invariably do it out of their own convictions and this involves some sacrifice on their own behalf, but even that can be limited too. You can start off on a project full of enthusiasm for it and pursue it and then, at a crucial stage, find that because of your other commitments you can't quite go through with it to the finality. It pretty much revolves around conviction on the particular issue involved. One which took up a lot of time and attention last year was the revaluation.[6] A lot of individuals spent a lot of time representing tenants in courts and arguing for reductions. It pretty much depended on having these kinds of people in the organisa-tions with the time available. You could have a bloke who was doing certain things during the day when he was on night shift, but then next month he's on day shift and so somebody else has to step in and there may not be anybody else available at that time. This is part of the difficulties of the organisation and I don't see any local organisation being in the position of having a full-time worker. Although some do have reasonable healthy funds and are prepared to pay for time off work, if they think the occasion is important enough. But this could not be as a once a week sort of thing.

RB This relates to another theme, namely the trend from social work departments and other social welfare agencies to employ what are loosely called 'community workers'. In many ways these community workers appear to be doing, at times, a similar type of work to your tenants' activists. How do you view this trend, given that the Gorbals has perhaps more 'outsiders' working as local community workers than anywhere else in Glasgow?

HL It's only in the last couple of years that I've become aware of the existence of community and social workers in this area or any other area, and what surprised me was to find that they were doing some of the work that I had been doing for some time previously, along with many others in the community. I was a little concerned at first as to their motives for being there. Were they genuinely concerned about the community or were they trying to establish some degree of authority in the community so that their concept of how things should be done, what changes should be made, might be the prevailing one as distinct from how the community themselves felt about it? Maybe also I felt a little piqued at one time, because they got paid for doing it whereas all the other members of the community, who had been doing it for years, were doing it in their leisure time. But since having developed better relations with the community workers and worked more closely with them, I've discovered that there's no reason why we shouldn't work together with the same aims in mind as long as they are prepared to respect the wishes of the community and their desires. My experience up to now is that this is pretty much what they have been doing. Maybe with not always the same degree of priority as we might have had, but nevertheless able to achieve certain things that were possible, that were available, but which we wouldn't have thought about, ourselves, because we were probably too concerned about what we thought were our first priorities, which weren't obtainable at the time. At least they get certain things done and by methods that they have much more technical expertise about than we have. Here we have people whose first concern is what they do for the community, as part of their normal everyday work. My views have changed to the extent that I think we could do with a lot more of this kind of activity and there's no reason at all why community organisations cannot work in close harmony and derive benefits from the special skills of the community and social workers, and in this way strengthen the development of the community. I think that certain developments would not take place, and could not take place, just by the tenants' associations alone if it were not for the assistance of professional people. I don't mean only assistance in terms of technical expertise but knowledge of how to go about getting things which we don't have, such as the most recent project that the tenants have become involved in, the development of our own Youth and Community Centre, as distinct from the Corporation's centres. Without the advice of people who know how to go about getting the cash, how to apply to the Scottish Education Department – and that included a lawyer, an architect, an ex-chief of police as treasurer and various people like that – we would never have been able to have made the kind of progress which has been made in this project. That assistance would not have been available to us if it were not for these professional people themselves being prepared to be socially identified with the development of the community and having this sort of social consciousness. I suppose the limitations on that will be pretty much the same as the limitations which are on the tenants' associations. It will be limited by the number of people like that who are prepared to involve themselves in this kind of activity. Maybe the reason for these limitations is that there are only a limited number of people involved. This is a reasonable explanation, I think, because while we're moving in the right direction in terms of professional people becoming more involved in social questions – and social questions mainly revolve around the poorer groups of the community – it's not exactly widespread. By their background and by their professions they may just develop along the traditional lines of the profession, which tends to be middle class and sheltered and limited to their own experience. I mean you can't expect these people to have the experience of having to lack this or lack that or go without this or go without that or to be confronted with some kinds of problem. It's surprising how sometimes small problems can turn into major tragedies; it's not always recognised by anyone other than the person who is directly involved.

RB Isn't there a danger of outsiders coming in and in many ways assuming some of the responsibilities of the local leaders? In my opinion there is a very delicate balance between the role of the outsider and the role of the local activist and it's a very difficult line to draw between where the outsider's work stops and the local's work begins. Where do you see this balance occurring, if that is not too hypothetical a question?

HL I think the role of the community worker would be best served by helping a community to develop its own organisations and help it, in a technical way, to advance the kinds of interests it wants to advance.

Rather than that the community worker should be a leader. I think there is a danger that they might try to get things done their way and they have more time to use their influence to ensure that they are done their way too. Up to now this hasn't been my experience, but it is certainly something which would have to be guarded against. It would be up to the organisations of the community to control their activities, although there is no way in which you can control them to the point of saying, 'Look, you can't do this or can't do that', because once they're involved in something, they're involved, and they will follow it through. The thing revolves around who gives these workers their edict, their licence about how far they can go and what activities they can involve themselves in. They can certainly play a tremendous role in helping the people to express themselves but at the end of the day it's got to revolve around the people expressing themselves. There is the danger that if people don't have to express themselves because they've only got to run round the corner to the 'social shop', this could be a retarding feature rather than a healthy feature. This is a possible danger, but as long as the social and community workers themselves *respect* the organisations and in fact know about them and know more about their policies and don't at any time attempt to cross the lines in terms of policy, then everything should work very satisfactorily. To what extent they can be involved in the more general political questions, I've got some reservations about, you know, because I don't think outsiders can come in and foist political views or attitudes towards political questions which the people may not be responding to. So I think the attitudes to political questions have very much got to come from the organisations themselves. I think the two can work very much together, but basically the organisations have got to have their grass roots in the community and mainly revolve around the community with all the help and assistance they can get from all other organisations which are prepared to identify themselves with the problems of the community. It's going to be a very difficult situation for any social or community worker who does understand the deeper political implications of the system and the need for a change in the system. They can help individuals and groups to improve their situation in the immediate sense, but it's unlikely that they will be able to go back to them a week or so later or a month or so later and explain to them the political reasons for the need for this and how to overcome it. Whereas someone in the community, who's there all the time, meets the people all the time, can always say, 'Well, that will maybe get you by for this week or next week', but it's not the ultimate solution and you can then have the opportunity to explain to them wh i you think the ultimate solution is in the political sense. In this, then, I think social and community workers will be very restricted. Unless of course they were part of the community and had the same standing as the long-standing members of the community who have been there for a long time.

RB   How do you think you achieve that, if it's at all possible?

HL   I don't think there are many short cuts to achieving ultimate political aims in any way. It can only come about by the hard work of the people who are dedicated to some kind of political change, and being dedicated doesn't mean doing it for the sake of the salary involved or conflict with employers as to what you're doing. I don't think there are any short cuts. It really revolves around the involvement of the people in political struggle, and the contribution that the paid professional social worker can make in that connection will be very limited, I should think, in so far as his job would be at risk, probably, if he weren't measuring up to the same political ideals as his employer. When we reach the stage when one employing body has people who are anxious for political change, then there will be much more scope for the community and social workers to express their ideals to the community without their job being at risk. This would be a great development, but it's not one which is near in the foreseeable future.

Notes

1 For example, see Calouste Gulbenkian Foundation, *Community Work and Social Change*, London, Longman, 1968.
2 See G. Popplestone, 'The ideology of professional social workers', *British Journal of Social Work*, 1 (1), April 1971.
3 See W. Gallacher, *Revolt on the Clyde*, London, Lawrence & Wishart, 1936, esp. chapter 4.
4 This refers to the Housing (Scotland) Act 1972.
5 The Glasgow Council of Tenants dates from 1926. The Scottish Council of Tenants was formed in 1948.
6 This is a revaluation of the housing stock which occurred in Glasgow in 1971, and which was contested by a number of the city's tenants' associations.

Part II Making Services Relevant and Responsive

David Jones

It is fortuitous that two of the contributions in this section relate to Camden. Yet Camden's services, both statutory and voluntary, probably compare very favourably with those in most areas. Although there are major exceptions, there is a tendency for those areas in which the need for change and development is greatest to be the least able and likely to generate new initiatives or to respond to them.

In the not too distant past the problems of community involvement were seen in terms of non-participation, apathy and lack of leadership, particularly among lower socio-economic groups and in areas of social deprivation. Recent experience of participation has still to be critically assessed but it is already evident that the issue has to be re-formulated. Given appropriate assistance, even seriously disadvantaged and handicapped populations have demonstrated an ability to organise themselves and take effective action. The extent and degree of participation remains problematic. Only a minority seem to participate in an active and sustained manner in any particular enterprise. But this is perhaps not unreasonable and applies to all social strata. While this is an important consideration it does not invalidate the idea of participation or its usefulness.

The more intractable problem which has been revealed is that when initiative appears and efforts are made to change the existing arrangements they tend too often to be undermined, discredited and side-tracked. The activities of community groups may sometimes be troublesome for those against whom they are directed. But the more important issue is the lack of responsiveness of organisations and of the normal decision-making machinery.

The contributions which discuss the situation from the grass-roots standpoint show a considerable ambivalence. On the one hand, action at the grass roots is seen as a potential solution to a wide range of social problems and a means to the transformation of society. On the other there is a deep pessimism about the possibility of any significant change at all, within the present social structure.

Additionally, experience at the grass roots has confirmed what should have been self-evident, that action solely at the local or small group level is unlikely to be the most effective way of bringing about major changes in social policy. Participation may overcome feelings of apathy, hopelessness and alienation. Self-help and mutual aid activities can be developed to the extent that those involved have the necessary resources. Neighbourhood action can deal with problems of a local nature or those that can be resolved by local decisions.

It becomes increasingly difficult, however, for action that is taken only at the level of the neighbourhood to have an impact on more general issues which affect many neighbourhoods or whole cities, and about which decisions are made by policy-makers far beyond the confines of the locality. Major problems facing social deprived areas – employment, housing, income maintenance, health services and education – require resources and decisions that cannot be made at local level.

In this section the issues are approached from the standpoint of some of the organisations and professions which exist to provide services and to meet people's needs. The contributions address themselves to what are recognisably the same problems. Without being facile or soporific, they add a further dimension of understanding, complexity and hope.

The Social Development Officers of New Towns were perhaps the first statutory officials with specified community work functions (community development, research, liaison with statutory and voluntary bodies, social planning), and the potential of their role has been authoritatively re-emphasised on a number of occasions. Harloe and Horrocks's suggestion that 'social development still has problems about establishing its legitimacy' is thus particularly disturbing. Interestingly, they point to greater professionalisation as one means of increasing effectiveness. More crucial, however, would seem to be the attitudes, assumptions and policies of New Town management.

John Crook considers developmental planning in another statutory context, the social services department of local authorities. Despite the complex political, intellectual and practical problems involved in planning, he argues that community participation is essential and should take place not only as problems arise (for 'the resources which can be manipulated at short notice are small'), but much earlier, when development proposals are being formulated and there is 'an opportunity to influence the balance of resources before decisions are made'. Crook also advocates flexible local plans which might 'not always bear a direct relationship to the overall plan, but may play an important role in clarifying developments and new issues which could lead to changes in the overall plan'. He also suggests that the development of corporate planning 'places the social services department in a powerful position to influence the policy of other departments by analysing the effects of these policies on vulnerable members of the community'.

Adah Kay, discussing some of these issues from the standpoint of the physical planner within the local authority, comes to more pessimistic conclusions.

Leissner and Joslin address themselves more to the actual delivery of services and show, with a wealth of illustration, that community work, as a logical and natural outgrowth of service responsibilities, is also feasible under local authority auspices. Most of the early work was initiated by Family Advice Centres under an action research mandate. The authors envisage the adoption of a similar community orientation by area teams of Social Services Departments including involvement in grass-roots community work. They argue that workers should not opt out but have the courage and stamina to work for change within the system.

A number of the developments discussed in this section in fact take the form of special projects. This can often be a most effective mechanism for initiating new developments, proving their value and practicality and gaining more general acceptance for them. Occasionally, however, a special project may be a way of encapsulating innovations and avoiding the need for more substantial and general changes in the host organisation.

As contrasted with the striving towards purity of role evident in some discussion of community work, Leissner and Joslin discuss an approach which integrates advice, guidance and assistance to individuals and families with the provision of community services, mutual aid, participation and community action although they do not indicate whether any problems arise from this combination.

Pam Warren, describing the work of a multi-purpose voluntary organisation, adopts a similar cavalier attitude towards categories. With a deceptively light touch she illustrates the inter-relationships and inter-actions between a wide range of services and community work activities, between many different organisations both statutory and voluntary, and between work at various levels – neighbourhood, district, borough, regional, national. She sees the Council of Social Service as primarily a broker – an honest broker – constantly crossing and re-crossing the boundaries. If community work is to grow and develop it 'must learn to live with ambiguities, paradoxes and untied ends'.

George and Teresa Smith discuss community work from the perspective of another major service – the schools. The parallels to developments in the social services are striking despite the important differences in the two settings. The authors argue that community work in terms of programmes extending out into the community and tailored to the local situation is a logical development for the school. They point, however, to 'the gulf between the way an ordinary school functions and that required for community work' and the 'conflicts which emerge as schools attempt to balance their traditional concern for individual children against their new role in community development.' The contribution which 'intermediate roles' and 'intermediate institutions' can make to change both within the school and in its relations with the community is demonstrated from the experience of a multi-purpose education centre. But the broader issue of the role of the schools as agents of social change remains to be explored.

Finally we have the Albany, a Victorian Settlement responding to the current situation in a depressed dockland area with a flexible, community-based programme embracing an extremely varied range of activities. Their contribution focuses on one aspect, a community arts project which is seen as 'central to the Albany's concern to provide opportunities for people to develop their potential in all aspects of their lives'. It speaks for itself. Unashamedly they wish to be Deptford's Entertainers, not missionaries of art, and quote a local housewife: 'after all, in art you don't need to be an expert – just simply to enjoy doing it is really its main purpose, and then gradually learning how to do it to one's own satisfaction, and from that comes a sense of achievement. And that's a very precious thing.'

7 Developmental planning in local authority services

John Crook

Social services are provided in a country increasingly subject to planning, and to demands for further planning. This is true of the physical environment and of the local authority context within which social services are provided. Planning has been fashionable for some time now, but recently we have become aware of the need for co-operation of the various separate plans which exist at the moment. The interdependence of problems and the interchangeability of resources have been recognised. Solutions to problems have been found to create additional problems, sometimes more intractable, although often more subtle than the original. In this complex world, the possibility and the relevance of planning must be considered.

The Seebohm Report argued the case for increased planning in the social services:[1]

> If the services are to meet effectively the complex range of
> individual, family and community problems, then effort devoted
> to investigating the needs of an area, and to overall planning
> and co-ordination of services and resources, both statutory and
> voluntary, is clearly of the utmost importance.

Such a conscious planning approach should lead to a number of improvements in the administration of services. The resources of the department would have to be reviewed in a systematic manner, any gaps or maldistribution would become obvious, and some indication of priorities for development obtained. But an examination of the department's resources can only sensibly be undertaken if prefaced by a consideration of the objectives to be achieved. This is a task which, in the pressure of daily administration, may receive little attention and yet proper consideration of objectives should show the relevance of policies to the current situation, highlight implicit conflicts, and identify inadequacies of resources. Objectives must be considered in relation to the needs which the department is trying to meet and, without a proper examination of these, the most sophisticated planning is wasted. The relationship of need to objectives is the prime management task and the most rational allocation of resources, the best co-operation between sections, is wasted if the wrong objectives are set.

The purposes and process of planning was examined by Parker during a recent speech[2] in which he discussed four themes. He suggested that plans were valuable because they expressed an intention on the part of the authority; this made crude measures of performance and the establishment of norms possible. Planning could lead to the second theme of co-ordination. Generally, services have developed in a piece-meal fashion with co-operation occurring in a bargaining situation; planning can make this more effective by building a basis of greater interdependence, which leads to more effective bargaining. Third, planning is concerned with 'instrumentality'; Parker suggests that rational planning can often fail at the implementation point because of a clash between political and rational solutions. Finally, forecasting is often an important part of planning but it is usually concerned with conditions outside the control of the department; it is therefore essentially reactive and, by its nature, fixed in the past and the present. Clearly there are considerable benefits to be achieved by rational planning but, as Parker points out, there are dangers of rigidity and lack of imagination.

A rational planning model is central to the current move to corporate management. Stewart,[3] strongly arguing the need for this approach, states that the management task 'is being increasingly recognised as involving an emphasis on general management – the management of the affairs of the authority in relation to its environment.' He argues that an overall approach cannot be achieved by using the traditional budget as a policy control because it only specifies resources, not objectives. Further, it does not encourage the analysis of alternative ways of achieving the organisations' objectives. He suggests a programme structure which classifies activities in relation to these objectives which are arranged in order of priority. This structure is analysed and alternative approaches to the achievement of objectives are evaluated so that the system is continually under review. A particular objective may require joint action by different departments or might be achieved independently; in this way the total effort allocated to different objectives can be analysed and the interactions of different departments become clear.

Unfortunately, objectives are very difficult to define in the field of social work and social policy. Donnison has analysed the difficulties very clearly[4] and has concluded: 'Thus there can be no generally and permanently valid "principles of social policy" and no book of rules for the social administration.' A co-ordinated approach to the authorities' administration is very attractive for it offers more effective use of limited resources – providing that the social services department is able to define its objectives, has full information about the effects of policies, or lack of policies, on vulnerable people and then is able to influence other departments through the management system.

The perception of need

The new management systems, with their promises of greater co-ordination and more effective use of resources, depend on statements of objectives which in turn depend on perceptions of need. Criticisms of the Seebohm Report by Sinfield[5] cast doubt on the reliability of social workers' perceptions of client need: 'However much reports emphasise the essential need for research, and social work text books stress client self-determination, there has been little energy devoted to finding out what recipients of social work help think of the services.' Research into the satisfaction of clients and into their understanding of the help offered to them by a casework agency forced Mayer and Timms[6] to 'an underlying suspicion that the conceptual differences between worker and client are . . . not wholly unlike the differences that separate the practitioners of Western medicine from the non-literate population they hope to serve.' Clearly, social workers' perceptions of need must be affected by the difficulties of communications which Mayer and Timms discuss. The first Gulbenkian Report suggested a corrective to this situation:[7] 'It is precisely at this gap between result and purpose that community work comes to interpret to the local authority how the services appear to the consumer.' Certainly, new modes of communication and assessment must be developed if adequate perception of need is to be achieved.

Need which is presented to social workers is not a true reflection of need in the community, for the service the department provided in the past – and provides in the present – very much affects the referrals received by the department – Donnison argues:[8]

> The number of and selection of clients served depends on the
> decisions of the provider responsible for accepting applications,
> the impression of their aims and capacities they convey to the
> public, the relations they establish with others who refer potential
> clients to them, and other activities on the boundary lines
> between provider and their clientele.

This has been recognised by the implementation of Section 1 of the Chronically Sick and Disabled Persons Act 1970 which requires local authorities to assess need in their areas rather than assume that the referrals they receive represent need.

Finally, the perception of need is not simply a matter of adequate survey techniques and good communication with the client. Packman found, in her investigation of the variation in numbers of children in care, that these variations could only be explained by taking into account the views of chief officers; she comments[9] that some chief officers were 'concerned about advertising their own service and smoothing the paths into care. There were at least some who felt if they went about their work quietly – even surreptitiously – the public would learn to get by without them.' She also suggests that moral judgments lie behind these views and Donnison brings this out quite explicitly:[10] 'The aims of each service and their practical application cannot be determined or reconciled without a continual exercise of moral judgment.' People in the community are affected by these moral decisions at times when they are in crisis situations; some justification and explanation of those views is necessary.

The limitation of social workers' perceptions and the moral element in a department's objectives indicate the need for a dialogue with the community, taking into account its perception of need and of the service provided. This approach much be supplemented by research into social worker–client communication and into referral process, but the moral nature of the exercise still requires explicit recognition.

Past planning and the current exercise

Local authority social services departments were asked by the Secretary of State to produce ten-year development plans[11] in September 1972. The plans expect local authorities to make detailed estimates of the resources needed to provide comprehensive services. The circular gives some estimates of the average standards of provision which are expected to be necessary. How successful is this exercise likely to be?

A detailed analysis by Davies of the ten-year plans produced by welfare departments in the 1960s is illuminating, but not encouraging.[12] He concludes that local authorities' planning would not result in a higher degree of correlation between standards and needs, when the completed plans are compared to the conditions existing at the time of planning. Despite the popular emphasis on community care, he found no tendency for local authorities to increase domiciliary services at a faster rate than residential homes. He concluded[13] that ideas were very vague about future need and horizons short – 'Principal determinant of future standards was to be current standards.'

The current circular gives more guidance to departments than was available to them in the 1960s; on the other hand, their task is much more complex and comprehensive. The difficulties in the planning exercise are discussed elsewhere[14] and possible solutions suggested. But it is important to consider the general issues involved and to relate them to the problems of perception discussed previously.

The most obvious difficulty facing any planner is the lack of adequate data. There can be few social services departments which have really adequate information about the referrals they receive, their current caseloads and the use they make of residential establishments. Usually what information is available is not comparable with information collected by the previously separate departments and so trends cannot be identified. The statistics collected at national level give little idea of the policies adopted by different authorities and no idea of their effectiveness. Another major difficulty is that information about the incidence and prevalence of problems is very limited. Only in the field of mental handicap and, more recently, physical handicap are there reasonably reliable figures which indicate the scale of the problem. The extent to which different services might be interchanged is not known – the 'trade off' in the provision of one service as against another cannot be calculated; consequently balanced expansion is difficult to achieve.

Yet planning must take place, and it will occur in an increasingly formalised structure as local government becomes more concerned with corporate management. There is a real danger that the techniques will overtake the objective – more effective planning based on sound information and the evaluation of alternatives. This is especially so in a department like social services, which is expanding rapidly and has not had an opportunity to consolidate. In any case, departments face legal and financial constraints on their planning but these, as Stewart[15] points out, often consist of constraints of attitude and fixed ways of working. The difficulty of defining alternatives, particularly where problems are subtle, can only be met by the development of what Parker calls a 'radical imagination'. He argues that this is usually absent from our attempts at planning which start in the present and work to the future instead of attempting the opposite. The only way to achieve this is to obtain a heterogeneity of experience which he suggests can be obtained from 'a greater variety of presents'. To do this, he suggests that planners must listen to outsiders, speak to young people at the formative stage of their development, and also be prepared to reinterpret their own experience; he quotes Szasz's view of mental illness as a significant reinterpretation of experience. Sinfield points out another danger when he argues[16] that social workers should not define their role in socio-psychological terms, but in social terms, which will move 'the emphasis away from the skills and techniques used and towards the objectives of the worker'.

Participation and responsibility

A 'radical imagination' could be fostered by obtaining a variety of presents from the community's involvement in planning. Stewart[17] acknowledges that 'the articulation of the attitudes and demands of those who live and work in the area is important for environmental analysis as for other parts of the authorities' work.' In another context, Mayer and Timms suggest that one way to overcome the lack of understanding between social worker and client would be to re-educate the client, but comment that 'a complementary approach – and one which we see as more productive in the long run – would involve prior efforts to learn more about the views of those who would on the former assumption have to be re-educated'. This latter approach conveys rather more humility!

The need to understand the environment is only one reason for participation. It has been suggested that many of the decisions taken by social workers and administrators cannot be seen only in a professional framework, but have a moral content. Sometimes this can be quite explicit, as in the case of a children's officer discussing an application by a married couple to have their child adopted:[18] 'For twelve months this had to be refused because a married couple *ought* to want to care for their child.' Other, less explicit, moral choices are behind many decisions in social work.

The very wide variation in the standard of provision between different authorities which Davies has analysed requires an explanation to the public. They should be aware of these differences and have an opportunity to comment on the standard of service they require. Until they do this, authorities themselves are unlikely to examine these variations critically. Davies argues[19] that a comprehensive set of criteria on which services can be assessed in relation to need are necessary, but that even then the 'degree to which the administration of social services take them into account will depend on the public vigilance, the supply of relevant information about services and a body of techniques which can help people to assess the success with which services are being organised to meet the needs for them.'

This is particularly necessary because in public organisations the two functions of the consumer – consumption and control[20] – are separated because payment, the main form of control, is compulsory. This situation easily leads to the assumption that those in control know what is best. If the people the organisation is to serve are to have any control, 'communication bridges' must be developed.

The Skeffington Report[21] discussed this in detail from the physical planning viewpoint. The report criticised the local authority for being more successful in informing than involving people, and for leaving the opportunity for comment too late. The Report suggested that the article could make use of community forums, advisory panels and co-option but that the less articulate needed a community development officer to give information, receive and transmit reactions. It is also suggested that participation by activity was valuable – arranging publicity, assisting in survey work, distributing material, etc. An attempt to do this is described by Plumridge[22] who used a town appraisal, questionnaires distributed at public meetings and planning surgeries. He concluded that there was an eagerness to participate but that there was a gap in communication, which indicated a need for education on the issues before participation. This is in some ways a dangerous conclusion as it stresses the role of the specialist. It may well be that the community development officer has a far more central role than in the experience described and that a much more personal form of communication is necessary for effective participation. Nevertheless, the experience of planning departments indicates that participation is possible on complex problems, and emphasises the failure of social services departments to attempt this.

Effective participation cannot be an activity which a team undertakes for a particular development plan and then moves on, since the social workers who provide the service are essential actors in any development. Donnison argues that the providers of the service are in a crucial position because they are in contact with both the controllers of resources and those who determine the demands on the resources. They are the people responsible for assessing the social problems presented to the department and so communication starts with them. Consequently they are particularly influential in influencing development, for 'The spark which ignites this process of innovation may come from various quarters, but the driving force that propels it comes from those deeply involved in providing the service'.[23] These are also the staff who are in the most personal contact with their areas. It is therefore they who must be involved in the participation process, first, if it is to be successful and, second, if the results are to affect practice.

The need to accept responsibility for the standards of the area, to discuss implicit moral discussions, to achieve effective participation and to affect the department's policies all focus on the role of the social worker. The social worker may be functioning in a community development role some of the time, and full-time community workers might be available, but the first emphasis must still be on the person most in contact with clients and with the community. The community worker may exert pressure on the administration over particular issues, but the long-term gains are likely to come from effecting the experience and perception of the social worker in the field.

The community and planning

The local authority clearly has a responsibility to improve its planning process. One of the most important developments would be an improvement in the management information services of the social services department, and a great deal of effort must be put into the development of expertise in their use. There is a paradox here, though; as more objective information is available, the essential 'feel' about problems faced by the department might escape and an important, though unmeasurable, element in the management process be lost. The on-going analysis which better information systems make possible must not be limited to the social services departments but linked to, and shared with, other departments which provide related services in the community. The resulting understanding of the department's operation should be shared with the community and the field-workers if the department is to be responsible to, and communicate with, the community.

People's expectations tend to rise and change with experience of reasonable quality services, consequently the perception of social need changes. The indeterminacy of this situation suggests that considerable attention should be given to the preservation of as much flexibility of resources as possible. The long-term aim should be to provide people who need services with a degree of choice as to the way in which their particular problem is met. This policy might emphasise the provision of community services which are less capital-intensive and therefore more flexible, as well as having advantages in keeping people independent. So far, social services have had to take what resources they could, but a continuation of this process will lead to in-built rigidities in the resources of departments and limitations on future choices.

At the moment, social services departments are primarily concerned with the preparation of plans for the development of the whole department. This is a necessary first step, but plans must also be related to the local community so that much smaller-scale plans are necessary. The more local plans serve a different purpose. They should have a shorter time-scale and may well include items which would not be appropriate to larger plans. Clearly there is a need for comparability between the overall plan and the area plan, but if the latter were just a scaled-down version of the former, participation would be ineffective. The area plan should suggest local and short-term targets and may well vary considerably in emphasis from year to year; it will not always bear a direct relationship to the overall plan, but may play an important role in clarifying developments and new issues which could lead to changes in the overall plan.

The small-scale plans would also have the advantage of starting a dialogue with field-workers and the community about short-term goals. This leads to a more fundamental point, which is the need for social workers to be aware of the detailed policy objectives of the department, to accept them, and to be prepared to implement them. For example, if the provision of the home help service has been increased at the expense of more places in old people's homes (usually departments cannot expand both), and social workers aware of the needs of the handicapped use the additional resources for them, then the welfare of the old people is likely to be reduced. It has already been argued that the providers of the service are in an influential position because they filter the information about need coming to the department and make independent professional decisions. Consequently, the implementation of a plan will depend on their involvement in its preparation and a commitment to the objectives of the plan. The social worker will then have consciously to differentiate between the needs which are presented to the department rather than give an average 'best possible' service to everyone. The alternative to this extremely difficult role is to be limited in the help given, as social workers are at the moment, but not in a conscious and controlled way; it should be more effective to adopt the planned approach although this places explicit limits on professional judgment rather than unspecified limits created by shortage of resources.

Ecw

The use of developmental planning gives the social worker an opportunity to be more effective in the roles described by Sinfield[24] as social investigator, mediator and interpreter. If the social worker is simply commenting on the resources of the authority as he is aware of them, the room for manœuvre in one year is limited because, characteristically, local authority budgets are largely committed to projects which cannot be easily cancelled; consequently the resources which can be manipulated at short notice are small. An informed and critical examination of development proposals, on the other hand, gives the social worker and the community an opportunity to influence the balance of resources before decisions are made.

Just as the social worker acts as an investigator, mediator and interpreter, so should the social services department. The development of corporate planning and the recognition of the interrelation and interdependence of local authority services place the social services department in a powerful position to influence the policy of other departments by analysing the effects of these policies on vulnerable members of the community. This potentially powerful and effective role will only be possible if the department itself is aware of the difficulties caused by particular policies. Once again, effective planning depends on communication with the people at the receiving end of policies, and hence the importance of the field-workers and community groups in the process of planning.

There are a number of groups in most communities which take an interest in particular social problems. In many areas the WRVS deliver meals on wheels and have considerable knowledge, seldom tapped, of the difficulties of old people in their area, and more particularly of local conditions or of policies which affect old people adversely. The Spastic Society have lively local groups with knowledge of this particular problem who can comment on the quantity and standard of local authority services. In most areas there are a considerable number of groups who could comment from experience on local authority plans and provide a valuable feedback. This has the advantage that people in vulnerable and dependent positions, perhaps badly needing the services they receive, can criticise them but be protected by the anonymity of the group.

The grass-roots organisations of tenants' and neighbourhood associations can comment on plans in a different way. They have a more general view of the area, its problems and their hopes for it. The discussion of development plans with them will test the relevance of the plan, but also may raise issues that they had not considered and give their concern some new direction. The local churches and youth clubs may see an involvement in the development plans for their areas as a practical way of expressing their pastoral concern. They may well find new needs in the community which would help them develop and extend their role. The idea of participation in planning is valuable here; they may be involved in surveys and the assessment of need as well as in disseminating information about plans and assessing local opinion.

Organisations which might not be directly involved in the community can be brought into the planning process. The local Chamber of Trade, the Post Office and local traders have great local knowledge. They are often aware of local conditions and difficulties which would be very relevant. The recent circular *Old and Cold*,[25] which stressed the dangers of hypothermia, has, in some areas, led to a much greater dialogue between public utilities and social workers than before. The social effects of commercial decisions, such as disconnecting electricity, are being considered more, and the public utilities seem to be interpreting their responsibilities much more widely.

The requirement that social services undertake developmental planning appears to offer the field-worker and community an important avenue by which policy can be affected before firm commitments are made. This seems to be very relevant to the functions of the community worker as discussed in the first Gulbenkian Report:[26]

> Thus his function is to clarify priorities of social need by fact finding and by encouraging members of the community to consider their own problems and attempt to relate these to other available services. He offers to groups in the community information which will educate, inform and enable them to perceive more accurately the nature of their own problems in relation to the commitments, obligations and limitations of the organisations and resources which they can call upon.

One might add the responsibility to assess and comment on the 'commitments, obligation and limitation' of organisations rather than simply consider their own problems in relation to the organisation.

The difficulties in planning, in particular the problem of the perception of need and the necessity of a radical imagination,[27] mean that the social services department must be more explicit about its objectives and look to the community for a 'variety of presents' on which to plan for the future. In this situation lie seeds of an interdependence which could foster effective consultation and the acceptance of a responsibility to justify the standard of service received by the community. Nevertheless,

it must be recognised that developmental planning is a new responsibility and that the first plans will only be tentative – fortunately
the plans are to be reviewed each year. Similarly, the techniques by
which plans are explained, discussed with, and modified by the community, are as yet untried and underdeveloped. However, explicit plans
offer the opportunity for effective participation, but there is also the
danger of rigidity being extended three or even more years forward;
the outcome will depend on the courage of social services departments
which will enable them to share their expectations and difficulties,
and the extent to which social workers and community workers use
the opportunity to open a fruitful dialogue between the community
and the department, so giving the plans a relevance to the needs of
people. Certainly not an easy task, but the potential benefits justify
some bold attempts, and the acceptance of early difficulties and failures.
The alternative is a detached but sophisticated planning system which
fails to connect with the needs of people in the community.

References

1 Committee on Local Authority and Allied Personal Social Services,
   Report, Cmnd 3703, London, HMSO, 1968, para 478.
2 Roy Parker, 'Reverence, ideas and planning', in Association of Directors
   of Social Services, *Expectations of the Social Services* (Proceedings of 1st
   Study Conference, 1972), Social Services Department, Somerset County
   Council, 1972.
3 J. D. Stewart, *New Approaches to Management in Local Government*,
   London, Knight, 1970, p. 21.
4 D. V. Donnison *et al.*, *Social Policy and Administration*, London, Allen
   & Unwin, 1965, p. 28.
5 A. Sinfield, 'Which way for social work?', in P. Townsend *et al.*, *The
   Fifth Social Service*, London, Fabian Society, 1970, pp. 23–59.
6 J. E. Mayer and N. Timms, *The Client Speaks*, London, Routledge &
   Kegan Paul, 1970, p. 46.
7 Calouste Gulbenkian Foundation, *Community Work and Social Change*,
   London, Longman, 1968, p. 29.
8 Donnison *et al.*, op. cit., p. 234.
9 J. Packman, *Child Care: Needs and Numbers*, London, Allen & Unwin,
   1968, p. 192.
10 Donnison *et al.*, op. cit., p. 28.
11 Department of Health and Social Security, *Local Authority Social Services
   Ten-Year Development Plans, 1973–1983*, Circular 35/72, London, HMSO,
   August 1972.
12 B. Davies, *Social Needs and Resources in Local Services*, London, Michael
   Joseph, chapter 10.

13 Ibid., p. 217.
14 J. Crook, *The Preparation of Ten-Year Plans*, Social Services Research Group, Social Services Department, Somerset County Council, 1972.
15 Stewart, op. cit.
16 Sinfield, op. cit., p. 31.
17 Stewart, op. cit., p. 85.
18 Packman, op. cit., p. 194.
19 Davies, op. cit., p. 217.
20 A. Etzioni, *Modern Organisations*, London and New York, Prentice-Hall, 1964.
21 Committee on Public Participation in Planning, *People and Planning*, London, HMSO, 1969.
22 A. Plumridge, 'Great Dunmow town appraisal: an exercise in public participation', *Journal of the Town Planning Institute*, 55, 1969, 214–15.
23 Donnison *et al.*, op. cit., p. 252.
24 Sinfield, op. cit.
25 Islington Task Force, Islington Poverty Action Group and Islington Consumers' Group, *Old and Cold in Islington . . . A question of survival*, Islington Task Force, 1971.
26 Calouste Gulbenkian Foundation, op. cit., p. 70.
27 Parker, op. cit.

8 Area team community work: achievement and crisis

Aryeh Leissner and Jennifer Joslin

An increasing number of local authorities have translated the emphasis of the Seebohm Report[1] upon the need for closer links between the social services departments and the community into de-centralisation of the services through the setting up of area teams located within the neighbourhoods they are intended to serve. The important function of such teams was stressed by several writers who deal with the post-Seebohm reorganisation of the social services. Foren and Brown, for instance, state that area teams must be community based and accessible,[2] and Kogan and Terry[3] hold that 'maximum responsibility should be placed on the area team to ensure that community and family resources are stimulated and used to the maximum and that cases are seen to be treated in their full family and neighbourhood content.'

Another report[4] cites accessibility as the first priority and citizen participation as one of the objectives of the area team, and speaks of

> the possibility of offering a community based service by allocating individual social workers to particular streets or estates where they can become well known and where they themselves can really get to know the dynamics of the community life. Indeed, one of the functions of a social worker in such a situation may be to create a sense of community among the residents, and help them in mobilising their own resources to meet needs in the area.

One Director of Social Services wrote[5] that the area office was conceived as 'the one door on which all could knock' (the original description of the family advice centre in the Ingleby Report), and that it would 'need to be linked closely with the community'.

The following pages will summarise the experience of a social services department area team which has made significant advances in establishing such close links with the community. This area team took part in the 1967–70 Home Office financed National Children's Bureau study of seven family advice centres and is now participating in the

118

Department of Health and Social Security financed National Children's Bureau action research study on community-based services for children and youth in detached family advice centre settings, which started in 1970 and is scheduled to end in 1975.[6] The staff of this area team was, from the outset, closely involved in the work of the family advice centre and adapted many of the community work methods of the centre to its own practice.

Community work as a social work discipline

A few weeks after the Association of Community Workers in the United Kingdom was founded, one of the writers of this paper noted[7] that, 'in the current confusion about definitions, goals and methods regarding social work with and in communities, any determined attempt to provide an incentive for defining and tightening what should be regarded as one of the most important social work methods is both timely and welcome.' Since then, little seems to have been done to end the confusion. One author, for instance,[8] holds that 'community work' and 'community organisation' are two different methods, and another seems to regard social and community work as different professions.[9] Still another writer separates the community work objectives of improving the socioeconomic conditions, the organisational structure and the social cohesion of the communty, assigning the former to 'community development' and the last to 'community organisation'.[10]

In September 1971 Ian Page took recourse to a December 1968 article by one of the writers of this paper[11] to offer a definition of community work,[12] but the latest report on community work in Britain[13] notes the persistence of 'uncertainty and doubt . . . about the meaning and function of community work and its proper place, both in training and practice'. The report makes a valiant attempt to define community work, but seems to add to the confusion by describing anything and everything, from 'preventive work' to 'group work with single parents', as community work.[14] At the 1973 Annual Conference of the British Association of Social Workers in Blackpool, a well-attended discussion group on community work reportedly left the participants 'with the conclusion that there were as many definitions [of community work] as people attempting to define it.' Mr Bill Taylor, who is described as a community worker of the Greenwich Community Project, is said to have posed the question, 'Who are these community workers?', and apparently confessed himself to be unable to give an answer.[15]

The picture is, perhaps, not as bleak as it looks at first sight. There seem to be some people in the social services field who have a fairly coherent conception of community work. This is indicated in an advertisement for community workers by the London Borough of Greenwich (apparently not drafted in consultation with Mr Taylor), which describes the tasks of the community workers as 'helping [communities] to organise, to define their own problems, and seek their own solutions, making full use of available local facilities and of statutory and voluntary agencies.' This advertisement appears in the same *Social Work Today* issue which reports the utter confusion regarding the goals and functions of community work which reigned at the BASW conference in Blackpool.

This paper will try to describe some of the pioneering attempts in community work carried out by a social services department area team and the detached family advice centre which operated under the team's auspices. However, before we proceed, we shall seek to dispel any doubts as to what we mean by community work by citing a recent article which offers a brief practice definition:[16]

> Community work is a social work discipline which has the overall task of enabling communities to function effectively as communities. This includes a wide range of specific tasks: helping a group of people to become aware of their identity as a community, to recognise the needs and problems they have in common; helping them to identify and to mobilise their own resources and providing them with professional guidance in utilising these resources in finding solutions to their problems; advising the community with regard to resources and services available to them by right, and helping them to make constructive use of these; helping the community to organise itself effectively in order to assist individuals, families or groups with special needs to obtain better social, economic and cultural conditions for the community as a whole and, if necessary, to engage in social action in order to prevail upon the authorities to fulfil their obligations towards the community. Community work also includes helping people to improve relations between neighbours and between different groups in the community, and to identify and acknowledge areas of conflict in order to resolve conflict and prevent it from spreading. An essential task of community work is to stimulate the interest of people in all aspects of community life, and to enable them to participate in the running of their own affairs, as well as in those policy decisions and

planning processes which are made outside the community, but which affect its well-being and determine its future. Finally, community work's objective is to enable the community to achieve a realistic degree of autonomy over its own social situation; an autonomy which enables the community to set up representative bodies to control its own activities, to participate in policy-making and planning relevant to the life of the community, and to represent the interests of the community within and outside its boundaries. . . .

In order to carry out his tasks the community worker adopts a number of complementary roles. He functions as a resource person to whom the community can come to seek information and advice. He may be called a social diagnostician in that he helps the community to identify and analyse its needs and its problems and to find realistic solutions. He provides guidance in the methods and techniques of problem solving and community organisation. He may have to become the arbitrator between different factions and interest groups in the community, and it is his task to ensure good communication between all members of the community. He functions as mediator between the community, the network of services and the authorities controlling these services. Under certain circumstances the community worker acts as the community's advocate, stating its case when the community itself is, as yet, unable to do so, interpreting needs and ensuring its rights.

The community worker's overall role of enabler, which he shares with all other social workers, cannot be restricted to a passively responsive non-directive one in deprived communities. He may have to accept the responsibility of initiating community action and, under certain circumstances, he may have to demonstrate that something can be done, and the manner in which it is most effectively done.

The neighbourhood-based family advice centre opens a door to community work

Nearly fifteen years ago the Ingleby Committee Report[17] recommended the setting up of family advice centres in the local authority children's departments, stressing the need to make the departments' services more accessible. The 1963 Children and Young Persons Act, which made the provision of 'advice, guidance and assistance' a statutory obligation, saw the objectives of the new service as 'diminishing the need to receive children into, or keep them in care ... or to bring children before a juvenile court'.[18] In 1966 the National Children's Bureau carried out an exploratory study of family advice service provisions in sixteen children's departments for the Home Office, which reported on a number of different adaptations of the Family Advice Centre approach. Most significant was the finding that 'detached centres or "outposts" serving a specific sub-area, neighbourhood or community had been established in high need communities. . . . These types of F.A.C. settings showed a marked tendency to regard the community as the basic client unit, and to allot much time and effort to community work.'[19] When the National Children's Bureau set out on a more detailed study of seven family advice centres in six local authorities in the summer of 1967, the research team had the potentialities of detached, community-based family advice centres very much in mind, and four such centres were included in the study.

Even in the early stages of FAC experience, it became apparent that the detached family advice centre would have to include the service functions as well as the organisational and social change tasks of community work.[20] At least some of the FAC functions of advice, guidance and assistance, mediation and liaison, referral and follow-up were already included in the practice of the local authority children's departments and of voluntary social service organisations, such as Family Service Units, the Family Welfare Association and Citizens' Advice Bureaux. 'Neighbourhood work' had a long and distinguished tradition in the work of the Settlement Houses and other voluntary agencies in Britain, and the concept of the detached neighbourhood project had been the subject of experiments in other countries for some years, mainly in the United States and Holland.[21] There was, in fact, a fund of experience upon which the detached family advice centres could draw. On the other hand, the statutory obligations of local authority children's departments were, in some instances, regarded as incompatible with the concept of accessibility and 'no-strings-attached', confidential service. Professional community work was still only a marginal subject in the social work training curricula in Britain, and given little or no recognition in the statutory social service agencies. Local authorities tended to regard community work as a disruptive influence. The action-research mandate of the National Children's Bureau research team offered a range of opportunities for experimenting with methods and techniques designed to make social services more accessible and effective in high-need areas; for the creative integration of social work methods geared to helping individuals, families and community groups; for community participation in the planning and provision of services and, last but not least, for testing the limits to which local authority agencies would tolerate and support new and sometimes somewhat unorthodox social work practice. Following the re-organisation of the statutory social services in accord with the recommendations of the Seebohm Report, the detached family advice centres assumed a new identity as 'reaching-out' community work units of the social services department area teams. In 1969 the Home Office applied the experience gained by the community-based family advice centres which took part in the National Children's Bureau study to the setting up of the first of twelve Community Development Projects. As Marjorie Mayo stated:[22] 'The Family Advice Centres have had a particular role in the development of local authority sponsorship of Community Work, and they have also had some considerable influence on the launching of C.D.P. in the first place.'

From advice, guidance and assistance to community work

The first hesitant experiments with detached family advice centres were given no explicit brief to engage in community work. The FAC workers found that, like the detached youth worker with a group of street corner boys, the achievement of their objectives would be determined by the worker's 'success in obtaining a second mandate for his service directly from the client group'.[23] As in the case of detached youth work, one can object to the FAC approach on the grounds that the service is being imposed, and that the people who become the target of the service have not asked for it. Elizabeth de Grooth, who served as FAC worker for a high-need London council estate over a period of two years, comments that 'very few tenants would have asked for a social worker to be planted in their midst'. But she also reports:[24] 'People made early contacts with me by coming to enquire why I was there and who I was. . . . I asked them to tell me how they thought they could use my services', and she adds: 'after a while and after many trials, a feeling of mutual trust and respect grew between many of us.' It may be added that this FAC worker provided direct helping services in the form of advice, guidance and assistance to 449 individuals of all ages out of a total of approximately 600 people living on the estate.[25] In the course of her two years' work, Mrs de Grooth also helped the community to revitalise a defunct tenants' association, to provide recreational services for children, teenagers and adults, to initiate self-help activities and neighbourly assistance for the elderly and to improve relations between the community and the handful of immigrant families living on the estate. Under this FAC worker's guidance, the community sent representatives to meetings of the Child Poverty Action Group and collectively submitted evidence on the allocation of council housing to the Cullingworth Committee. Organised community action, including petitions, meetings with councillors and newspaper publicity, induced the housing department to heed the community's demands for information and for more adequate arrangements with regard to the planned rehousing of the tenants of the estate.

The pre-Seebohm local authority children's departments set up detached family advice centres in flats, empty shops, or any other suitable accommodation in neighbourhoods regarded as high-need areas. Among the criteria for the designation of such areas were a high percentage of low-income, unskilled or semi-skilled workers' families, a great number of large families and many families in the area receiving state income supplements. High-need criteria also included a high incidence of truancy, learning difficulties, retardation, other physical and emotional handicaps and delinquency among the children of the area, a high percentage of one-parent families, inadequate school facilities and a high rate of teacher turnover, as well as a significant proportion of immigrant families, substandard, overcrowded and badly maintained housing and a lack of adequate and easily accessible shopping facilities. Insufficient adaptability, accessibility and co-ordination of social service provisions and non-use of the existing provisions because of lack of information, social isolation or local attitudes of distrust of the statutory services were among the major determinants.[26] A feasibility study for the setting up of a family advice centre commissioned by one children's department[27] states that the proposed target area

> contains a multiplicity of problems, some of which have come to the surface, some we feel it absolutely essential should be brought to the surface if we are to provide the sort of help which people find either difficult to define or are unable to crystallise in any verbal sense. One has in mind such problems as isolation through a lack of understanding of what is available, or the lack of communication through language problems particularly with regard to the immigrants, and an insufficiency of opportunity and time to look for the deeper rooted difficulties that may in fact lurk in the background.

Initially staffed by one FAC worker, usually a child care officer with some community work experience, and a part-time clerical assistant, detached family advice centres now comprise a team consisting of the FAC worker, an FAC assistant, two to four youth workers and play leaders, a project secretary and several indigenous workers recruited in the community.

Community work in the detached centres grows out of the advice, guidance and assistance and the mediation and liaison functions. For instance, when a number of mothers express concern about the lack of pre-school play facilities, a mothers' group is formed in order to set up a community pre-school playgroup and to raise funds for this purpose. In a number of cases, the mothers' group then becomes concerned with other community needs, such as the lack of social activities for parents, after-school and holiday recreational programmes for children and the plight of old age pensioners. As a result, a parents' association is formed which appoints several sub-committees, engages in a wider range of fund-raising activities and organises social events, such as community holiday outings and an annual sports day. To give another example: a substantial number of complaints about housing problems leads to the formation of a tenants' or residents' association which opens negotiations with the relevant authorities, such as the housing and health departments. Representative community groups are eventually formed to discuss traffic problems with the police and the need for an adventure playground, youth club facilities or a football pitch with the area youth officer, the social services and the parks departments. Fund-raising by the community association makes it possible to purchase a bus for a community transport scheme. As the advice, guidance and assistance, mediation and liaison functions become integrated with community work, a two-fold process takes place: on the one hand the people of the community become more directly involved in the work of the family advice centre and the FAC staff find themselves increasingly accountable to the people they serve; on the other hand, individuals and groups in the community become more self sufficient and autonomous in planning and providing community services and in representing the interests of the community.

Community work in the family advice centre setting combines three overlapping and mutually reinforcing patterns. The first of these consists of community services, the second may be called community organisation, the third is community action.

Community services

Services to the community provided by the staff of the detached family
advice centre are, in all cases, initiated in response to the need for
such services by the community. Our action research study has recorded
a wide range of such services including pre-school play groups, arts
and crafts centres, after-school and school holiday recreational programmes for children, camping and sports programmes for teenagers,
detached youth work with 'hard-to-reach' youngsters, tutoring and
recreational programmes for slow learners, recreational programmes for
adults, and recreational and helping services for the elderly. A number
of services are set up in co-operation with other professionals and
agencies, such as legal, housing and youth employment advisory services.
In all cases it is regarded as preferable to let the community itself
initiate these services, even if this means considerable delays. The centre
staff takes the initiative only when it becomes apparent that it has
become necessary to 'demonstrate by doing' how a specific service or
programme works, or when a specific service clearly requires trained
professionals in order to be effective. As the report on the Family
Advice Services Study explains:[28]

> the F.A.S. workers function as initiators and consultants, as
> advisors, resource persons, mediators and enablers. In order to
> meet existing needs, the family advice centre may have to make
> the services of a number of 'special task' workers available, such
> as youth club leaders, detached youth workers, playground
> supervisors, arts and crafts teachers, playgroup and nursery
> school staff, and community home helpers. These may be
> professionals, indigenous workers, volunteers or staff members
> of other voluntary or statutory agencies who co-operate
> with the family advice centre.

The objective is to provide a service which has been recognised as a
necessity by the community, to involve members of the community at
the earliest possible stage in the planning and provision of the service,
and to transfer responsibility for the service to a representative community body as soon as possible.

Community organisation

Community organisation in the areas served by the detached family
advice centres has a two-fold purpose: to enable the inhabitants of a

neighbourhood to gain cohesion and self-confidence as a community, and to gain a measure of influence and control as a community over the services and provisions which affect their daily lives. To achieve this, the community worker 'operates through the people with whom he comes into contact; he helps them to identify problems or opportunities which they may well have felt but have not necessarily thought about, and to set up and achieve possible solutions or objectives of their own choosing.'[29] The objective is social change within the community and with regard to the relations between the community and the local authority power structure.

The process may start with the gradual involvement of members of the community in the planning and provision of community services initiated and staffed by the family advice centre, or through the formation of a mothers' group originally meeting over a cup of tea to have a break from the daily household chores, but becoming concerned with the need for play facilities and the lack of social activities for the neighbourhood's elderly people. It may gain impetus from the need to deal with a crisis situation, such as anxiety over rumours of redevelopment plans, a sudden increase in vandalism in the area, a series of accidents resulting from unguarded building sites or heavy traffic. Quite often people are brought together in order to do something to curb the usual chaos of the school holidays, or to ensure the safety of their children by organising a supervised fireworks display for bonfire night. Even middle-age spread can be the cause for organising a group; in one centre a slimming and exercise club was set up by a group of local housewives and joined by one of the husbands. Community newspapers help to involve people in developing a discussion of community problems and issues. The early stages of fund-raising activities are usually successful because they involve the inhabitants of the neighbourhood in traditional activities such as jumble sales and clothing and furniture swop-shops. In one of the centres, funds for the acquisition of a canal barge were raised at a strip-club benefit party. More sophisticated and lasting organisational activities often result from such modest beginnings. Parents', tenants' and residents' associations learn to deal with a wide range of community problems and to negotiate with the authorities on the community's behalf. Fund-raising committees mobilise community resources and obtain grants from local authority sources and private trusts. Management committees assume responsibility for youth clubs, adventure playgrounds and pre-school playgroups. As the community gains self-confidence and organisational experience, the family advice centre staff begin to be regarded as accountable to the representative bodies of the community. At the same time, members of the community take a more active part in the running of the centre and its range of services, either as paid indigenous workers, or as volunteer helpers. In one centre, members of the local parents' association employed as indigenous workers were ready and able to run the family advice centre in consultation with social workers from the social service department area team.

In many of the high-need areas served by detached family advice centres the main task of community organisation is to enable the inhabitants of a neighbourhood to acquire, or regain, the ability to function as a community. The function of the centre in these areas is to help the inhabitants to realise their own potentialities and to activate their own resources as a community, as well as to enable them to make the statutory authorities aware of their obligations with regard to the needs and the rights of the community.

Community action

Community action in the frame of reference of the detached family advice centre can be defined as any organised activity by community groups which is intended to meet a legitimate community need, to provide a service or to ensure the provision of a service by the appropriate agency, or any action taken by the community to resolve or alleviate problem situations affecting the well-being of members of the community to obtain and safeguard the rights of individuals and groups, and to prevent, protest and avert any infringements of the rights of the community and its members. Community action may consist of a request to the authorities to appoint 'lollypop-men' at a dangerous road-crossing, or it may take the form of a protest vigil at the home of a family threatened with eviction. Community action may find expression in a petition to a housing department requesting that the community be given precise information as to the redevelopment plans for the area, or it may be a working weekend during which a piece of wasteland is cleaned up and equipped as an adventure playground. A meeting with police officials to discuss tension between the police and immigrant groups in the neighbourhood is community action, just as is the setting up of a working party of local fathers and teenagers to board up an abandoned building which has become a hazard to adventurous youngsters or to provide firewood for old age pensioners in a fuel crisis. Community action may consist of the appointment of a committee to plan and provide assistance for a needy family in the community, or, all other means having failed, it may result in a demonstration on the steps of the City Hall.

Community action is social action at the grass-roots level. Social action has been defined as aimed at achieving objectives which are legal and socially desirable, and which seek a better adaptation of social policy to social needs. In its broader effects, social action consists of 'those organised and planned activities that attempt to influence the social distribution of status, power and resources'.[30] In the context of the detached family advice centre, the staff function directly related to community action is that of the professional social worker who 'imparts information about rights, makes services available, helps to communicate needs to those in authority, and encourages action by the individual, family and group on their own behalf as well as on the behalf of the community'.[31]

In the process of helping the population of a high-need area to obtain the services it needs, to gain cohesion as a community and to acquire the organisational strength and experience needed to engage in community action, the family advice centre teams at times find themselves cast in the roles of advocates. This may entail stating the case for the needs and the rights of the community clearly and forcefully when the community itself is not yet able to speak out on its own behalf. It can mean taking the side of the community in situations of conflict with the statutory power structure. As an early report stated: 'The Family Advice Centres must act and be seen to act entirely in the interests of those who come to them for help. They must never become yet another agency which can be identified with "the authorities" or with "them" in the "us and them" controversy.'[32]

In an approach which integrates advice, guidance and assistance to individuals and families in high-need areas with community work, the concept of advocacy is directly related to the entire range of functions of the family advice centre team. As one writer observed: 'Users of social services need, above all, adequate information about what is available, what their rights are and how to get them . . . but the more inarticulate and timid clients of the social services need spokesmen, negotiators and sometimes advocates.'[33] The degree to which the local authorities are able to accept the advocate's role can be regarded as a reliable indicator of the authority's readiness to accept community work as a professional social work discipline, and to recognise the creative, constructive dynamics of community action.

Community participation

The report on the FAC study emphasises that 'the initiation of, and the support for, community participation in the identification and meeting of community needs and the solving of community problems must be regarded as the foremost objective of community work.' The report also notes: 'The very location of the centre (within the neighbourhood it serves) brought about a process of involvement between the centre and the community.'[34] This kind of informal involvement, mainly caused by the proximity and the accessibility of the detached family advice centre, is the first step towards the development of community participation in the planning and provision of community services, in community organisation, and in community action. The aim is to bring about a partnership between the local people and the professional staff 'so that the external interference may be legitimised'.[35] In the high-need areas served by the family advice centres, long-established patterns of apathy and dependence and lack of community cohesion often make the development of community participation a slow and frustrating process. The question has indeed been raised as to whether such a process can take place in areas regarded as 'socially incompetent'.[36] The experience of the National Children's Bureau studies of family advice centres show that there are good chances of participation in even the most deprived and disorganised areas, if opportunities for participation are provided at the earliest possible stages of planning and throughout every phase of service and organisation. Within the frame of reference of the detached family advice centre, urgently needed services may have to be initiated by professional staff, but members of the community must be involved as soon as possible. It is self-evident that any form of community organisation, whether this involves the formation of a group to hold a fund-raising jumble sale, the setting up of a rota system to help to supervise a playground, or the election of a management committee for a community centre, presupposes community participation. If community participation fails to develop within a reasonable period of time (and in some areas this may be as long as one year), then the validity of the family advice centre's presence, or the competence of its staff, must be closely examined. So far this has not become necessary. Of the eleven detached centres which participated in the two National Children's Bureau studies, all have shown that some measure of community participation gets under way fairly rapidly.

The methods and objectives of participation adopted by the family advice centres have been summed up as follows:[37]

> The objectives of participation in deprived areas can be divided into three broad categories: 1. the improvement of material and environmental conditions; 2. changes in psychological and social attitudes; 3. changes in the power structure. One may also speak of different stages of participation: Stage One is concerned with the identification and the alleviation of needs. Stage Two aims at bringing about community cohesion and organisation. Stage Three consists of establishing channels of communication and structures which will bring about a realistic degree of autonomy in the management of the community's own affairs, and which will ensure the representation and the participation of the community in the planning and decision-making processes in matters which affect the community's present and future situations. These are, of course, artificial divisions. In practice the objectives are inter-dependent, the processes leading to their achievement are closely interwoven, and the various stages overlap. Moreover, over-emphasis or neglect of one objective must, of necessity, affect the chances for the realisation of the others, and too much pressure or procrastination in one stage of the process will have repercussions in another.

Community participation brings with it a gradual increase in the accountability of the family advice centre staff to the community. As Betty de Grooth noted, she 'became increasingly accountable to and aligned with the residents' who provided 'much realistic help, advice and encouragement'. Mrs de Grooth adds: 'Some were hard taskmasters, too.' The experience of the detached family advice centre shows that, once the principle of community participation is established, the community develops the ability not only to share to take over the professional's tasks, but also to assert some authority over his activities and objectives in relation to the community. This change in the client–worker relationship often causes discomfort to statutory and voluntary service workers alike. A health visitor was quite shocked when she found out that a letter from an FAC worker delivered to her by a client and dealing with this client's problems had, in fact, been written with the client's consent and in her presence and was read to her. A group of enthusiastic young volunteers who came into a slum area to organise a school holiday programme was equally taken aback when the FAC worker in that area told them that they would have to submit their plans to the local parents' association and obtain the approval and co-operation of the community.

Community youth work

The findings of the Family Advice Services study showed that the demands for services for children and teenagers had become one of the major concerns of the centres. 'In many cases this need was the first incentive for organising community groups and community action.'[38] The report on the study noted that: 'For the delinquent as well as for the withdrawn youngsters, and for their families, the family advice centre's potentialities for an integrated availability of recreational programming, advice, guidance and assistance and community work can provide a very valuable service.'[39] The findings of the study took on special significance in the light of the experience of detached youth work, the growing interest in community-based youth work, and the recommendations for the provisions of 'intermediate treatment services' within the community. As a result of these findings, the National Children's Bureau is now carrying out our current action research study. The basic suppositions of this study have been defined as 'inherent in the objectives of community work and of detached youth work: that it is beneficial for the community to participate in and to share the responsibility for providing services for children and the young people in the community – and that it is of the foremost importance to help young people to maintain satisfactory relations with the community, and to take an active interest in the activities and the problems of their own neighbourhood.'[40] The goal is community autonomy in the provision of services to the community's children and young people. 'The process by which this may be achieved is community participation in the planning and the operation of the services. The method is that of professional advice, guidance and assistance by community and youth workers' who work as a team in the detached neighboorhood-based centre.[41] To give but one example of the variety of community youth work in the context of the family advice centre approach: one of the detached centres which participated in the FAS study and is now taking part in the study on community-based services to children and youth was involved in the following activities as listed in a National Children's Bureau interim report of 30 April 1972:

Advice, guidance, assistance and referral services for individuals and families.

Close co-operation with a Legal Advice Centre initiated by the family advice centre.

Guidance and support for three council housing estate tenants' associations.

Guidance and support for two pre-school playgroups initiated by the centre and staffed by indigenous workers, the provision of training facilities for these workers, with the setting up of other playgroups in the area in co-operation with other agencies.

Guidance and support for two adventure playgrounds initiated by the centre and supervised by F.A.C. staff and members of the community.

Close co-operation with a camping association partly initiated by the centre.

Detached youth work and club programmes with a group of ca. forty 15–19-year-old boys, most of them delinquent.

Club programming and detached youth work with a group of ca. ten 16–21-year-old delinquent boys.

Recreational programming and camping for ca. forty 11–14-year-old boys and girls.

Club programming for ca. seventy 11–15-year-old boys and girls in co-operation with community volunteers.

A camping and leadership training programme for 11–12-year-old boys and girls.

Guidance and support for under-14, under-13 and under-11 football teams in co-operation with community volunteers and other youth work agencies.

The organisation of an annual inter-estate sports festival in co-operation with local tenants' associations and playground management committees.

School holidays programming in co-operation with community groups.

Personal counselling and help with legal, employment and educational problems for a fluctuating number of young people in the neighbourhood.

Initiation of, and support for, community fund-raising activities to finance services for children and youth.

The staff of this centre consisted of one FAC worker (who also supervised three other family advice centres in the borough not part of the NCB study), one FAC assistant, one youth worker, two youth work assistants (untrained) and one project secretary.

The area team and the family advice centre

The area team became closely involved with the setting up and the running of its family advice centre at the very start of the National Children's Bureau study in September 1967, when the area team was still a section in the central offices of the children's department, and the team's senior social worker was appointed as supervisor and liaison officer to the centre. The team shared the ups and downs of the family advice centre through its four and a half years of existence in a redevelopment area consisting of a cluster of streets with terraced private-landlord-owned houses and a 'notorious' high-need housing estate. During these years the centre had to change its location three times because of the demolition of its building, and towards the end of 1969 services had to be suspended for a period of five months, some of the most essential work being carried on by FAC staff and area team social workers. By the beginning of 1972 the neighbourhood served by the area team had, with the exception of the estate, been demolished and the centre, having become redundant in its old location, moved to offices on a large estate in another sector of the team area. Several of the FAC workers joined forces with area team social workers in continuing to provide services for the population remnants in the redevelopment area and for the tenants of the estate, while the rest of the FAC team began to establish themselves as a community work project for the new estate and the surrounding area with the support of the area team.

In July 1970, nearly a year before the implementation of the Seebohm reforms, the family advice centre joined the NCB study on community-based services for children and youth and, about the same time, the area team, then consisting of six child care officers, one administrative assistant and the team leader, moved out of the department's central offices and into the area it served, occupying office space in a public swimming bath (which had served the people of the neighbourhood since 1892) on 1 April 1971, on Seebohm-'D'-Day; four additional social workers and a second administrative assistant joined the team, and the senior appointments were made. This group of fifteen workers served an area with a population of approximately 30,000. The family advice centre team, supervised by the area team leader, consisted of one FAC worker, a project secretary, three community youth workers and one playgroup leader.

The staff of the area team had helped to organise an adventure playground for the family advice centre, and assumed responsibility for a mothers' and children's group which met in the premises of the centre. The members of the team had responded very positively to the experience of working with children and their parents in the informal setting of the centre and the playground. They were enthusiastic about the new approach to the problems of a deprived community and about the wider opportunities for 'grass-roots' contacts with their clients offered by the community-based setting. The members of the team also enjoyed a range of opportunities for making informal contacts with the people of the area; there were frequent day-outings, excursions and week-end trips organised by the centre or initiated by the area team itself, with the participation of FAC staff.

Area team community work

When the team moved out of the department's central offices into the building locally known as 'The Baths', it immediately set out to create a friendly and comfortable centre which people could use as a meeting place, and to which people would enjoy coming. The aim was to provide a place to which the inhabitants of the area would come regardless of whether they had 'a problem', and where workers and clients could meet informally. This attempt succeeded beyond all expectations: people came to have a coffee and a chat, to discuss their affairs with the workers or with each other, or simply to sit a while in warmth and comfort. For a substantial number of people of the neighbourhood this became the most important service the area team had to offer. There were, of course, also interviewing rooms which afforded privacy. One room was reserved for group activities, but it had to be turned into a second-hand clothes and furniture exchange where weekly sales were held.

The team was already involved in a number of experimental group and community work activities before the move to the new location, and these were continued and extended. A mothers' and children's group met weekly at the family advice centre and provided for ten mothers and about twenty-five children. Five members of the team were directly involved with this group, with the objective of offering support and practical assistance, and counteracting the social isolation of some of the most deprived mothers of the community. In addition to this, one of the team members met with a group of fourteen- to sixteen-year-old girls, some of them in care, some under supervision orders, the rest under voluntary supervision. The meetings took place in the area office once a week and afforded the girls the opportunity to discuss common problems with each other and with the worker. After moving into the area, the team doubled their efforts to 'reach' the tenants in a welfare accommodation block. A twice-a-week advice centre was set up in the block. It was found that most of the problems of this community were connected with the housing situation, financial difficulties and the lack of play space for children. The team's workers helped the tenants to channel and assert their demands for housing improvements, and co-operated in setting up a local branch of the Claimants' Union to assist in negotiations with the Social Security Benefits Office. A mothers' group met regularly in the two-room flat of the advice centre, and holiday outings and social events were organised. The tenants formed a representative group to discuss offers of rehousing when the block was finally demolished. Many of these tenants still live in the area and meet regularly at the area team office. It should be pointed out that one of the four team members assigned to this project was a pre-Seebohm mental health worker, now a senior social worker in the area team.

One of the objectives of the area team was to break down the barriers between clients and those people who did not seek, or sought only rarely, the help of professionals, in order to establish a relationship between the area team and the community as a whole. Partly with this aim in mind, community volunteers were recruited among clients as well as among people who had no need of professional social work services. The volunteers, under the supervision of members of the team, made home visits, assisted with baby-sitting and carried out various other helping functions. In some instances small payments for this work were made from Section 1, Children and Young Persons Act 1963 funds but from April 1972 a project fund was provided by the social services department for this purpose. The volunteer group consists of forty-five people, and has set up its own organisation and registered as a charity, so as to be able to apply for funds independently of the social services department. This community group runs a club at a local church hall for about 100 elderly and handicapped people with the guidance and support of the area team, and raises funds for outings, parties and other social events. The close co-operation with this community volunteer group, and other 'detached' work carried out by members of the area team, have resulted in a network of relationships between the social workers and the inhabitants of the neighbourhood. Four members of the team also provide a service consisting of group work and recreational programming in a hostel for mentally ill or retarded men in the area. Other members worked closely with a newly formed tenants' association in one of the 'high-need' estates, helping to set up play activities for the estate's children in co-operation with a member of the family advice centre team. There are also plans to open an advice centre on the estate and to provide a club for the elderly. It may be added that, while the family advice centre is engaged in community work in the biggest estate in the area, there are four other estates which have been pin-pointed for attention by the area team. In order to put the com-munity work of this team in perspective, it should be noted that the team reported the following 'caseload' in April 1972: 152 children in care; 106 preventive family and child care cases; 356 registered handi-capped persons; 85 mentally ill or subnormal persons; 20 children under supervision; about 100 elderly people in need of help; the supervision of 8 foster mothers, 13 child-minders, 5 playgroups and 45 volunteers.

By the end of the first community-based year, the open-door policy of the area team office resulting in some degree of chaos in the office, the increasing demands made upon the team by community groups, and the workers' own growing realisation of the size and the range of the problems confronting them – problems which may well be beyond the scope of any social work approach because they demand far-reaching socio-economic and political solutions – all this has served to put the members of the team under considerable strain. Far from becoming overwhelmed and considering a retreat to the older safer methods, they began to plan youth club facilities in conjunction with the youth service to be located in the area office building, a playroom for pre-school children on the premises, a playgroup for physically handicapped children, and a financial-assistance first-aid service for the many vagrants who drift into the office in need of immediate help. While some social workers have left the statutory services because they feel that the local authority setting prevents them from engaging in radical action on behalf of their clients, declaring that they are 'sick and tired of being apologists for policies we don't believe in',[42] the workers of this area team, as those in the detached family advice centres and perhaps many others in the statutory services, continue to test the limits the 'system' sets.

Tasks, problems and frustrations

The family advice centre can be said to have provided a community work model for the area team, and the team's participation in the centre's activities provided opportunities to learn new methods, often by trial and error, and to experiment with new attitudes and relationships. It became soon clear, however, that a number of serious problems arose due to the fact that this experience was not shared by the professional and administrative 'higher echelons' of the social services department, upon whom the area team has to rely for support. Although considerable efforts were made by the team leader and the National Children's Bureau research team to feed back information and recommendations for changes in policy and practice to the department, a gap in communication remained. While the department and the local authority rarely objected to the innovations introduced by the area team, and was generous with its financial support, there were many instances of lack of consultation with regard to policy decisions affecting the team's community-oriented services. But perhaps more significant, and most important in its effects upon the team, has been the lack of moral support, of encouragement to persist in the difficult and demanding work, and of tangible official recognition of the team's achievements in implementing not only the organisational changes, but the spirit of the Seebohm reforms. To some degree, the local authority system itself is responsible for this situation, because of the limitations it puts upon the social services departments' flexibility and freedom of action. The 'Chairman's Address' to the 1973 BASW conference expressed the exasperation felt in the profession. Terry Cooper said:[43]

> What, I question, is the role of establishment committees and management service units in local authority social services departments? It is a source of constant amazement to me that a director of social services, who controls an operation costing many millions a year and whose own salary could be around £10,000 is not empowered to increase his secretarial or junior administrative staff without first getting approval from another department in the authority. We have a situation in which the decision to employ one more social worker or one more secretary in an area team is taken by a committee outside the department, by members who cannot know what the pressures are like, on the advice of people who have never worked in the department. And all this in a situation where there already exists a financial control system accountable to yet another committee.

The need for moral and practical support is great, because the tasks facing the area team which sets out to create a community-based service are formidable, especially if we take into account the fact that there is, as yet, very little formal training for professional community work available, and neither the family advice centre nor the area team can employ trained community workers freed from all other tasks to direct the team's community work approach. All the members of the team, including the team leader, had to learn new methods and acquire new skills 'on the job', by doing, while the caseload of each worker is not lessened, but increased, by the successes achieved in 'reaching the unreached' through community work methods and the accessibility of the neighbourhood-based area team premises and its family advice services.

In order to establish its new identity, its new 'image' as a community service, the area team faces a number of major tasks:

It must demonstrate its accessibility and the effectiveness of its services to those people in the area who are in need of social work support. This was done by providing a comfortable, 'open' setting in the limited space available, by the informal, accepting atmosphere created by the staff, and by the readiness of the workers to go out into the community to meet the needs of people who, for a variety of reasons, had not been 'reached' by the social service provisions.

The team must seek the active involvement of the people of the area by giving up some of the traditional defences of 'professional mythos' and secretiveness and by letting the greatest possible number of people in the community participate in the planning and provision of services. Significant progress in this direction was made by enlisting the services of community volunteers and part-time paid indigenous workers, many of them social service clients, all residents of the area.

The team must identify the influence network and the indigenous leadership of the area, learn to understand its community structures and characteristics and accumulate a fund of information regarding the needs and the resources, the limitations and the potentialities of the local population. This was done by the assignment of team members to support existing, or initiate new community groups and organisations (such as mothers' groups, parents' associations and tenants' associations), and by participating in or initiating community social events and recreational programmes and activities.

The achievement of these objectives was seen to be directly related to the professional competence, the personal commitment and the resourcefulness of the staff of the area team and the family advice centre, the leadership provided by the team leader, and the ability of the team to adapt its methods and to gear its objectives to the socio-economic realities and the socio-cultural milieu of the area. Limitations to the achievement of these objectives were mainly set by the unmet need for adequate physical working conditions.

The area team and the community in 1973

The mothers' group (which started in the early stages of the family advice centre with the help of the area team, and then moved to the area team offices) is now in its fourth year of existence. The mothers' group plans and takes its annual holidays together and organises a variety of social events throughout the year. The group's 1973 Christmas party was attended by fifty parents and children. The Community volunteer group, which started with two local mothers in January 1971, has grown into a vigorous group of forty-five, managed by its own committee, registered as a charity and engaged in a range of fund-raising activities throughout the year. This group sees itself as part of the area team, without any noticeable change in its community identity. The volunteer group now maintains a regular visiting system for 120 people in the area, most of them housebound and/or handicapped, runs a social club for old people which has over 100 members and supports social activities and other services for a group of blind people and for the men of a hostel for the mentally ill in the neighbourhood. Affiliated to the volunteer group is a smaller group of tenants from one of the 'multi-problem' estates in the area where the team has tried unsuccessfully for the past two years to help a handful of people to form a tenants' association. A very high percentage of the team's overall caseload comes from this estate. While apathy is the dominant reaction to all attempts at stimulating community involvement on this estate, the above-mentioned group of tenants are helping to provide services for children and for old people with the help of members of the team and the family advice centre. The tenants' group has helped to persuade the local authority housing department (with considerable difficulty) to permit the use of the estate's community hall for children's and old people's club programmes, and a playgroup which operated in the community hall, but did not serve the children of the estate, was induced to move elsewhere. The core group of a tenants' association has now been formed, and its chairman helps to provide a club programme for a group of teenagers whose delinquency records have made them notorious in the area. The sole source of income for the community activities on this estate is a weekly tea and jumble sale held by the tenants' association.

Other community work attempts focused on a block of welfare

accommodation in the area. Four area team workers took turns in providing a call-in advice centre in one of the blocks with the help of the FAC worker. The flat in which this service was accommodated became the base for a mothers' and children's group and for a branch of the Claimants' Union. This advice centre, and the uses to which it was put, caused considerable conflict with the housing department, who regarded it as a nest of troublemakers. There is no doubt that the centre's activities succeeded in counteracting the ghetto mood of apathy and sullen despair which prevailed in the block, and helped the tenants to assert their rights with regards to living conditions and rehousing. At present the area team is asking the housing department for the use of a groundfloor flat in another, much larger, estate which has been turned into welfare accommodation. Four team workers have been assigned responsibility for this project and plan to start out by helping a group of local mothers to set up a pre-school playgroup for this estate.

An important development of the past year has been a community boarding-out scheme for the mentally ill which grew out of the area team's and the community volunteer group's work with a number of mentally handicapped men in a private boarding-house in the neighbourhood. This boarding-house, subsidised by the local authority at considerable expense, was clearly shown to offer sub-standard conditions to its inhabitants. The team proposed that these men would do much better looking after themselves in shared flats, with the support of community volunteers supervised by the area team. The proposal was accepted and the funds for the rent of four flats were provided by the authority for boarding-house tenants, as well as for a number of men to be discharged from a nearby mental hospital. The men meet every week for a social evening, alternately in a local pub and in the area office. The mental and physical condition of the men has improved markedly since the beginning of the scheme, and they have become more independent and more involved in the life of the community.

A group of handicapped people met at the area office once a week throughout the year for an arts and crafts session. This group has become self supporting, not only able to sell its work at a profit, but also giving work to a number of housebound handicapped people in the area. It is backed up by two area team social workers and a community volunteer, and has recently begun to form several smaller 'satellite' groups in other sectors of the area.

Throughout the year, the area team gave its support to the community organisation effort of the family advice centre, and the team leader frequently had to present its demands and fight its battles with the social services department and the local authority. In mid-1972 the FAC team and the tenants' association of the large estate served by the centre began a campaign to demand the purchase of a disused factory site by the local authority for the setting up of an adventure playground and a purpose-built youth and community centre. That summer, a parents' committee of the tenants' association and a group of youngsters took over the site and cleaned and equipped it for temporary use as an adventure playground. At the same time, the area team and the FAC staff jointly organised three weeks of camping holidays for the children of the previously mentioned 'multi-problem' estate. In August the area team took part in a community festival organised by the FAC team, the tenants' association and local youngsters. In September the local authority Arts and Recreation Committee agreed to the tenants' association's demand and purchased the factory site. The area team leader, FAC staff and tenants' association members began a series of meetings with the borough planning and architects' departments to work out plans for the building of the youth and community centre, and a special committee of local tenants was formed to take charge of the development of the factory site and the building of the centre. Work started in spring 1973 and is scheduled to be completed by spring 1974.

Crisis

There is no doubt that much more could have been achieved in the area team's community work efforts, but for a crisis situation which arose and disrupted work during the past year. In December 1972 a structural fault was discovered in the 'Baths' which rendered dangerous that part of the building occupied by the area team. The team was forced to vacate two-thirds of its accommodation, leaving it with one large and one small room for its fifteen workers and its entire range of services. The team had to inform the Director of Social Services of the obvious fact that it would very soon become impossible to maintain effective services under these circumstances. The local authority was informed of the situation, but apparently saw no urgency in the matter. After further remonstrations by the team leader a prefabricated ramshackle hut was put up in the courtyard, which was so damp, dark and cold that it was unusable during the winter months. In July the team was permitted to move into a small six-room building in the area, with the promise that suitable office space would be provided shortly. The building was filthy and abandoned and had to be cleaned from top to bottom by the social workers and community volunteers. The windows were broken, there was no electricity and no telephone, and the basement was flooded every time it rained. For the next few months the team and the volunteer group, both increasingly distressed and angry, struggled to maintain the building and to continue to provide services. In August the team leader was told that the promised new accommodation would not be ready before the coming spring and the team decided to consult its union (NALGO). By September the building had deteriorated to such a degree that work became impossible, and, according to a health department official who inspected the premises, was uninhabitable. The team protested that it could not spend another winter in impossible working conditions. The decision was taken to withdraw labour until suitable accommodation was provided. The strike was supported by 90 per cent of the department's social work and residential care staff, by many people in the area and by the volunteer group whose part-time paid members refused any payment for their services. At the end of the first week of the strike temporary accommodation for the team was found. This, too, was highly inadequate and, a week before Christmas, with the team working frantically to meet the new needs of the national crisis situation, the electricity broke down, leaving the team to continue working without light, heat or telephone.

The year ended with the staff of the area team exhausted and depressed after an extremely difficult twelve months. Worst of all, throughout this year of crisis there had been no effective expressions of concern from the leaders of the social services department and the local authority. For the moment, at least, the enthusiasm and commitment with which this area team set out to become a truly community-based service has greatly diminished. As the temporary accommodation does not have room enough for a 'drop-in-and-chat' approach to clients and for group meetings, a great deal of the basic accessibility and the work with community groups – most important of all the relationship with the volunteer group – has deteriorated. Many of the team members are speaking of leaving the department, and all feel that, at least in this local authority, decentralisation has resulted in the isolation of the central office and its alienation from the fieldwork staff. Rightly or wrongly, there is also the feeling among the workers and the volunteers that the department has very little sympathy for their community work achievements and may even be hostile to this approach, and that the lack of central office support for the team in its time of crisis must be regarded as a manifestation of this negative attitude.

Concluding remarks

A recent article on the state of the social services three years after Seebohm warns of the growing depersonalisation of the management structures of the departments:[44]

> What is required is a structure that is more flexible and adaptable, one in which the personal qualities and expertise of individuals is made accessible to the clients. Rather than the social worker being engaged in what is still basically an individual task, he is likely to become more a part of a group that is tackling a problem. In a social work setting it would not be the field-worker alone who would be seen helping the client – a group of people with diverse skills would be the helper. A client could participate in discussion and share in decisions reached. Workers of all kinds could feel a sense of value and commitment in seeing their skills and personal qualities put to their best use.
>
> It is not an easy task to set up such a new structure. I am convinced that social work managers must tackle it to avoid planning a service which, within the next decade, will fail to meet the needs of its clients. Rapid change in our society requires flexibility – not more bureaucracy.

The area team described in this paper represents, in our view, an example of what a team work approach can set out to achieve in putting into practice the community involvement principles of the Seebohm recommendations. The experience of the community-based family advice centres, as well as the experience of this area team, have also shown that it is the team work approach which offers the best chances for success in community work in priority, high-need areas. We have also learned one important lesson: the experience gained by a detached family advice centre can become the basis for the community-oriented approach of a social services area team. But if the principles, the objectives and the long-term benefits of community work are not accepted and supported by the local authority power structure and its managerial and administrative arms, community work under local authority auspices may be rendered impossible. If that is the verdict that has to be reached, it will become the verdict on the Seebohm reforms: A noble attempt, but our society was not ready for it.

References

1 Committee on Local Authority and Allied Personal Social Services, *Report*, Cmnd 3703, HMSO, 1968.
2 R. Foren and M. J. Brown, *Planning for Services*, Charles Knight, 1971, p. 44.
3 M. Kogan and J. Terry, *The Organisation of a Social Services Department: A Blueprint*, London, Bookstall Publications, 1971, p. 26.
4 N. Johnson, C. Richardson and J. Warner, 'A local authority social services department', Department of Sociology, University of Keele, August 1970 (mimeographed).
5 M. G. Speed, 'The first eight months in a county', in K. Jones (ed.), *The Year Book of Social Policy in Britain, 1971*, Routledge & Kegan Paul, 1972, p. 65.
6 For brief descriptions of both studies, see: A. Leissner, 'Family advice centres', *Social Work Today*, 2 (24), 1972, pp. 3–4; A. Leissner, 'Developments in community-based youth work', *British Hospital Journal and Social Service Review*, 82 (4300), 1972, pp. 2068–9; A. Leissner, 'How youth work can involve the community', *Youth Review*, no. 25, winter 1972, pp. 3–7; T. A. Powley, 'Family advice centres', *British Hospital Journal and Social Service Review*, 81 (4234), 1971, pp. 1164–5; T. A. Powley, 'Neighbourhood youth work', *Concern* (National Children's Bureau), no. 12, summer 1973, pp. 19–23.
7 A. Leissner, 'Association of Community Workers', *British Hospital Journal and Social Service Review*, 78 (4106), 1968, pp. 2407–8.
8 R. A. B. Leaper, *Community Work*, National Council of Social Service, rev. ed., London, 1971, pp. 162–7.
9 G. Popplestone, 'The ideology of professional community workers', *British Journal of Social Work*, 1 (1), April 1971, pp. 85–104.
10 G. F. Thomason, *The Professional Approach to Community Work*, London, Sands, 1969, p. 14.
11 A. Leissner, 'Association of Community Workers'.
12 I. Page, 'Social services scenario', *Social Work Today*, 2 (11), 1971, pp. 7–9.
13 Lord Boyle of Handsworth, E. A. O. G. Weddell and Dame Eileen Younghusband, *Current Issues in Community Work: A study by the community work group*, Routledge & Kegan Paul, 1973, p. 2.
14 Ibid., chapter 2.
15 Report on the 1973 BASW Conference, 'Living with change', *Social Work Today*, 4 (17), 1973, p. 522.
16 A. Leissner, 'Community work – a professional approach', *Social Services Quarterly*, 47 (1), 1973, pp. 3–5; see also J. Cheetham and M. J. Hill, 'Community work: social realities and ethical dilemmas', *British Journal of Social Work*, 3 (3), 1973, pp. 331–48.
17 Home Office, Committee on Children and Young Persons, *Report* (Ingleby Report), HMSO, 1960.

Fcw

18 Children and Young Persons Act, 1963, Section I, Part 1.

19 A. Leissner, *Family Advice Services* (2nd ed.), Longman, 1968, pp. 79–80; see also D. S. Runnicles, 'The development of a detached family advice centre in a high problem area', *Case Conference*, 14 (7), 1967, pp. 252–7.

20 A. Leissner, 'Association of Community Workers', pp. 18–19.

21 For more detailed information, see: R. Perlman and D. Jones, *Neighborhood Service Centers*, Department of Health, Education and Welfare, Office of Juvenile Delinquency and Youth Development, Washington, D.C., 1967; J. Rae Price, 'The Netherlands – some models for Britain?', *British Hospital Journal and Social Service Review*, 78, 27 September 1968, pp. 1802–4; A. Leissner, 'Report on a study tour of community-based advice centres and community-based services for children and youth in eight European cities' (submitted to the Department of Education and Science and the National Children's Bureau), London, December 1973 (mimeographed).

22 M. Mayo, Background paper, European study group on community development and urban deprivation, Oxford, 6–16 September 1973, United Nations Office at Geneva, Division of Social Affairs, p. 7.

23 A. Leissner, *Street Club Work in Tel Aviv and New York*, Longman, 1969, p. 122.

24 E. De Grooth, 'Family advice?', *Social Work Today*, 2 (24), 1972, p. 7.

25 A. Leissner, K. A. M. Herdman and E. V. Davies, *Advice, Guidance and Assistance*, Longman, 1971, pp. 48–55.

26 Ibid., p. 300.

27 P. A. Evens, 'A feasibility study on organisational change in a Children's Department', County Borough of Luton, n.d. (mimeographed), p. 58.

28 Leissner, Herdman and Davies, op. cit., p. 313.

29 R. Guthrie, 'Local authorities and social change', in A. Lapping (ed.), *Community Action*, Fabian Tract no. 400, 1971, p. 18.

30 J. E. Paull, 'Social action for a different decade', *Social Service Review* (USA), 45 (1), March 1971, pp. 34–5.

31 A. Sinfield, 'Which way for social work?', in P. Townsend *et al.*, *The Fifth Social Service*, Fabian Society, 1970, p. 31.

32 Council for Children's Welfare Study Group, *A Family Service and a Family Court*, London, 1965.

33 R. Brooks, 'Civic rights and social services', in W. A. Robson and B. Crick (eds), *The Future of the Social Services*, Penguin, 1970, p. 41.

34 Leissner, Herdman and Davies, op. cit., p. 248.

35 Thomason, op. cit., p. 36.

36 R. Short and J. W. McCulloch, 'Health, welfare and advice centre', *Case Conference*, 15 (3), 1968, pp. 107–8.

37 A. Leissner, 'Participation: issues of strategy and tactics', in P. Evens (ed.), *Readings in Social Change*, vol. 1, Oxford, Alistair Schurnach, 1974.

38 T. A. Powley, 'Family advice centres'.

39 Leissner, Herdman and Davies, op. cit., p. 317.

40 A. Leissner, 'Developments in community youth work'.

41 A. Leissner, 'Participation and pseudo-participation', *International Child Welfare Review*, no. 11–12, 1971, pp. 81–6.
42 D. Carter and J. Carter, 'Climbing off the fence', *Social Work Today*, 3 (10), 1972, pp. 4–6.
43 T. Cooper, Chairman's Address, *Social Work Today*, 4 (17), 1973, pp. 514–19.
44 P. Keogh, 'Planning for persons', *New Society*, no. 577, 25 October 1973, pp. 210–11.

9 Responsibility without power: the case of social development*

Michael Harloe and Meryl Horrocks

Social development

The new towns provided one of the earliest opportunities for officially supported community work in Britain and the corps of social development officers (SDOs) can lay good claim to being among the most experienced community workers. It was over twenty-five years ago that the Harlow Development Corporation advertised for an SDO to 'be responsible for directing and co-ordinating the development of the town into a balanced and self-contained community' and even before this the Welwyn Garden City Company Ltd – then a private concern – had employed a similar official. Furthermore, the new towns have often been referred to as great social experiments and they are clearly places where those with social work and related skills are likely to have a major role to play.

This might lead one to expect that the justification for social development and the status and role of its practitioners would be by now firmly established. At a first glance this certainly seems to be the case. In *The Needs of New Communities*, published in 1967, a sub-committee of the Central Housing Advisory Committee headed by Barry Cullingworth commended the practice of appointing SDOs in new towns and went on to suggest that other forms of new communities such as expanding towns, peripheral housing estates and even large redevelopment areas could benefit from the application of such skills.[1] In 1968 the Seebohm Report also laid great emphasis on the extension of what might broadly be described as social development work to a whole variety of situations within existing urban areas.[2] A study of these and similar official pronouncements would suggest that social development is well on the way

* Since this was written in October 1972, both the situation in social development and our own thinking have naturally changed. This contribution must now therefore be seen as being to some extent historical rather than reflecting current realities.

to becoming an established and important element of the country's social services.

However, this impression is at some variance with the picture of social development which emerges from any acquaintance, however brief, with its work in the new towns. A strong feeling of insecurity pervades the comments and attitudes of SDOs, and there appears to be a lack of clear-cut objectives and methods of operation. The opportunities offered by the above-mentioned reports for a consolidation and expansion of the work to other situations seem to have been largely ignored, and the general air of confusion and pessimism suggests that, far from being in a position to exert any form of leadership in the emerging profession of community work, SDOs are marginal men whose future is far from secure.

Recent studies by the Centre for Urban and Regional Studies at the University of Birmingham illustrate these points.[3] Despite general agreement in official reports about the importance of social development in new towns, only twenty of the thirty new towns had such officers at the end of 1970 although it must be stressed that most of the more recently designated towns had made such an appointment. Some measure of the status and powers of SDOs, or their lack of it, can be gained from the fact that in only eight of these towns was social development an autonomous department and in only one of them did the SDO have unequivocal chief officer status. The size of the social development departments or sections also varied widely and not wholly in accordance with the size or stage of development of the town. In one town the SDO had twenty professional and ten administrative staff in 1971–2, but this was exceptionally large.[4]

One reason for this variation in size and status of departments relates to the widely differing functions which are given to social development in the various towns. The Birmingham study listed five main areas of concern:

1   community development and arrivals work,
2   public relations and information,
3   social planning,
4   research,
5   liaison with statutory and voluntary bodies.

No single department is likely to do all these tasks, but all of them can be found located in one or another of the new town social development departments.

Not only is there no generally applicable list of social development operations but there is only limited agreement among SDOs as to what this list might contain. The Birmingham researchers held a seminar attended by many of those working in this field, and their lack of unanimity was evident.[5] For example, some advocated the social planning role whereas others denied even the possibility of such a role. Some observers felt that the key task should be that of a 'facilitator' or political manipulator, fighting the bureaucratic development corporation on behalf of the residents, but others suggested that the arm-twisting days were over.

The same seminar also revealed widely differing opinions concerning the future of the SDO. Some participants were convinced that greater thought about the goals of social development and its status could be aided by more professionalisation – university training courses and a professional association – whereas others felt that this would lead to a weakening of what should be the overwhelming motivation of social development, that of helping people.

One of the present authors has concluded that the influence that an individual SDO will have on the new town planning process will depend on a number of factors.[6] These include:

1   the stage of development at which an SDO is appointed,
2   the seniority of the appointment,
3   the quality and nature of the officer's contribution,
4   the receptiveness of other departments to his work,
5   the attitude of the General Manager of the development corporation to his work,
6   the extent to which work is delegated to consultants.

The important point about this list is that it confirms the impression that, whatever outsiders may think, there is no *generally* accepted need for the SDO to play a major role in the planning of the new towns and their administration and that, where this does occur, the nature of the task is often largely defined by people and bodies other than the SDO and his department. Another way of stating this is to say that social development still has a problem about establishing its legitimacy. And yet, if social development has the importance that official reports such as those mentioned above seem to cloak it with, it seems necessary that it should emerge from this position of weakness and uncertainty and establish itself on a firmer footing. The question of how this might be achieved must await an analysis of the current situation, to which we now turn.

There seem to be two important interlinked areas for analysis. The first centres on the content of the SDO's role, its importance and the extent to which this importance is recognised and accepted by others. The second concerns the relationships between the SDO and the development corporation for which he works and the new town residents. The very considerable sociological literature on the professions and on social work enables some useful comparisons and conclusions to be made. Etzioni and his associates have characterised social work as a 'semi-profession'.[7] They point out that the professions by and large share the following characteristics: they have a body of theoretical knowledge and their members have special skills, often the product of long training, in applying this knowledge. They are guided by a code of ethics, the focus of which is the client, and their authority to prescribe solutions within this area of competence is usually accepted by their employers, clients and the community at large.[8] Together with these attributes goes a professional culture, professional associations and the principle of judgment by one's professional equals. Medicine, the law, the church and university teaching are obvious examples of occupations in which these rules apply. By comparison the semi-professions lack some or all of these attributes and so lack the power and freedom of action within their own sphere that the full professions enjoy.

In discussing the detailed case of social work, both Etzioni and his colleagues and Heraud, in a more recent study, refer to the limitations of the organisation of this semi-professional occupation in comparison with the outline of professional organisation stated above and add some points that refer more specifically to the nature of social work.[9] One of the common features of the development of all the professions is an increasingly clear and precise definition of their content, and the scope of the competence and responsibilities of their practitioners. Social work as a whole still has a long way to go in this direction and, as we saw above, social development is hardly in the forefront here. One of the features of a profession which aids its task of self-definition is the existence of constant discussion and criticism of their work by the professionals. The volume of such literature as a whole in social work is on the increase but there have been few contributions made by those engaged in new town social development. As Goodey has remarked, 'there is already a substantial literature on social development and planning in new communities but too often this consists of short articles or effusive commentaries, useful ideas seem a little thinner on the ground.'[10] Of course, one way in which many professions develop their corpus of knowledge is by research. Social development officers often have 'research' listed as one of their duties but, as the Birmingham project discovered, 'few SDOs seemed to be keenly interested in research or the whole area of social planning.'[11]

It is perhaps not surprising that, with few exceptions, social development officers should have ignored or rejected these trappings of professionalism. As Toren has pointed out, social workers tend to resist professionalisation and even to be actively opposed to it.[12] In social development, at least, this is also highlighted by the lack of an effective programme for a formal course of training. Despite the recommendation contained in *The Needs of New Communities* that such courses would be valuable, the response from all but a few at the Birmingham seminar to such a proposal was poor and even scornful. As one SDO remarked, 'in my opinion, there was far too much emphasis placed by the speaker on the question of professionalism. A person may be a very well qualified person . . . but not a very successful operator. I am not always that much impressed by people who have a long string of letters after their names.'[13] The fundamental reason for this attitude appears to be the factor mentioned earlier, namely that SDOs feel that any formal training might weaken their strong commitment to helping people but, as Heraud remarks, 'those social workers who have not been exposed to professional acculturation through training courses are most likely to take on bureaucratic characteristics, in particular to think about their clients in bureaucratic rather than professional ways.'[14]

Professions are also marked by the emergence of a common culture usually presided over by one or more formal associations. Heraud has pointed to the fragmentation of social work – largely a product of the varying bureaucratic context in which its different aspects first arise – as the main factor standing in the way of this coming together. This problem is marked in the case of social development – while some SDOs belong to the ACW or other associations, there is no body to which they all affiliate. Their only common meeting-place is the Social Development Officer's Group. Membership of this is, however, restricted solely to new town officers as, significantly, it is a sub-committee of the new town General Managers' Group to whom it is wholly responsible. So the only association which exists has its membership and terms of reference decided by another group and is not even able to include people performing almost identical tasks in expanding towns, let alone those operating in wider spheres outlined in the Seebohm and Cullingworth reports. The contrast with a self-governing professional association could not be more acute.

So far as the specific content of the SDO's role is concerned, two factors stand out. First, some of the elements in his work conflict and as a whole

they call for widely differing skills. An obvious example is the difficulty
of being a public relations man and community developer although, to
be fair, many SDOs dislike and resist carrying out the former role and it
seems that this is gradually being detached from their duties. Second,
social development, and social work more generally, suffers in comparison
with the professions from a lack of general agreement by outsiders, be
they employers or clients, as to the special nature of their skills and therefore their special competence to solve the problems they face. According
to Wilensky, 'the types of problems dealt with are part of everyday
living. The lay public cannot recognise the need for special competence
in an area where everyone is "expert".'[15] In the semi-professions'
state of internal weakness and lack of cohesion, many of their goals
will be formulated and imposed on them by lay personnel (particularly
of course the employers), and the occupation will be subject to a considerable degree of lay control. Social development is in this situation
in most towns and, as we saw, the significance of its contribution to
social planning at least is largely determined by the attitudes and
actions of others. The General Manager of the new town is of key
importance as a controller – the Birmingham seminar was littered with
references to this fact. Horrocks also reports: 'members of the research
team were also told that the existence of social development at all, and
certainly its relative power, depends on the attitudes of the general
manager. In places where there was no SDO the reasons given were
almost uniformly that either the general manager positively did not
approve of social development, or more moderately, did not see its
usefulness at that state or scale of development.'[16]

The relationship of SDOs to their employers, the development corporation, raises the second major area for analysis that we referred to above.
But before this is explored, this relationship is also involved in another
issue which arises from consideration of the content of social development.

Professionals exist to serve clearly defined clients, but there is some
doubt about who the SDO's real client is. Despite expressed concern for
people, the SDO is an official of the development corporation and subject,
to a greater or lesser degree, to its goals which often appear to find
expression in physical or financial terms. The introduction of modern
methods of management, such as planning, programming and budgeting
systems which tend to use physical and financial measures of effectiveness,
makes it even more difficult to integrate the social concerns of the SDO
with the overall goals of the development corporation, as the following
remark by an SDO shows: 'You can work at a great big project and

apportion costs entirely and you can discipline administrative costs and design fees and all the rest of it. And you get to the end of that lovely exercise and you've got social development sitting on the end doing nothing, just twiddling its thumbs – absolutely unquantifiable.'[17]

The relationship of social development to the development corporation lies at the core of much of the insecurity and lack of coherence that characterises this job. In the series of studies edited by Etzioni, Scott shows how the professional whose outlook is dominated by professional associations and training comes into conflict with the bureaucracies in which he works which are pursuing organisational goals. He comments: 'in many respects the professional person employed by a bureaucratic organisation is the modern marginal man, his feet uncertainly planted in two different and partially conflicting environments'.[18] He examined a welfare agency to see whether this conflict is apparent in social work, and concluded that the higher the level of professional training of the individual worker the more likely he is to find fault with the agency's programme. Conversely, social workers with little training tended to accept the bureaucratic definition of goals that dominated the agency. In the new towns situation where formal training in social development work is non-existent and, as we have seen, the nature of one's job is often determined by one's brother officers, one can predict that a considerable distance will exist between the social development department and the people it is trying to serve. Alternatively, if he tries to become a tenants' advocate (which was suggested as a possible future role in the Birmingham seminar), the SDO will come into conflict with the corporation. Since he lacks the status and power conferred by professionalism, this is likely to be a rather one-sided contest.

Therefore there must be considerable doubt about whether social development is recognised by a majority of new town residents as having an important role to play. The lack of further evidence prevents any definite conclusion here, but several indications are available that this may be so. Horrocks quotes the director of a company who had just moved to a new town, who commented: 'I will bet most of our employees have never heard of a social development officer.'[19] The Birmingham seminar contains several references to the SDO's role as an anti-bureaucrat or as the only person who is available to argue for social goals in the inner councils of the development corporation. However it is clear from the same seminar that the SDO's ability to make this a continuous function is almost wholly dependent on the goodwill and co-operation of the General Manager. The limitations of this support are probably well illustrated by a comment from the General Manager of one of the new towns which has done most to integrate social development into its work, having an SDO with chief officer status and a large supporting staff:[20]

> The essential thing is to try and create an atmosphere in which the individual inhabitant feels that the development organisation is concerned personally with the inhabitant's welfare. . . . At the same time this must not be confused with a wishy-washy attitude such as that which, in our opinion, is inevitable if the excesses of so-called 'public participation' are followed. A paternal attitude can, in many cases, be wrong, but provided that it is genuine and motivated entirely by an interest in and caring for the people in a new development, then in our opinion it is both desirable and essential to the social well-being of that community. Somebody has to take the responsibility for preparing the plans and for carrying out the work, and in respect of every project there is a point where discussion must stop and a decision must be taken.

This article has attempted to explain at least some of the reasons why the increasing emphasis that has been put on the need for social development work in a wide range of urban situations contrast sharply with the adverse picture received of some aspects of such work as it is being carried out in some of the British new towns. The degree of pessimism and insecurity is perhaps best summed up by the following conclusion: 'One of the more surprising observations from our research is that doubt about the present structure and for the future viability of social development was expressed, not by one-man teams fighting a losing battle, but by articulate officers in large and apparently influential departments.'[21] Whenever those who on the face of it are in the strongest position express such doubts, the future does indeed seem bleak.

Yet the role of the SDO as the human face of bureaucracy attempting to ensure that social priorities are paramount in what after all is, or should be, primarily a social policy seems to be as important as ever and increasingly recognised by outside authorities as such. What changes might serve to reduce the insecurity and improve the level of effectiveness of social development in the new towns? It is clear from the discussion above that what social development lacks above all is a sufficiently established and powerful position in the process of planning and implementing new towns. In an article entitled 'Social planning: the search for legitimacy', Rein has discussed where the reform-oriented planner gets his authority to propose social change, and his analysis can usefully be brought to bear on the problems faced by SDOs.[22] Rein's article related mainly to city planners but, adapting it to the particular situation discussed here, there would seem to be three possible power bases for social development.

First, the SDO could attain influence by seeking to identify himself with the goals of the bureaucracy for which he works, in this case the development corporation, and attempting to pursue socially oriented policies within the limitations which that situation imposes. Heraud has suggested that this may be a viable method for many social workers in a bureaucratic setting:[23]

> if the organisation is seen in terms of individuals or groups who attempt to gain acceptance for rather differing goals, and where rules relate to the resolution of potential conflict, then it is possible to be much more optimistic about the effects of the bureaucratic action of social work, and of the chances that social workers may have in future of influencing or changing the goals of their agencies.

The one case study Heraud quotes which supports this view concerned a local authority children's department incorporating new legislation. In a complex organisation, such as a local authority which has a strong 'social' aspect to its total operations and a mixture of control by official and elected representatives, it is easy to see that there may well be sufficient 'give' in the organisation to enable such changes to occur. Unfortunately most development corporations seem to have a rather clearly defined set of goals which are not social ones, and a hierarchical structure dominated by the General Manager – or sometimes the Chairman. One SDO summed up the situation in conversation when he referred to the corporations as basically being estate development companies who often, if not always, had the good grace to hire someone to look after social matters. If this is in practice (as opposed to in theory) the order of priorities, Heraud's suggestion seems likely to be less applicable in the new town situation than in any other in which social workers are currently operating.

The second possibility is that social development will gain power by increased professionalisation. By attaining a level of expertise which is accepted by the community and by their fellow officers, the SDOs will be given more security and freedom to effect planning and implementation. We have seen how far the existing body of SDOs are from arriving at a consensus in favour of this future possibility. Disagreement on training, goals, formal association and other prerequisites for increased professionalisation is almost total.

The third possibility is for social development to become community based. It seems doubtful whether this is feasible in a situation where SDOs are employed and have their role very largely determined by a completely different set of people who contain few, if any, recognised representatives of the local residents.

In his article Rein points out the limitations on seeking legitimacy exclusively from any one of the three sources referred to above. Too close an identification with bureaucratic goals facilitates legitimation, but may divert social development from attempting to serve social goals to serving purely economic, physical or organisational/political goals. Similarly too great a concentration on professionalisation might – and this is what social workers tend to fear – divert effect and attention towards the search for prestige or irrelevant knowledge, e.g. community power might strengthen the SDO's ability to raise relevant issues but at the cost of cutting himself off from the powerful organisation whose goals and policies he would be attempting to modify or alter.

Rein concluded that neither source nor legitimacy is by itself sufficient, and that organisations and the people employed by them must choose between the various strategies as the situation demands. Conflict is inherent in the situation that Rein is examining and this is also the case in the situation that the SDO finds himself in. It would be naive to suggest that this could be eliminated.

However, to intervene effectively, social development needs a more assured status than at present, and therefore must be able to appeal to one or more sources to legitimise its actions, but at the moment social development seems to be in a particularly weak position to appeal effectively to any of these sources of legitimacy. A number of changes might improve the position. A social development department headed by a chief officer should be statutory requirement of all new town development corporations and it should be a matter of course that the SDO participates on an equal footing with his brother officers on all major policy decisions which have social implications. The SDOs themselves urgently need to discuss and define the goals and techniques of their work and by research, publication and training raise the level of their professionalism. A formal association, analogous perhaps to the Institute of Housing Managers, would be an appropriate forum for this work but alternatively a special section of one of the emergent social work associations might be preferable. Finally, social development must move closer to the people it exists to serve; this is perhaps the most difficult problem of all while it continues to be a part of a rather remote and undemocratically based organisation. Social develop- ment could become the responsibility of the new town local authorities which, being elected bodies, are at least one step closer to the people, but this gain might be outweighted by the removal of the 'human face' from the bureaucracy. What really seems necessary is that the develop- ment corporation itself be democratised by the inclusion of a substantial number of locally elected representatives on the corporation and possibly by a far closer working association between the local authority and the development corporation departments, with far more effective arrange- ments for the joint generation and implementation of policy than occurs in most new towns today.

Notes

1 Central Housing Advisory Committee, *The Needs of New Communities* (Cullingworth Report), HMSO, 1967.
2 Committee on Local Authority and Allied Personal Social Services, *Report*, Cmnd 3703, HMSO, 1968.
3 The preparation of this paper would have been impossible without reference to the work of the New Communities Team at the Centre for Urban and Regional Studies, University of Birmingham. Much of the supporting material has been drawn from their works and from dis- cussions with them but they do not, necessarily, wish to be identified with the conclusions of this paper. The data come from a Social Science Research Council Supported Study (1969–72), which was concerned with a number of aspects of social development in new communities. Working papers and other reports are available from the Publications Secretary at the Centre.
4 Personal communication to M. Harloe.
5 George Smith, 'The future of social development', in *Social Development in New Communities: Proceedings of a Seminar . . . in the University of Birmingham, 1972*, ed. Brian Goodey *et al.* (SDNC), Research Memoran- dum no. 12, Birmingham, Centre for Urban and Regional Studies, pp. 39–61.
6 Meryl Horrocks, 'The organisation of social development in new towns', paper presented at Social Planning Seminar, University of Sheffield, December 1971. A revised version of this paper, from which the present authors have abstracted frequently, appeared as 'Social planning in new communities', *Built Environment* (November 1972). A final version of this material is now available: Meryl Horrocks, *Social Development Work in New Communities*, University of Birmingham, Centre for Urban and Regional Studies, Occasional Paper no. 27, CURS, 1973.
7 A. Etzioni (ed.), *The Semi-Professionals and their Organisation*, Collier- Macmillan, 1969, p. 5.

8 N. Toren, 'Semi-professionalism and social work', in ibid., pp. 142–4.
9 B. Heraud, *Sociology and Social Work*, Pergamon, 1970.
10 Brian Goodey, 'Tenants of life's middle stage, securely placed between the small and great', in SDNC, p. 10.
11 Horrocks, op. cit., pp. 11–12.
12 Toren, op. cit., p. 148.
13 SDNC, pp. 49–50. The speaker was the Public and Social Relations Officer of Craigavon Development Commission, Northern Ireland.
14 Heraud, op. cit., p. 237.
15 Quoted in ibid., p. 230.
16 Horrocks, op. cit., p. 13.
17 Ibid., p. 12.
18 W. R. Scott, 'Professional employees in a bureaucratic structure – social work', in Etzioni, op. cit., p. 89.
19 Horrocks, op. cit., p. 16.
20 Personal communication to M. Harloe.
21 Horrocks, op. cit., p. 16.
22 M. Rein, 'Social planning: the search for legitimacy', in M. Rein, *Social Policy*, Random House, 1970, pp. 193–217.
23 Heraud, op. cit., pp. 262–3.

10 Three-dimensional noughts and crosses: the work of a Council of Social Service

Pamela Warren

As an organisation concerned with community work in a London borough, we are often made to feel 'impure' by visitors and students because we are constantly crossing and recrossing the boundaries of work between the intensive local level (say, a network of about a dozen streets), work at a district level, and work at the borough, regional or national level. We are also constantly shuttling between the techniques of community organisation, community service and community development.

Creative work of any kind is seldom tidy and community work, if it is open to growth and development, must learn to live with ambiguities, paradoxes and untied ends. For communities are living and dynamic forces, not abstract statistics to be filed and tidily stored away.

There is an expensive adult toy called Three-Dimensional Noughts and Crosses which perfectly illustrates what I mean about community work. For it, too, is a game played at several levels simultaneously. In community work, what happens locally is at the same time affecting both the national and the regional scene and vice versa; similarly the methods of approach are also almost imperceptibly changing from one technique to another.

A Council of Social Service is primarily a broker, bringing together disparate members of the community network who may be mutually helpful. Identifying need and, to use Professor Kathleen Jones's phrase, 'releasing the resources that exist within every community to enable it to heal itself'. It may do this in three different ways: through community organisation, by offering community services, and through the techniques of community development. Community organisation is inherent in its structure. Its Council (which elects the Executive Committee) is made up of representatives of member voluntary organisations, the ex-officio membership of the chief officers of the statutory services and members of the borough council. Thrice yearly Council meetings deal with the matters of common concern – the single homeless, the needs of unsupported women, the disabled – and go on to form working parties for action. The Executive Committee, a representative group of both statutory and voluntary agencies, makes the policy of the Council of Social Service.

But community organisation (with voluntary agencies at least) must nearly always be oblique in its approach. It is not a phrase which gladdens many hearts (least of all voluntary English hearts). People like to do their thing and not be tidied into seemly administrative patterns. The response to a straightforward invitation to be organised will nearly always be a lemon. 'Who wants it?' 'What do they want badly enough to co-operate with each other for?' and 'What do they care enough about to want to do something about?' are all good questions for the community worker to ask himself.

Working together over matters of common interest is an unselfconscious means of co-ordination. Recently, the Camden Council of Social Service has been working with a number of groups concerned with territory. After all, everyone is an expert on the place where he lives or works. Neighbourhood study groups, made up of local residents and professional workers, are brought together to consider the needs of an area. It is imperative in the early stages of such a group to clearly identify the geographical boundaries of an area so that the neighbourhood discussed is meaningful to the participants.

One such group came into being at the behest of the borough youth officer. Worried by a high delinquency rate and repeated outbreaks of vandalism in a neighbourhood, she came to the Council of Social Service to ask what was known about its history. The answer was, 'Not enough by half', and so a study group was set up. Among those invited were representatives of local voluntary organisations, a housing society, tenants' associations, the police, the probation service, ward councillors, clergy, school teachers, youth leaders and members of the social services department.

The initial invitation asked for help from those with special knowledge of the area, and clearly indicated that the meeting (held at 6.30 p.m.) would not last for more than an hour and a half and that refreshments would be available. Those invited were also asked to nominate others, known to them, who had special knowledge of the neighbourhood. Over 80 per cent of those asked to the first meeting turned up. After a careful explanation of the Council of Social Service's function, which was merely to act as a catalyst for their views, and an initial discussion on the needs of the area, they were asked to let the css have in writing not more than 300 words on the views of the needs of the neighbourhood as they saw them and ways in which those needs might be met. Gradually a picture began to emerge.

This was an area which had housed the workers of the Industrial Revolution. By the end of the nineteenth century it had become one of the worst industrial slums in central London. In the 1920s social reformers had cleared away the slums and replaced them by blocks of flats. But in their zeal (and we in our time have as surely made our own mistakes) they forgot to ask the actual people what they felt about the area. Consequently, they were rehoused in bright new homes but never really felt that they were personally involved with the place or had much responsibility for it. In addition, the barrack-room lawyers, showing early signs of leadership through grumbles and protests, were thought to be troublemakers by the social workers who had worked so hard to rehouse them and were firmly discouraged. As a result there was apparently very little indigenous leadership and energy was dispersed in violence and vandalism.

The people were no longer financially deprived, but the legacy of hard times remained in cultural deprivation. Their vocabularies were limited. (Perhaps 150 words, 6 swear-words and then violence.) In this neighbourhood the family who shouted loudest and hit hardest was king. In a population of 5,000 epople – 1,600 of whom where children – there were no play facilities. Many of the local workers had not met until they came together in the study group (the success of any neighbourhood study group may best be judged by the volume of the buzz of conversation which goes on *after* a meeting). People were sitting back and saying, 'It's high time they did something.' There were few trees or recreational facilities (the pubs were drinking-shops rather than social meeting·places), some people longed for a swimming-pool or (if that wasn't possible) a paddling pool.

From the mosaic of information provided by the members of the study group, the Council of Social Service ventured a diagnosis. 'What we think you are saying is that you need a place to meet, you need to work more closely together, you need more local leadership, you need something for the kids. Is this right?' And gradually and tentatively the group began to prescribe. There was to be a café – a welcoming and friendly place where everyone could meet – and two workers based in the café whose job it would be to identify and encourage local leadership and co-ordinate the activities of the neighbourhood. The project would be sponsored by the study group so that by the time it became operational it would already have people in the area who were working towards its ends.

Grants were negotiated with the borough council and the Youth Service. There followed an interlude for a summer play-scheme. The high delinquency rate seemed to be directly related to the boredom of the children during the long summer holiday. A well run play-scheme would keep many children out of trouble. But what was a well run play-scheme? And wouldn't the css, by providing one, turn into yet another interventionist agency in the area? Still, there were the children, there was the boredom and the high rate of juvenile delinquency. These couldn't be ignored.

A site was found and borrowed from the Greater London Council. Here the support of the Leader of the Council and the local representatives of the Metropolitan Water Board saved months of negotiation and unnecessary expense. But the site had been used as a rubbish dump. It must be cleared. The planners decided against seeking the help of the borough council. It would be better if the site could be cleared by the local people. Anonymous workmen from official sources were all too familiar in the neighbourhood. So, one hot Saturday morning, a group of workers appeared on the site. They came from the css, the study group, local young people's organisations, and from the police cadet force. Posters were stuck up, inviting passers by to 'Watch this site', and leaflets were handed to enquirers inviting them to join in and help. By the end of the day there was an additional work-force of local children and mothers and fathers. Hard rubbish was piled high (it cost over £300 to cart away). Other things (like maggot-infested carpets and dead animals) perished in huge bonfires gleefully fed by the children. Food was provided by the parish church, and outsiders and local workers ate together. It was the beginning of the formation of many relationships.

Local people were suspicious at first ('We thought you was a lot of hippies') but were soon setting to with a will, 'to get something done for the kids this summer'. Staff and volunteers for the play-scheme were most carefully selected and four Monday evenings in July were allocated to a preparatory training.

The play-scheme proved to be the entrée to the long-term community development project planned by the study group. Mothers began to ask why the playground should only have six weeks of life. 'Our kids want to play all the year round.' The Council of Social Service agreed that this was so but explained that they couldn't afford to keep the playground open any longer. (Money for the summer scheme had been found through an emergency grant from the education authority and from the css's own voluntary funds.) If money could be found, they would certainly continue the playground while the light evenings lasted. Mothers and fathers ran a carnival, whist drives and dances and raised over £100. The balance was found by the education authority and the CSS.

But now the summer was over and the children were resenting the withdrawal of their friends. Luckily, it could be explained to them that some of the workers, at any rate, would be back when the café opened. Premises had been found on the main shopping street of the neighbourhood – an ex-laundry office owned by the GLC. An architect was consulted and a bright, simply furnished little café appeared (at least on paper). But money was running short. In the end the plans were simplified and a group made up of local volunteer craftsmen, boys from the play-scheme and the two community workers (who had been on the staff of the summer playground) did 50 per cent of the work, leaving only the most difficult jobs to be done by a building contractor.

The project is now in its third year. It has become a meeting-place for local adults and children and, over informal cups of tea, plans have been made for outings, parties and a three-day summer festival. The old play-site is being transformed into a recreation ground for the neighbourhood with an adventure playground, a sitting-out area and a *paddling* pool. The local workers have formed themselves into a community association and are slowly being joined by caretakers, tenants' associations and representatives of local opinion. A monthly community newspaper and a local directory have helped to improve communications. Our workers plan to withdraw at the end of this year leaving the management of the centre to a local group.

This project has involved work at the local level, at borough level and at regional level (to obtain resources), and has used the methods of community organisation, community service and community development over its three years of life.

Another group called together by the Council of Social Service has been involved in studying the management and deployment of volunteers in hospitals. The volunteer industry is a booming one and more and more 'organisers' are being employed. This is a comparatively new job and so a group was formed to bring together the experienced and the inexperienced to consider the recruitment, selection, accountability, development and supervision of volunteers. Organisers came from the hospitals, the social service department and the voluntary agencies. Their shared experience was published in a joint report. This was community organisation at borough level, but the report drawn up by the organisers of volunteers has implications to those involved in work of this kind all over the country.

Community organisation also means being in the information business, letting each agency know what the others are doing, keeping them informed of developments on the national or regional scene. It means helping new organisations come into being – helping to prepare a planning brief or application for grant – and helping organisations with hardened arteries to change their role or perhaps to go out of business. It is the dread of every Council of Social Service Secretary that they will inform the Elizabeth Fry of the twentieth century that there is no future in her ideas.

The community services offered by the Camden Council of Social Service cover a wide range, but they are often planned with primary and secondary functions. Its five Citizens' Advice Bureaux (which last year dealt with 54,000 callers) are primarily concerned with offering a first-class information service: 'My landlord won't give me a rent book. What can I do?' 'I've had notice to quit.' 'Can you find a home for my dog if I go to prison?' 'My daughter hasn't been home since last Sunday.' 'Can I take beer on the plane to the Costa Brava?' 'My son was murdered in Hamburg three months ago and the authorities won't let me have his personal effects.' 'I bought a carpet and after a month it's covered in a kind of green fungus. . . .' 'I need a solicitor/dentist/doctor.'

All these enquirers must be helped to find the answer they need. But the community-work-based CAB has at least two functions. First the unfiltered problems streaming over its counter are invaluable material in making the CAB an intelligence unit. From the study of the quarterly reports and record cards you can pick up quite easily the emerging problems – What's worrying people? What are the rackets? What are the pressures? One CAB showed a sharp rise in the number of quarrelling neighbours. This was traced back to hot, early summer evenings and the lack of play-space in the district. The CSS made representations to the local authority for play provision in the area and found itself involved in yet another summer play-scheme.

The CABs, decentralised as they are throughout the borough, can act as a base for services designed to reach minority groups who may be at risk. A CAB in an area which houses many Greek Cypriots provides a Greek-speaking CAB and casework service, but this service has come to be used by Cypriots from all over London. Representation has been made to the London Boroughs' Association in order to ensure that Cypriots living in other parts of London may be offered such a service.

Professional men and women giving their services voluntarily also provide first-class professional services for CAB clients. There are, of course, all the usual legal services, including representation at tribunals but, lately, honorary accountants have offered an invaluable service to those who find themselves on the wrong side of the tax man.

Another CAB has been responsible for a pilot scheme to help the bereaved. Death has become the taboo of the mid-twentieth century, and workers were aware of many clients in deep emotional distress with apparently no one to turn to. Sometimes close relatives can be of little help when the first shock is over, by the very reason of their closeness. Thanks to the co-operation of the Medical Officer of Health, the CAB is notified of all deaths in the district. The organiser sends a letter of sympathy to the next of kin, neighbour or flat mate with an offer of practical help (dying these days is a very complicated business and such things as wills or tenancies can be daunting to deal with alone) or, if the need is felt, a visit from a sympathetic stranger to talk things over with. This letter has had a 20 per cent take-up. The visitors are all carefully selected voluntary workers and the project is supervised by the Unit for the Study of Psycho-Social Transitions of The Tavistock Institute of Human Relations.

If they are to survive in the post-Seebohm era, Citizens' Advice Bureaux must become much more than information posts. They must use the knowledge gained in their work for the wider benefit of the community, using more than one dimension in the service they give and, with other community work agencies and their clients, widening the scope of their work.

The Volunteer Bureau came about because CAB workers and other agencies were concerned by the hit-and-miss approach to those wishing to give their spare time to the community. After a two-year research project a Bureau was set up to recruit and place volunteers in the social services. Great emphasis is placed on matching volunteer to job. The Bureau also sets out to build up a store of knowledge on all matters concerning volunteers and their management for work. Agencies are asked to draw up a job description when seeking a volunteer – How many hours a week? What skills are needed? What temperament? Are expenses paid? To whom is the volunteer accountable? Volunteers are interviewed in order to find out the amount of time they can give (always accept the minimum); their skills and experience; their inclinations and, as far as possible, their motivation. In the year 1972–3 the Camden Bureau placed 864 volunteers with 90 different agencies, both statutory and voluntary. It is closely and informally in touch with the plans and activities of all these organisations and others all over the borough, and thus acts as a valuable instrument of community organisation for the CSS.

To date the Bureau has mainly been concerned with established agencies, sending volunteers to the hospitals, the Social Services and Health departments, to youth clubs, playgrounds and voluntary organisations. Now in co-operation with the community development projects, it is engaged in organising groups to give neighbourly help in the place where they live. Popping in for a chat, running an errand or sharing a meal. It seems likely that the two branches of the Bureau's work will continue to function side by side.

The Volunteer Bureau is also concerning itself with the training and preparation of volunteers and has set up a representative steering committee to plan a systematic training programme for volunteers and their supervisors.

Playgrounds, whether as temporary holiday schemes or as permanent sites, also offer many opportunities for building a community. Children are often willing and eager to be involved in work such as building, digging, distributing leaflets or helping at bazaars, jumble sales and parties. It is a salutary experience to be cross-questioned by a fourteen-year-old as to just why you want to raise money for an organisation. Parents can become involved in the life and work of a playground through their children, and through this involvement begin to ask questions about the place where they live. Why isn't there a swimming-pool or a roller skating rink? Why can't there be a road crossing at those traffic lights? Why don't we organise an outing to Boulogne for all of us? Social workers, the police, probation officers and other professionals can be available for informal contact or counselling and so encourage the children and their parents to make readier use of the services on offer.

Professional caseworkers are available to the rest of the Council of Social Service through its Personal Consultation Centre which, while offering a skilled counselling service to those with emotional problems, offers a supportive advisory function to other voluntary agencies. The social workers also act as tutors to volunteers or staff wishing to understand a situation in greater depth (the CAB's honorary legal advisers once became disturbed by their encounters with too many aggressive clients!) or to gain a new skill.

All these departments are constantly cross-fertilising each other. The CAB will deal with a practical matter for a client of the Personal Consultation Centre. A CAB worker will ring up the PCC for advice as how best to deal with an emotionally disturbed client. The playgrounds will seek the PCC's help in dealing with an over-demanding child. The Volunteer Bureau will provide workers for all these activities. The barriers between community organisation, community services and community development are here again constantly being crossed and recrossed.

Community development is the primary concern of three Camden projects. One of these has been described earlier. But it might be added that this, too, has become concerned, in co-operation with other departments of the css, to offer some specialised services. A CAB worker spends a morning a week in the café dealing with problems too technical for the community workers; honorary legal advisers provide a walk-in legal advice session on Monday evenings and the education authority's senior Careers' Officer has experimented in providing job counselling for adolescents.

Another project set up a neighbourhood centre in an area swept by the rumours and counter-rumours of a redevelopment plan. The Centre began by offering information and then helped its callers who shared a problem in common to form into groups to negotiate with the authorities. As new residents moved in, surveys were taken to find out their reactions to their new homes after three months of living in them. The findings were relayed back to the planners and architects. Now in its fourth year of life, the Centre is still heavily used for information, but after the community development process had produced action groups, a neighbourhood forum was established to begin the work of community organisation. This involves the Centre in co-ordinating the groups and agencies it helped to foster, keeping people informed through the community newspaper, launching working parties on local issues such as play facilities, traffic or the care of the elderly.

A third centre, also in a redevelopment area after the initial phase of helping groups to organise for better negotiation and communication, found itself caught in the crossfire between what was left of the indigenous community and the 'welfare families,' and squatters living in short-life accommodation. Here the workers are thrown back for the present to providing services jointly with the local authority, including information, case work and a playground. As the new population moves in, the Centre will once again take up its role in community development.

Neighbourhood study groups remain a most valuable method of introduction to new projects. People enjoy talking about what they know about and will eagerly respond to plans for action arrived at together. But if pushed too hard they will sometimes confront you with disconcerting results. One group in a densely populated, inner urban area set off well. They identified special areas of need in the following categories: the old and lonely; the children with nowhere to play; the lack of shopping and recreational facilities (those offered were metropolitan rather than local in character); the prostitutes and drifters attracted by main line termini; the anxiety of private tenants as to their security of tenure or ability to pay inflated rents; the noise suffered by all from traffic, children and late night football revellers. Urged on by the local councillors in the group, they set out to create a community association to act as an umbrella for those undertaking to deal with all these ills. After six months, four key people in the association were showing definite signs of strain, and the group had to drop from a sprint to a trot to a walk to a crawl. Very slowly, new leaders have begun to emerge and the existing leaders have lightened their loads and steadied their pace. They are now wary of 'enthusiasts' in the eighteenth-century sense and have learned that patience and ideals must be evenly balanced in trying to create a new Jerusalem.

But out of this struggling group has already come a scheme for street wardens to keep a friendly eye on the elderly; a summer play-scheme in a dusty square bounded by London's plane trees, using the crypt of the local church when it rains, and a Wednesday evening social club. Serious negotiations are now taking place with the local authority on ways in which their environment might be improved.

A Council of Social Service stands in the centre between statutory and voluntary services. It is politically neutral so far as party politics are concerned and, therefore, can be a meeting ground for people from many widely differing backgrounds. It has no power, no authority, only influence. All those concerned with its work must set great store by the theories of administration through personal relationships. It is the ability to seek and gain favours from the Medical Officer of Health, the lady who keeps the corner shop, the Head of the Adult Education Institute, the Mayor, the police, the local villains or the caretaker of the primary school which makes the css worker a successful broker. At times they grow weary of saying 'Thank you' (but 'thank you' must always be said), and too often identify with the famous Thurber drawing whose caption runs, 'She's so damn charming she gives me the creeps.'

One day a visitor to our office watched in a rather bemused way its frantic comings and goings – the local Round Table returning collecting tins; two members of a club for mentally disturbed people chatting to the secretaries; two volunteers waiting to be interviewed; an Ethiopian psychiatrist on a visit of observation; two students; jumble arriving for a forthcoming sale; a ward councillor to discuss an agenda; play leaders borrowing camping equipment and the secretary of a tenants' association calling for advice on the wording of a petition – leaned back on his heels and said, 'This place is the hub of Camden, isn't it?' 'No', we said, 'but it is the hub of unofficial Camden.' And it is this unofficial quality which remains our greatest strength. Like the Queen on the chessboard we can move to either side or backwards and forwards at will. Sometimes, too, we can start something and then, when the balloon goes up, be like Eliot's Macavity mysteriously 'Not there'. Although we have to mind we don't get our tail trapped in the door.

The Camden Council of Social Service is fortunate in its many resources. It has the goodwill and generous support of the local authority, skilled workers and an intricate pattern of local networks built up over the years. Its chief resource is the people of Camden, and contacts with them must constantly be replenished and renewed.

The work of the CSS has become so irrevocably intertwined that it is almost impossible to write of the work of one department without mentioning the work of another. Scratch a play-scheme and you find a lawyer, rub a neighbourhood centre and you find a play-leader, cut open a club and you find a pre-retirement tutor or a caseworker. A purposeful mobilisation of local resources to meet local needs while relating these to the regional and national scene. But this, after all, is what community work is about.

11 Community arts

Sharon Collins, Paul Curno, Jenny Harris and John Turner

The Albany is an independent voluntary community centre. Its range is wide: it houses pre-school playgroups, housing scheme using short-life property for single-parent families, intermediate treatment programme, a truancy project (a kind of free-school after school for hardened truants and latch-key children), claimants' union, women's action group, squatting association, youth clubs, coffee bar, social workers, clubs for old people, for ESN children, for people with problems.

We have been attempting to employ a multifaceted approach in our work with the community, to integrate and reinforce a variety of interventions through several different methods. Our overall aim has been to enable people to have more control over situations around them, to bring about changes where needed, to offer support services to families, individuals and community groups, and to work towards enriching the quality of life.

A part of our work, however, has nothing specifically to do with these projects but is instead co-ordinating with existing local community groups, such as tenants' associations. We try and be a resource centre. An advice centre. An encouragement centre. We have fundamental things to offer, space to hold meetings, duplicating and secretarial facilities.

The Albany is in Deptford, a depressed dockland area in south-east London, where the housing shortage is severe. The accommodation that does exist falls into two distinct categories: the new council developments, dominated by high-rise blocks:

Idea

take snaps of families living on one face of a tower block. Blow up to window size. Stick on window, faces out. From outside the block – meet your neighbours on the Heavenly High Street.

And the old council slums – overcrowded rodent-ridden black lumps of flats built around concrete courtyards.

Event

Block party. Ugly courtyard at night, lit by theatre lights and blazing bonfire, festooned with bunting, ringing with loud music, a bar on the first balcony, kids, parents, old folks raving. Organised by Crossfield Tenants' Association. Gear and disco by the Combination.

'The time is right for Dancing in the Streets' – Martha and the Vandellas.

A large proportion of the Deptford population are dependent on social security for their income.

Event

Combination Street Theatre 'stage' National Assistance Board Show in local Department of Health and Social Security offices. A row of brightly coloured bowler-hatted clerks, high stepping, chant–

> We are the men from the S.S.
> And we come to relieve distress
> So confess, the truth, now confess
> You *know* you could live on less.

Commissioned by South East London Claimants' Union. (In one door, out the other. Preceded by leaflets. Followed up by discussion.) All part of a membership campaign, 'Never Meet the Enemy Alone.'

Many older people feel increasingly isolated as the younger members of families move out of the borough. A much higher than average percentage of local schoolchildren are serious truants; vandalism and petty theft are more interesting than school. These are the concerns that the Albany must involve itself in.

What then has art to do with this? This chapter describes a programme of arts community work and attempts to identify the patterns that are emerging from it.

Priority: Cheer the place up!

The Albany, September 1971: looming Victorian building/battle-scarred with graffiti and broken windows and city grime.

The Albany, November 1971: scaffolding/John Upton – painter/half the wall covered with mural brightly painted in Woolworths 'household gloss'/paintings of the people inside the building showing those outside what goes on, paintings of local kids, mums, dads, of the football team, of the bike boys and John Upton Lewisham-born ex-prizefighter becoming a local celebrity.

The Albany, New Year's Eve 1971: torchlight procession lighting up the mural, now finished 50' by 30' the biggest in London? John and wife masked and costumed for the procession.

January–September 1972: local people and associations asking if John could come and paint walls in their blocks.

October 1972: an offer from the Greater London Arts Association of a grant of about £200 for John to carry out one or two of these murals.

August 1973: mural wins *Evening Standard* 'Brighter London' Award.

Note: This mural has not been defaced.

The arts programme is central to the Albany's concern to provide opportunities for people to develop their potential in all aspects of their lives, and so is at least partially counteracting the sterile tendency to over-emphasise any single aspect of life – be it work or social action. It also helps defy the prevalent notion that there is no room for art until there is a better society.

Perhaps it would be helpful here to illustrate some of the ways in which a community arts programme can contribute to social change. At the Albany there have been three main areas of interaction between arts work and community work:

1 Two-way referrals or the social work–community involvement continuum.

2 Arts programme back-up in community work interventions.

3 Arts work developing into community work issues.

The first category is a continuum from the point of view of the individuals or family, and ideally looks something like this:

person faced with a crisis calls at the Albany
↓
worker responds to crisis situation, giving some credibility to workers of agency
↓
worker and community person discuss crisis in relation to factors in community
↓
worker puts person in touch with other users or staff
↓
community person becomes involved in Workshop or project or group

In this way we attempt to move from a situation where a person is seeking help in a dependent relationship to a situation where that person is functioning on his own behalf. The advantage for the social worker here is that he is not restricted to problem-centred relationships. He can refer people on to situations of more positive involvements.

A recent campaign with a group of council tenants provides an example of the second type of interaction – arts programme back-up in a community work intervention. The Albany's contact with the Crossfield Estate – a drab, pre-war council development, lacking amenities – had been through arts workers' involvement in organising street parties/entertainments. These workers therefore were in a position to identify a pattern of concern building up among tenants on the Estate and focusing on problems that would arise out of redevelopment proposals for the area. The Albany's community worker was then consulted on the matter and she and the arts development officer built up a full picture of the issues involved. The arts worker then contacted several people and gave the community worker the names of others who had expressed concern at the council's proposals. This led to a small group of tenants attending a council committee meeting and the beginning of what the tenants eventually called 'the Crossfield Campaign'. At this point the community worker took over as the main worker in relation to the issue, and the arts staff made resources available at appropriate points in **the Campaign:**

1   **Tenants decide it's important to present their case to councillors and public in readable, convincing way . . .**
    . . . arts programme workers (writer, photographer, designer) help in the layout, writing and production of 'A Deliberate Act of Policy?' – a booklet detailing the issues involved and the action the tenants are seeking.
2   **Crossfield tenants use Workshop to make banners and posters for MP's visit to Estate.**
3   **Combination (resident theatre group) song-writer helps tenants compose songs, slogans, limericks for event on the Estate designed to stimulate interest in the issue.**
4   **Combination prepare music and street theatre programme, dramatising the issues involved, to accompany street demonstration . . .**
    . . . performance in fact serves to alleviate tensions and to offset feelings of failure after potentially demoralising confrontation with police.

At other times, arts work provides more than the initial identification of a community work concern:

Summer playscheme

joint arts programme/youthwork venture becomes focus for community organisation.

The arts programme staff were heavily involved in the presentation of the play-scheme. Three sites in Deptford were taken over as temporary adventure playgrounds. In the area served by one site, parents were enthusiastic about continuing the site on a permanent basis. The community worker became involved and a parents' association was formed. As a result of their negotiations with the council, the parents' association now receives a grant and employs two full-time playground leaders.

The argument

There is a prevailing tendency to devalue Entertainment for its own sake. Either it must be breaking new boundaries in art or it must be saying something – socially or politically relevant.

In fact, it is in itself socially and politically relevant.

In an area where there is no cinema, no theatre, no dance hall, no club, no amusement arcade, no nothing!

Entertainment is Needed!

And at a party, or over a beer, people do not always want information stuffed down their gullets.

Never devalue Entertainment. Live Entertainment. We are Deptford's Entertainers. Not Missionaries of Art.

The name of the game is DEMYSTIFICATION.

Art and politics

The implicit divorce of art and politics is at best a misleading concept. Art is always the expression of a particular culture. It is not some kind of creation of man in the abstract but it is made by particular artists in response to specific social conditions and in a class society, art – both its selection and its creation – will always be marked by the expression of different classes.

Far from being the separate and somehow counter-productive endeavour that many socialists perceive it as, authentic art . . .

Argument: Authentic? What criteria are being used here?

We are DEPTFORD'S ENTERTAINERS, *not* **missionaries of Art.**

Redefine your art before you bombard anyone else with it. Does it include graffiti? Is jazz a dirty word? And pop? And films? And video? And market slang?

What are we trying to prove anyway?

Everyman is an artist!

Authentic art does in fact tend to mirror and extend political awareness.

Cultural poverty

The New Cross Empire, 'A Palace of Varieties', still has very strong memories for Deptford people. Today, with no place of live entertainment locally, and no cinema, concert-hall or gallery, the old pub song tradition is still very important, even among the young. The changing environment takes away the natural street entertainments: there are no streets, merely a street of front doors and direct access onto the street. Barrel organs, dancing bears or monkeys, the old practice of singing for your supper, and even busking for queues (no live entertainment – no queues) have all died out.

Sociologists have quite properly noted this disintegration of working-class culture, but often rather too dramatically in terms of the breakdown of economic environmental structures, at the expense of any detailed analysis of cultural forfeitures.

Clobbering a culture

The decision to make most of south east London a monolithic end-to-end housing estate was taken soon after the war, and though enclaves of the middle class have put up stout resistance here and there, the original plan is just beginning to really run amok in the heartlands of New Cross and Deptford. Entire networks of streets now run between corrugated iron walls or smashed-up terraces of decent little stock brick houses. Those inhabitants who linger on sometimes have the paving stones stripped from outside their front doors. Stories about old ladies whose homes have accidentally been demolished over their heads, or who have been found wandering the streets afraid to stay home alone in the company of dossers and rats, appear regularly in the local Press. Having destroyed a community, devastated trade, and broken up a good deal of workable low level housing the planners have just completed one of the alternatives: an awesome complex in which people are simply refusing to live. Fears about tower-block living die hard in south east London since the Ronan Point disaster across the river. The reluctant tenants are also aware that the supporting community buildings that might make life less bleak will not be ready until 1975. Brochures are being sent out to persuade tenants to live in the blocks, which, as every tidy-minded person knows, are much more suitable than a little house in a terraced street with a friendly Irish off-licence on the corner and a street market nearby. – Peter Way, *Sunday Times*, 1972

Deprivation

Even of the experience of large family parties; overcrowded inadequate flats, old people, babies complaints from neighbours. The result – isolation and the TV.

Introducing a tradition of aesthetic appreciation to a community is a more difficult task in many ways than establishing a political tradition.

Deptford Market in Douglas Way: the Albany Workshop stall selling pottery, candles, bags, paintings, paper flowers, collages, etc. £6.95 made the first day. The people who make the stuff for sale give 20% to the stall for overheads and equipment. The second week the stall made £10.34. The response from the people wandering through the market is one of interest: who makes this stuff? Where? It's not bad, is it? That little vase would be good for me old girl . . .
Can anyone go down there and make this stuff . . .
See you next week.

In the arts, as in any aspect of community work, the worker must start from where the community's at.

A community worker who wishes to stimulate a reaction in a tenants' association to, say, the Housing Finance Act, will not succeed if the members are in fact more aware of and concerned about a lift that has not been repaired. He will far more usefully encourage the association to organise around the minor issue first.

Similarly in arts community work, it is necessary to extend and build on what is worth while in current values rather than to attempt to impose new ones.

Technology and mechanisation predominate at work and in the
Gcw

community. This leads to a situation where less and less scope is available for the human contact and individual responsibility. At work, it is, for many people, becoming increasingly difficult to see clearly the contribution of their own labour to the end product or to the service they help to provide.

> I can't describe how good I feel making something myself
> instead of going into a shop and plonking me money down.

Art, with a capital A, is regarded as something that happens in museums, galleries or theatres, and is isolated from community life in that it is neither constantly available in the home (like TV or radio) nor an integral part of an outing or social occasion (like dance music or film). Art then is regarded as the property of the privileged, the talented or, more alien still, the effeminate.

> 'You load of bummers!' Terry (ten)

The norm of aesthetic taste has settled contentedly on sentimentalised pictures of children or animals and three-dimensional plastic Christs – which are unreal enough not to engage the intellect, idealised enough to prohibit analysis.

Development of argument

People have no choice. In Deptford stores and market there is little choice when buying goods. Plastic art is all that is sold. There is no opportunity of comparing different qualities of design. The workshop attempts to reverse this trend.

A creation not only has a value for the artist himself, but also influences his family and his friends – and the influence is a more subtle, more demanding one than mass-produced art can exercise. The object is a part of the artist's life: real and meaningful; art of that kind can no longer be undemanding, alien, or merely pretty.

An industrialised society which conceives of the value of an individual largely in terms of his capacity for work forces utilitarian standards of assessment on all experiences.

> 'Painting is no use' – an instinctive resistance to the Workshop.

Working-class parents tend, for example to see education as a means of obtaining qualifications for better jobs, and not as an essential ingredient of a fulfilling and stimulating existence.

Education? For what!

The qualifications the school offers as well as the education it gives are seen as useless: twenty-five-year-old betting-shop manager: 'I've got four "O" levels and you tell me what bloody good they are?' School is often totally irrelevant to the way people live. It offers no help in survival techniques in a poor urban area, no help in grafting, totting, buying and selling, docking, having a good laugh. Instead, school hands out a jumble of middle-class aims and values which are rejected.

> We're hop hop hopping the wag
> 'cos the schooling that we're tooling with
> is just a big drag.
> We're tearing up the textbooks
> their facts are a sham
> we can't get a job
> so wot's the point of exams. – a chorus from a Combination
> show on truancy (popular with the kids).

Children see much that is taught at school as irrelevant to their lives outside the classroom. This is not always because the relationship does not exist, but sometimes it is concealed in the basic premise of school routine. The schools, or the examinations, are necessary in terms of employment potential. Only art is a curriculum subject, outside that assessment. Art exams are relevant only if the pupil intends to become an artist. It is not an 'academic' subject, nor is it usually related to job qualifications. Its relevance is not stressed or defended, and perhaps because of this, it is the subject in which self-direction is most acceptable. Thought discipline is necessarily less rigid, and it is a class which is regarded by many pupils more as recreation than any other. It is expressive, and seen least as relating to life – because it does not relate to work. The idea that an art lesson in school can form taste, or influence an idea of beauty, is rarely explored.

Factor ...

A high proportion of schools in working-class areas have very poor art facilities. Therefore, children of the users of the Workshop want to come to the Workshop with their parents because they don't have the opportunity at school.

But apart from that ...

Art, then, suffers a double stigma: it is part of school, and therefore suspect to the majority; but in the schools themselves it is not seen or treated as a 'respectable' or 'useful' subject – because it does not directly affect employment potential.

Recreation = RE-CREATION
the re-creation of self
from the cog in the machine to the acting individual.

Recreation undermines the work ETHIC.

In Deptford the emergence of creative endeavours is at times regarded with equal suspicion because it is dependent on the enforced leisure of housewives, old people or the unemployed. It is one of the saddest comments on our society that the products of our 'leisure' are so undervalued, and those of our 'work' regarded as of virtually exclusive importance.

No, for success, start here:

The Workshop

'Recreation = RE-CREATION'

The Workshop is not subject biased. People can wander in any time between ten and four or seven and nine three evenings a week and do any type of activity. There are classes in specific subjects held at specific times, but people can come at other times and do these subjects themselves. It is important to have someone in the Workshop all the time to greet people, chat, make coffee, put out materials, help and instruct if needed, to act as a catalyst to peoples' needs and talents. The base worker must be able to refer to other services in the Albany and in the borough.

This implies basing our approach in the Albany Workshop (which provides a home base for the arts programme) on work-related utilitarian values, developing the skills necessary to produce objects which can be used. Only when this base for respect has been established can aesthetic awareness begin to grow.

A syndrome

Given that achievement is measured principally as achievement at work, and that for most people work does not offer the opportunity for achievement, the population of a deprived urban area by society's definition are automatically failures.

But . . . Deptford community has its own different set of value judgments. Middle-class people may judge a totter as a failure, whereas working-class people often see teachers as suckers on low wages.

But . . . Old Tom retired, felt he had no more to offer the community, became very lethargic, came to the workshop and started doing pottery, found out he could do it well and as an added incentive he was able to sell his mugs on the stall, earning money for doing a pleasurable thing.

So . . . the Albany Workshop is individual expression, having a good time, group work. Alternative attainment in a natural harmonious atmosphere. Non-structured. Non-competitive.

Art and you!

Before a person can fully explore his physical and social environment and his capacity to relate to it or to change it – to gain greater control over it, he must first explore himself.

Does this mean art therapy is vital before social revolution is possible?
No.
The *act* of Creation is Therapeutic and Revolutionary at one and the same time – in the context of mass production.

> I felt trapped in my flat, my little world of shopping in the High Street, visits to the park and, thank God, my television, then one day I realised that I now felt happy – not nervous or depressed any more. It doesn't sound possible that painting could do that, but I've lived it, so I know. After all, in art you don't need to be an expert – just simply to enjoy doing it is really its main purpose, and then gradually learning how to do it to one's own satisfaction, and from that comes a sense of achievement. And that's a very precious thing.

The Workshop aims to rebuild lost confidence through a progression of seemingly small achievements, through a gradual process of self-development which regenerates the confidence to create and do.

People are deterred from attempting to paint/pot, etc., because their criteria of what is good is a mass product for an artificially stimulated demand: a plastic gnome. People feel that they cannot produce anything as perfect. They value the finished product and only gradually value the intrinsic value of creating an object. We have found with people who have a talent for making carbon copies that they do this first and gradually become interested in experimenting or doodling with materials and then start creating for themselves a totally new perspective.

Dressmaking is popular because it is seen as a practical technical skill worth acquiring.

However, because of the structure of the Workshop, the people attending dressmaking classes see others doing different activities around them, e.g. painting a picture. Although the person did not come intending to paint, they can get drawn in: 'If he can do it, I might as well have a bash.' If they had been dressmaking in isolation, in a special room, they would never have been inspired to do anything else. Because of the wide range of activities and the non-specialist casual approach and the implicit belief that the workers have that anyone can do anything well, the Workshop experience tends to demystify art.

Others come into the Workshop and immediately begin to use the materials to create a whole fantasy world within the structure of a utilitarian approach, e.g. teapots styled like fishes.

The Albany Workshop provides not only stimulus, but support – a warm, friendly atmosphere, and a flexible full group which is capable of expanding to welcome newcomers and of encouraging the formation of relationships and friendships which are so much hindered by the physical structure of Deptford.

A possible process:

making a pot = helping on the stall = making decorations for a party = organising a party = involvement with local action groups.

In terms of education, the learning has been found to be faster and more efficient where the pressure of competition and the inevitable connotations of failure do not apply, and where the process of social interaction and mutual aid has advantages both for the helper and the helped.

Training in the creative arts, and group experiences in neighbourhood craft production, appeal strongly to the need for positive identity. Finding new media of communication through the arts or contributing to meaningful social action goes far towards countering feelings of isolation and impotence and encouraging the establishment of autonomy and social competence. And, encouragingly, members of social groups have gained artistic confidence through political achievements.

South East London Claimants' Union decide that they should have their own guerrilla theatre group. Rehearsed in chants of National Assistance Board Show, they then raid their local social security offices:

> 'Good morning,
> Here's your money.
> Thanks a lot,
> It's not enough!
> Pay a visit to your local S.S.'

The denial of artistic expression is a negative limitation of human potential. Creating a work of art involves self-assertion, self-affirmation and self-control.

Recreation = RE-CREATION
The other arm of the arts programme is Theatre!
What kind of Theatre?

If live theatre is to do anything more than survive, those involved in the medium must dispense with the notion that for 'art' to succeed, it merely has to *be*.

Nor is it enough to point to the full houses in a few heavily subsidised London theatres, for who are they full of? A 'new' audience?

Theatre is no longer a first-class entertainment. It is locked, isolated in an unexciting environment. It is literary based, it comments little upon what is happening at this moment, it denies its very 'liveliness', it is snobbish and class-ridden and clings to its rituals and mystification like an old maid to her underwear. The exceptions are vital, immensely stimulating and few.

If live theatre wishes, really wants, to communicate with its future potential audience, it must find its public. It cannot (literally) afford to wait. It must go where its audience naturally congregates. Not to seduce it back into the museums, but to stay there and to allow itself to be re-created by that audience. If necessary, it must create the ambiance that the new audience will flock to.

In practice

Street Processions: with Bands/Masks/Floats/Torches/Pub Shows; Old Time Music Hall, Melodrama, Pop Music, Live Bands/ Discos/Modern Day Mummers' Plays; Inflatables; Political Theatre for local action groups; Participational Kids' Theatre; plays for the struggle.

Conversations between actors in character are minimised. Use is made of chants, dances, routines, songs, tricks, props, jokes. A stress on performing skills rather than *acting*.

Entertainment – pure hedonistic entertainment

A statement in itself as the bingo halls take over all the old music halls and dance halls and cinemas!
Non-Literary Theatre.

Theatre drawn from the shared experience of the community. About the High Streets, the dole offices, the pub, the police, the tower blocks, the good times, the celebrations, the hard times, the kids, the work, the mates. Theatre that reacts to what you do. Non-alienating, involving theatre. Public holidays, holiday periods, festival times, street parties, good weather, evenings, bright Saturday market days, a demonstration at the Town Hall/social security office. These are the occasions for performance.

First things first

Theatre is an environmental form. A visual art. Therefore the first production became the redecoration and rejuvenation of the *inside* of the Community Centre.

Creating the building as an open fairly flexible environment where people can wander in, look around and join in with something that takes their fancy, versus the everlasting problem of keys/vandalism/kicked doors/security.

Repainting doors as fast as the paint was kicked off. Renewing locks. Creating the illusion of flexibility which gradually turned into more of a reality.

Giving the basement to the kids and keeping the upper floors for adults, and a reasonably strict 'no kids in the building in school hours' policy.

Important to make the adults feel at home/feel it is an adult place/ feel they are not being elbowed out by kids.

And with the closing of all live entertainment in Deptford – to create a space in the Albany.

– A Community Theatre!

A new 'Palace of Varieties'

A dance hall, an ice-cream parlour, a saloon and gambling

house if you want, a community centre at its best. This will provide the context for both the audience and performers. For the context of the play is as vital as the content.

Introducing live theatre to an audience whose experience has been limited to a mass media synthesis of the form has not, of course, been easy. The Combination has taken its impetus from, and linked its work closely to, important local issues, in order both to promote a greater awareness in the audience of its physical and cultural focus, and to extend the means of communication available to clarify complex issues and to restate them in more immediately available terms.

The NAB Show – a propaganda piece for claimants' unions. 'Frying Tonight' or 'The Crime-Does-Not-Pay Show' – dedicated to all the criminals in the police force and judiciary.

The Combination's popular pub show, Will the Old Place Ever be the Same Again?, deals with town planning and the local housing situation and acts as a catalyst for discussion and social action. Often the meaning of a play or a piece of street theatre has been emphasised by the performance's location. The NAB Show has been performed in social security offices, and The Monster of the Blocks – a children's play about tower block living – has been performed on housing estates, adventure playgrounds and in the streets.

Discussion

Direct experience of 'live theatre' may in fact be rare but this is overcome by broadening our theatre:

thus for old people we incorporate that which *is* in their experience – music hall, melodrama, old time dancing

for kids we use as a structure adventure games – 'you chase me but I see you coming and trip you up, etc.'

in pubs we make much use of stand-up cabaret entertainment: sex, songs, suggestive jokes

Theatre is implicit in any human situation; exploited and enlarged it is recognised and enjoyed as ENTERTAINMENT.

We are Deptford's Entertainers!

12 The community school - a base for community development?

George and Teresa Smith

In the final report of their action-research programme (Halsey, 1972), the Educational Priority Areas projects called for six major educational developments in EPAs.[1] With the publication at the end of 1972 of Mrs Thatcher's White Paper, *Education: A Framework for Expansion*, it looks as if the score after the first round is – two positive, three doubtful, and one nil response to these proposals. On the positive side is the expansion of pre-school education with priority for EPAs, and the acceptance of the principle of 'positive discrimination' and its extension to certain rural areas, small towns and new housing estates as well as the inner city. Successful implementation will not be easy; the White Paper says nothing about the criteria for identifying EPAs, and is vague about how to ensure that parental involvement on a wide scale becomes a characteristic of pre-school education. It is encouraging that research will monitor the expansion.

On the negative side, the White Paper has nothing to say on another of the EPA recommendations – the development of 'community schools'. This is perhaps not unexpected. Pre-schooling has a long history of development, a relatively clear-cut institutional form, and a powerful lobby of supporters. Even with the addition of parental involvement it could without difficulty be translated into administrative proposals – what more radical educational reformers have dismissed as 'an addition to the system', though, we would argue, none the worse for that. But 'community schools' are a very different animal – one that implies new directions and changing roles for existing institutions. Despite the claim of the EPA Report to have developed the idea of the 'community school' from the sketchy and restricted description in Plowden – 'a school which is open beyond the ordinary school hours for the use of children, their parents and, exceptionally, for other members of the community' (para. 121) – the concept still remains vague, a long way from any neat administrative package. Perhaps the very different 'community school' experiments set up by various EPA projects have increased the confusion; what looked like a simple proposal to extend school opening hours is shown to be complex and far-reaching.

In this paper we want to re-examine the idea of the 'community school', using evidence from the EPA programme, in particular the setting up of a multi-purpose education centre, Red House, by the West Riding project. By placing description of a practical development against a background of more general debate, we hope to show some of the reasons for the slow, and, for many, unsatisfactory development of 'community schools' so far. It is not our purpose to specify in detail what a community school should be like; over-concern with detail rather than broad objectives may be one reason for the lack of progress. A major lesson of EPA was the importance of tailoring developments to fit the local situation. Thus the aim of writing on 'community schools' should be to set out general guidelines, and a range of possible institutional forms, rather than a single model.

With feet in both the EPA and Community Development Project (CDP) camps, our concern is with the question of how far education, in the shape of 'community schools', can become a base for wider community development; the focus is on institutions that seek a wide range of involvement with the community, not merely the extension of their opening hours. Clearly with such frequent use of the word 'community' and phrases like 'community development' and 'community school', we cannot slip by without offering some indication of what we mean by these terms. This is not the place for a strict definition, even if one were possible; we suspect that the strength and attractiveness of 'community' to us and to others, lies partly in its Protean character, unlike some of the more precise, but short-lived, technical concepts that social science proliferates. Sociologists who plead for a moratorium on the use of 'community' have, like Canute, clearly got it wrong; they need instead to analyse how 'community' is used in social situations and by different social groups.

In projects like EPA and CDP, terms such as 'community' and 'community development' imply a number of related assumptions, even though these may not be well articulated. First, 'community' refers to a relatively small area, characterised by a high degree of face-to-face interaction, with some degree of shared value patterns. Second, it implies concern with the total group in any category, rather than a selected sub-group. Schools in EPA's, for example, clearly fulfil a creaming function, still formalised in some areas with selective secondary education for a minority; community education, in contrast, aims at the complete group, developing a curriculum relevant to the needs of those likely to remain in EPAS. Third, it emphasises a broad, non-specialist approach to the services in the area; social or individual problems are seen to be the result of a complex set of factors, and therefore not best tackled by a series of unco-ordinated and highly specialised agencies. Fourth, for the same reason it emphasises linkage and integration among organisations servicing an area; and fifth, it stresses the importance of participation and development of the community's own institutions on the basis that the community is a viable entity, independent of the administrative structures created to service it. Community development, then, is the broad process which embodies this approach, rather than the bit of social life that is left over, when education, health, social services and the other big battalions have been taken out.

With the 'community school' we are on a well-trodden path. Usually four or five types are identified – each article on the subject perhaps stepping out a little further to add something extra to the final, most attractive variety. First, it can apply to a school which serves an entire neighbourhood; most primary schools and more and more secondary 'neighbourhood' schools would qualify. A second definition is a school which shares its premises with the community. This has been a long-standing arrangement in many areas, and in the West Riding EPA one of the primary schools had been carefully designed with this purpose in mind – in 1893. Large modern comprehensive schools obviously have bigger and better facilities to offer, such as swimming pools and libraries. But size can be a problem, as the catchment area of the school will also be large, and this may conflict with the need to develop links with a relatively small area. We would also like to place a query against a strategy which attempted to draw the community into the school as its main objective. Sharing buildings may be economically sound, but both groups may function side by side with comparative autonomy: school content and organisation do not necessarily become more community-oriented or responsive by opening the doors to community-run activities for adults.

A third possibility is a school which develops a curriculum of community study, arguing for the social and educational relevancy of local and familiar material. Much of the work of Eric Midwinter in the Liverpool EPA (1972) has centred on this theme. To the charge that this type of education will produce increased conformity and second-class citizenship, Midwinter replies that 'community education is about moving on, not standing still'; the aim is to produce 'constructive discontent'. Yet there is plenty of evidence that curriculum is nearly always used in ways unintended by its authors. The problem remains of ensuring that socially relevant material is used to weaken rather than confirm social divisions.

A fourth type is a school where there is some degree of community control. This is familiar in the United States, particularly following the Ford Foundation-supported programmes for community control of inner city schools in the late 1960s; but less so in this country, outside a few Free Schools and LEAs experimenting with greater community participation on governing boards. A fifth and final possibility is a school which seeks to involve itself directly in promoting social change within the local community. This type incorporates some of the earlier varieties, as it could well include longer opening hours, community use of buildings, and community participation. Schools have considerable advantages in taking the initiative in social change. First, they are institutions acceptable to the community, in contrast to other social agencies which may be stigmatised by their association with problem groups. Second, there is the sheer number of schools and teachers which are already present in the area. In the West Riding EPA, as an example, there were 130 to 140 teachers at eleven separate primary and secondary schools, yet the social services had no base in the area, and there were perhaps two or three social workers, part of whose territory included the EPA. Such considerations make the idea of the community school as an agent of social change within the community powerfully attractive. Yet the problems of turning this into a reality have hardly been examined at all.

Most practical examples of 'community schools' have been of the first four types, and though there are examples of the last type, these are often drawn from developing countries, where the relationship between school and community is likely to be very different. Examples closer to home often cite activities such as surveys of the neighbourhood and similar studies, but these by themselves hardly constitute an adequate community school programme. There is a wide gap between these practical examples and the attractive theoretical picture of the school as an agent of social change. We can all accept the proposition that 'community minded and community-competent teachers are essential at all levels . . .' (Olsen, 1963), but the problem is to translate into practice the exhortation typical of writing on community schools. Further training is a favourite suggestion. But first we need to examine whether the problem is more basic than mere lack of training. As S. M. Miller argues (1967), more education tends to become the standard panacea for a number of problems, 'whether those of racial prejudice, sexual unhappiness or economic conflict'. Even in education itself, the belief that further training will bring about change is often an illusion.

A basic problem which has been overlooked by those anxious to develop the idea of the school as an agent of social change, is the gulf between the way an ordinary school functions, and that required for community work. Even in its most progressive format, schooling remains a highly structured activity; there are set times of day, week and year when schools operate. Pupils are divided into class groups, and work with specific teachers for set periods of time; the content of what is done may be defined by outside bodies, external exams and so on. Community work is at the other end of the spectrum: there is no fixed group of clients, place or time of operation, and the type of work may change dramatically as new groups or problems crop up.

The difference is underlined by looking at the experience of workers who attempt to span the gap. A youth or community worker attached to a school has to develop a flexible programme to deal with events outside the school, but may be constrained by the within school require-ments of class groupings, timetables and school organisation. A study of secondary school teachers running community service projects (Smith, 1969) demonstrated the problem of conflicting interests. Despite differences of organising community service in academic and non-academic schools, teachers saw it primarily in terms of benefit to their pupils – a way of developing a sense of responsibility, self-confidence and maturity: the work was defined in individual moral terms, as a problem which 'one had to do something about' in personal action. It was not clear whether teachers in the study failed to see the significance of community service for the role and position of the school in the community, or whether they rejected this approach because it would have taken time from what they saw as their main objective, the develop-ment of individual children. 'Free Schools' could be another response to the same problem. Frustration with the inability of existing schools to develop a suitably flexible programme for the local community was a major reason in setting up the Liverpool Free School, which has planned extensive community development work linked to the school.

Though we need more evidence about the problems of developing community work from a school base, these examples show that not enough attention has been paid to conflicts that emerge as schools attempt to balance their traditional concern for individual children against their new role in community development. This ought to be the type of problem that action-research experiments investigate – can the organisation of schools tolerate the kind of relationships demanded by community work, or do they require new organisational forms? Are schools or other educational institutions in fact capable of initiating programmes of social change, or is the growing pessimism about the role of the school as an agent of change justified? Practical experiments of this nature might be more useful than further exhortations to teachers about the importance of 'community orientation', or even training courses to develop new attitudes.

As a first shot at what such experiments might be like, we turn to a description of the education centre set up by the West Riding project, and the experience gained in running it over three years.[2] It is important to make clear that the centre was not developed as a 'community school'; in fact the label was resisted – it was not a 'school' in the accepted sense, and those who ran it tried to avoid identification with community schools whose objective was to absorb the community into the school building. The project area was a small, socially isolated mining community in the Don Valley – a community in the strong traditional sense – a stable population with shared experience in the work place and in social life. Roughly 60 per cent of the men worked in the local pit, and there was a close-knit pattern of friendship and marriage within the area. But the decline of the mining industry meant that the driving force of the community was gradually running down. The general picture of a stable area was underlined by the schools, where in contrast to many other EPAs there was an extremely low level of teacher turnover: many teachers had also taught the parents of their present generation of children.

The EPA project focused on education. Though it could analyse the more basic changes threatening the area, it was clearly powerless with its small resources to make any impression on them directly. In the educational field, the programmes set up by the project were of two types: first, specific pieces of action meeting an obvious need – the provision of preschool places, or a remedial reading scheme; second, and more fundamental, there was a need for more general exploration of the ways schools could be stimulated into change, and for ways of extending the role of education.

The project team saw a multi-purpose education centre as one possible strategy for change in the area. But different groups had different expectations about how this could be realised in practice. First, there was the idea of a centre attached to a school with short-term residential accommodation for children during periods of crisis in the home put forward by the Chief Education Officer of the West Riding, Sir Alec Clegg (Clegg and Megson, 1968). Second, some schools were anxious to have a centre outside the area, partly for residential purposes and partly as a base for project work: their concern was to remove the child at least temporarily from his environment. Third, the aim of the project team was to set up a multi-purpose base, linking schools, the social services, and the community.

The objectives would be broad ranging, and mainly institutional in form. The centre would work closely with schools and colleges as well as with parents and the community. It would act as a demonstration and resource centre which could experiment with pilot schemes, cutting across the age grouping which characterises most educational institutions, and trying out schemes that involved children of different ages, and adults from different sources – from schools, colleges, or the local community. It would be able to operate outside the normal school day and term timetable, offering courses in the evening, at weekends, and during the holidays. The centre had to be accessible to the community at all times, and therefore locally based. Community involvement was to be a high priority. This did not mean the formal trappings of participation – committees of local people – but an institution that could respond to local needs and had flexible enough resources to meet them. For this reason, staff and facilities could not be tied to a strictly specialist role, but had to adapt rapidly to radically different demands. Residential provision was to be one of a range of facilities available to the community.

The actual development of Red House was a combination of these various strands. With the help of the West Riding, and a generous grant from the Rowntree Trust, a large house in the community was bought and converted into an education centre. This included limited residential accommodation and space for a resident warden and family.

Red House opened in January 1970. In describing the work of the centre since then, merely to list the activities set up would not be helpful for our purposes: it has become characteristic for the centre to be used throughout the day and evening by many different groups of children and adults. One activity grew out of another: we propose to concentrate on these growth points. Activities have almost always been organised for limited numbers, ranging from three or four children in residence to a school class or pre-school group of twenty-five to thirty-five children; over the school year large numbers will have taken part in various courses. The purpose was to act as a 'demonstration' centre, to show what could be done and what additional resources could be tapped: success therefore depended on how far other groups took up ideas developed at the centre.

The first stage was to develop local confidence and show that the centre could meet school and community needs. The 'intensive courses' were designed in response to requests from local schools for a programme for junior age children. Initially, groups from three separate schools came to the centre every morning for half a term. At the centre the children were mixed up and split into groups of four or five, each group working with a teacher-training student, following its own programme in the centre, or making field trips to collect material for environmental study. A problem found in the first year was that class teachers could not be fully involved. In the second year, the scheme covered complete school classes instead of groups from different schools: class teachers could work alongside students with small groups from their own class, giving advice where necessary. At the same time, a pre-school group was set up. The policy was to make places available to all children in a particular age range and school catchment area, to avoid problems of selection; to ensure that everybody was approached, home visits to all families with young children in the area were made and the scheme explained. Parental involvement was encouraged from the start, at first by operating an open door policy.

The pre-school programme and its parental involvement sparked off a series of further developments. Early on, the main objective of this form of pre-school work came to be seen as strengthening the educational resources of home and community rather than merely getting parents into schools. This resulted in a shift of emphasis in the pre-school group itself, towards the role of parents as teachers, or the training potential for this purpose of the pre-school group. As some parents gained confidence in teaching skills, they were able to take control of groups of children, and the teacher could spend time working with other parents. Confidence gained here increased awareness among parents of their role as educators outside the school context. Out of the pre-school have grown parent groups meeting in the evenings as a general discussion group rather than with invited speakers.

Raising the level of educational resources in the home and the community led directly to the development of home visiting. This had become part of the pre-school programme, with the teacher taking materials into the home to work with parent and child together. It was also turned into a separate programme. Here the home visitor worked with younger children and their parents, making weekly visits over a year or more: with suitable educational material she could show the skills that young children develop, and equipment was left in the home for parents to experiment with. A weekly stall run by the project, selling educational books and toys, was another way of adding to the area's resources. A pitch in the local open market was a place to display children's work, to show films and slides of projects such as holiday schemes, and to serve as an advice point on education and welfare rights. These developments placed the project in a position to improve support for the growing number of playgroups in the district with advice, materials, and training courses.

Another growth point was the development of schemes using one group in a learning situation to help another. A new form of the 'intensive courses' was set up for infant children, using fourth- and fifth-year secondary school pupils instead of students to run the small groups. Similar aged pupils had worked in the pre-school group, and in other courses at the centre where they could develop practical skills such as cooking and serving a regular meal for old people or pre-school children. In the evening, week-end, and holiday courses, the project relied heavily on the help given by students and local volunteers.

Residential work had to develop slowly if the community was to accept that the centre had a broad role to play. The accommodation was useful for other groups such as students on placement, but its main purpose was to provide short-term residential care for children during periods of difficulty in the home. The centre had no statutory powers. As the centre was local, children in residence continued to go to their local schools and maintained contact with their families. Most children were already familiar with the centre, where they had attended various courses. This contact meant that a system of 'self-referral' developed, as children and parents became aware that the centre had residential space available for a crisis such as a parent going into hospital. Relatively small numbers of children have stayed in the centre. Short-term residence was not seen as a way of 'curing' the particular problem, but one of a number of strategies the centre could adopt to strengthen contact with a child or his family. For some situations, a residential stay was not appropriate; in others, it could be a support for the child at a time of acute family crisis; or it might put the child in contact with adults sympathetic to his difficulties. It might produce information about the family situation which enabled the centre to call upon the other services for specialist support. Children who had been in residence could and did return to the centre, which was within easy reach, for example for a weekly meal or evening course.

More important, perhaps, than a brief description of the programmes are the underlying trends. First, there is a clear shift from the educational starting point to social and community work, though from an educational perspective. This is a logical development. If the child's experience outside school influences classroom performance, then clearly the field of education has to be extended. In many cases this must go beyond merely visiting families, or making parents welcome in school. Residential work at the centre emphasised the need for wider involvement as it brought staff into more intensive contact with families and the community. The growth points at the centre are now social and community work. At a more tentative stage are explorations of work and employment, the idea of a community workshop – perhaps a future growth point.

A second theme is linkage – reducing the distance between different age levels and levels of education as well as between education and related social and welfare services. This is partly a matter of unused resources which can be realised by linking levels or institutions – students can staff courses for junior children, or secondary school pupils work with infants; parents or other community members can develop teaching skills. Not surprisingly, some of these links had their organisational problems, which underlines the importance of an independent group or institution whose role it is to create such links. Similarly there is the reinforcement that one programme can provide for another: for example, the market stall supplying a need stimulated by the home visiting or pre-school projects.

A third and related theme is the type of role that this method of working demanded from the team at the centre – one with no clear boundaries, but with overlapping functions of teacher, social worker, counsellor, as the situation demanded. There was also the creation of 'intermediate roles', when students, secondary pupils, parents, and others adopted teaching positions. This meant that although the team at the centre numbered only six or seven, the effective number was always far larger. The role of the central team was to organise and plan for the use of these resources as well as to work directly on the courses.

The final point and most important is the changing conception of the relationship between school and community. Instead of trying to improve the educational process in school by encouraging parental involvement, the direction was reversed: the aim should rather be to strengthen the educational resources of home and community. This meant that the centre increasingly became a base for programmes extending out into the community, rather than drawing the community into the centre as an end in itself.

We have deliberately kept this outline of the work at Red House at a general level. Obviously in practice there were successes and failures: schemes were piloted, modified with experience, and launched on a

larger scale. In general the approaches adopted were shown to be viable
in practice, and the response from schools and community encouraged
the centre to continue along its path. For the two years of the centre's
running by the EPA project, it was supported by a group with independent resources and the flexibility to use them as it decided best. Since
1972 the centre has been taken over by the West Riding LEA though
largely retaining the same staff and continuing with similar programmes.

In this final section, we turn back to some of the general questions
set out at the beginning, using the development of Red House as an
example. First, the assumption that education is a well-placed starting
point for wider social and community development is supported.
Though research may emphasise the gap between home and school
values in working-class areas, nevertheless, in contrast to other services
which are selective and associated with problem groups, education is
universal and an accepted institution. The logic, too, of extending
work from an educational base into the community is easily understood;
for the objective of improving educational standards remains the same,
though the field of operation is enlarged.

Red House, however, is not a school; and though education in its
broadest sense may be the starting point for community development,
we cannot say from the example whether a school could undertake a
role of this kind. Comparing the centre with a small school on the five
elements we identified as characteristic of a community development
approach, we find a number of differences. Both may service a small
area, and try to avoid any selection, except that demanded by age or
catchment area; but on the remaining three characteristics the flexible
organisation of the centre clearly gives it an advantage: it had no
statutory obligations or set programme, and its resources could be
committed where appropriate. It was thus better placed to develop a
flexible role to meet changing needs, and to stimulate links among
other institutions. As the centre was small, and staff limited, there was
an incentive to tap community and other resources, and develop work
out in the community rather than attempt to get the community into
the building.

As we argued in examining the fifth type of community school – one
that seeks to act as an agent of social change in the local community –
the central problem is one of institutional form and its related roles.
We identified the wide gap between the typical role of teacher and of
community worker. The set-up at Red House can be seen as an institution intermediate between schools and community, with obligations
to both groups. Clearly this was a feasible role, though one which at

times brought almost intolerable shifts of style to deal in rapid succession with, for example, a teacher planning a course, a social worker following up a case, a class of children working on a project, a youth in trouble, and a visitor wanting an account of the centre's operations. These shifts of role meant inefficiency in traditional terms, though this may be a necessary feature of any multi-purpose centre where roles cannot be highly specialised. Specialisation by restricting the range of problems that a professional has to deal with may seem efficient. But issues are usually complex, and at the local level it is essential to have a group prepared to tackle a wide range of problems, who can bring in specialist help where necessary. Though obviously such roles will be demanding, it may be that the development of a suitable institutional context will provide a measure of insulation and support.

In the same way that Red House developed intermediate teaching roles as one way of breaking down the teacher/learner distinction, we may need 'intermediate institutions' to link school and community. It is important to develop the necessary roles and institutional framework to take advantage of their links with schools, yet provide enough autonomy to prevent them becoming merely satellites. Again, individual appointments such as teacher/social workers or teacher/youth leaders to this intermediate position have demonstrated the problems of individuals in this situation. As Craft suggests for social workers in his account of the school welfare team (1972), the need is to push for the appointment of teams or groups, rather than of isolated individuals.

One of the major lessons of EPA was the importance of tailoring institutions to their setting. Red House was planned and developed in response to what were seen as the needs of an area and its schools, not as a general answer to the problem of setting up 'community schools'. Red House could be one way of developing links between education and community work. But there may well be other, more appropriate forms, more closely linked to an individual school. What is needed is further experiment to try out some of these possible variations. If this were to take place, preferably in an action-research context, then the debate on 'community schools' might be based on more practical examples and increasing knowledge about the problems and possibilities of the community school as an agent of change. Unfortunately we seem reluctant to experiment. The first director of the Parkway Project in Philadelphia, one of the most imaginative community school developments in the USA – which has no school buildings as such but uses the resources of the city centre, libraries, museums, and firms to provide courses for its students – was asked how as an Englishman he came to be running such a project in the States. In reply, he asked which local education authority in England would have given backing on this scale to such an innovation.

Now that pre-school education is to be expanded on a wide scale, that part of the Urban Programme previously reserved for playgroups and nurseries should become available for other educational projects, as indeed has happened with Phase 9 in 1973, which has funded several similar schemes. If the Urban Programme is to continue its role of piloting future developments, 'community schools' of the type we have outlined ought to be strong candidates for these funds. If so, we should quickly see a more realistic debate about 'community schools', more examples, and more information about the potential of these centres for wider community development.

Notes

1 The recommendations were, in outline: (i) the extension of the EPA policy of 'positive discrimination'; (ii) the expansion of pre-schooling in EPAs; (iii) the development of 'community schools'; (iv) improved home–school relations; (v) improved teaching methods and resources and (vi) more action-research projects. A final non-educational recommendation was for a comprehensive programme of community development to accompany these educational changes.
2 Though we were both members of the West Riding EPA team, the conception of the centre and its development were the work of Mike Harvey, the project director, and Geoff and Lin Poulton, the first wardens. A longer account of the centre and of other project work in the West Riding was published in the project's final report: *Educational Priority*, vol. 4, *The West Riding EPA Project*, HMSO, 1974.

References

Central Advisory Council for Education (England), *Children and their Primary Schools* (Plowden Report), HMSO, 1967.
Clegg, A. and Megson, B., *Children in Distress*, Penguin Books, 1968.
Craft, M., 'The school welfare team', in Craft, M., Raynor, J. and Cohen, L. (eds), *Linking Home and School*, 2nd ed., Longman, 1972.
Halsey, A. H. (ed.), *Educational Priority*, vol. 1, *EPA Problems and Policies*, HMSO, 1972.
Midwinter, Eric, *Priority Education*, Penguin Books, 1972.
Miller, S. M., 'Dropouts – a political problem', in Schreiber, D. (ed.), *Profile of the School Dropout*, New York, Vintage Books, 1967.
Olsen, E. G. (ed.), *The School and Community Reader*, Macmillan, 1963.
Smith, T., 'Community service and the school', unpublished thesis for Diploma in Social and Administrative Studies, University of Oxford, 1969.

13 Planning, participation and planners

Adah Kay

The problem

The contradictions of a society like Britain which practises partial state intervention in the economy highlights the need for a discussion of participation in planning. People experience the results of planning (and failure to plan) at points of production, such as the location of industry, investment in regional development, legislation for office development or plans for the use of obsolete dockland. People also experience planned intervention at points of consumption, for example in the provision of housing, health, social and education services. Despite the growing importance of the 'public sector' in Britain (in common with other advanced capitalist economies), economic activity is still predominantly controlled by economic elites. These elites, composed of owners and managers of a vast amount of personal wealth, are married to the goals of accumulation of capital for private profit.

Demands for participation in Town and Country Planning (T&CP) are part of a growing public awareness of the failure of the welfare state and T&CP in their assault on the structural inequalities of British society. Successive governments have responded to these demands in documents[1] which demonstrate an entrenched unwillingness to confront the basic issues at stake. This is because the public sector has been so subjected to pressure from industry and finance capital that little has been done to substantially alter the existing pattern of distribution of wealth and economic power.[2] Capitalism itself needs planning in order to achieve its own goals. T&CP is implicated in this process, for example in setting policies for subsidising industry and supporting infrastructure, or for the distribution of people through housing provision.[3] Participation in planning therefore calls into question the representative nature of a social democracy whose government colludes by default with vested economic interests.[4] Participation also challenges myths of bureaucratic and professional expertise and impartiality, and

199

the possibility of achieving accountability to the electorate and recall of public servants and politicians.

To discuss participation in planning, one needs to view it as an aspect of a class struggle in which vast sections of the population are excluded from any control over decisions affecting themselves. One also needs to relate experiences of community involvement in planning issues to a wider political awareness; the act of collective engagement which may initially stem from a reaction to bureaucratic intransigence can be a step towards a broader political awareness of social, political and economic inequalities. Within this process, professional planners are as deeply involved as their public. Indeed a growing number of planners are questioning the legitimacy of their actions, are deeply concerned about the relationship of Town and Country Planning in stabilising and supporting the goals of capitalism and are seeking to evolve new roles for themselves.

Democracy and the role of participation in government

A great deal of confusion surrounds the theoretical notion of participation within democratic theory. This is a result of ambiguities arising from the notion of classical democracy,[5] and of the various critiques to which it has been subjected in the light of empirical evidence.[6] These critiques in turn have evolved the big red herring of pluralism.[7] Since the concept of participation in planning, as statutorily defined,[8] is based on pluralist assumptions, a brief look at the theory is necessary.

One can distinguish three main theoretical traditions concerning the nature of government and democracy. The classical notion of participatory democracy (Rousseau, J. S. Mill) emphasised the importance of participation in all aspects of public life for the development of man's individual capabilities. The quality of government is judged not only by the soundness of decisions reached but by the manner in which they are reached. 'Rousseau's Ideal System is designed to develop responsible individual social and political action through the effect of the participatory process.'[9] The two other strands, elite theories of governments and reformulations of classical notions of democratic theory, arose as reactions to classical democratic theory. Elite theories postulated that since, empirically, the complexity and size of modern society make the attainment of the classical ideal impossible and, since the majority of people were inherently incompetent to rule anyway,[10] in every society an elite must rule:

in all societies . . . two classes of people appear . . . a class
that rules and a class that is ruled. The first class, always the
less numerous, performs all political functions, monopolises
power and enjoys the advantages that power brings, while the
second, the more numerous class, is directed and controlled by
the first, in a manner that is now more or less legal, now more
or less arbitrary and violent.

Modifications of democratic theory have, in the main, resulted in forms
of representative democracy which emphasise the accountability of
the governing officials to their electorate. In theory, the electorate
wields influence by choosing among different contenders for political
office at regular intervals. Emphasis is placed on stability and constitutional arrangements. Theorists like Schumpeter and Dahl argue that
it is unrealistic to expect all people to be involved in government through
decision-making and that the crucial point is to ensure that adequate
institutional arrangements for competition by decision-makers for
people's votes are made.[11] These writers base their theory largely on
descriptions of currently operating 'democratic' systems. Participation
is reduced to a choice between different decision-makers. The pluralist
concept is central to this. 'What is generally meant by the phrase is
something like this: power in America is distributed among a variety
of groups and institutions in such a manner as to guarantee that no one
institution can lord it over the collectivity of others.'[12] The pluralists
thus claim that equality of political opportunity is possible, despite
barriers of inequalities in income, wealth, status and education and is,
therefore, non-cumulative. They contend that there is no alternative
but to recast democracy and to stress the stable, constitutional and
liberal nature of the system of elite pluralism since the accountability
to the electorate, the open election system and the many points of
access available to pressure groups ensure the non-abuse of power.[13]

The relevance of this theory to planning in Britain is twofold. First,
since the pluralists have concentrated in their empirical research on
studies of local community power,[14] their subject-matter is of particular
interest to community involvement in planning decisions. Second, and
more important, the Skeffington Report, by leaning heavily on the
experience of community action projects from the USA (themselves
founded on a pluralist ethic), has implicitly accepted the validity of
pluralism as applied to Britain.

The Skeffington Report has, on closer analysis, been shown to accept
pluralism on the following counts. By advocating the formation of a

community forum[15] and the employment of community development officers[16] to stimulate the formation of interest groups, the need for organised pressure groups is accepted. In common with the American advocates of pluralism, this approach accepts the validity of the current system of democratic control, but points to the 'slack'[17] in the system, which enables any group or individual to organise and enter into the political arena with other competing interests. Thus, the irrelevance of the current political system to many people (dubbed 'inarticulate'[18] in the Skeffington Report) is dismissed as an argument for non-involvement, although this sense of futility may be the real reason behind their inactivity. Furthermore, when saying that the function of community forum should be 'to bring together in discussion the active units in the community',[19] the Report does not state how conflicting interests would be resolved, or how the dominance of powerful interests can be counteracted. Finally, the Report is naive in its assumption that all decisions occur within the arena of formal government. In reality, decision-making is limited to relatively safe issues, reinforcing existing political and social attitudes – thus curtailing the field of discussion.[20]

Planning: redistribution or conservatism?

Town and Country Planning (together with other aspects of state intervention in the economy) has done little to alter, either the underlying pattern of resource distribution, or the balance of class interests in society through participation by pluralistic means. This can be borne out by a brief look at planners and their achievements.

Planners in Britain (working mainly in local government as part of the highly centralised hierarchy of national administration) have predominantly been custodians of the status quo, apart from a brief period in the nineteenth century.[21] Thus claims of political neutrality or resource redistribution lose credence when one considers the planners' acceptance of the goals of capitalism and the constraints of the market situation. The seeds of a new analysis are given by John Palmer,[22] who deals with the various stages through which regional, economic and social planning in Britain has evolved since the end of the nineteenth century. Palmer explicitly links planning to phases in the development of capitalism.

Phase one, the nineteenth-century period of industrial expansion, brought about piecemeal health and housing reforms needed both to prevent social upheaval following events in Europe in 1848 and to maintain a healthy labour force. Phase two, the interwar period, saw attempts at planning retreat in the light of the need to save the £ and to promote internal economic growth.[23] In this period the stark inequalities in British society were highlighted by areas of industrial decline and attendant mass unemployment. Phase three, the postwar period, saw partial nationalisation, the creation of the welfare state and, in planning, attempts to tackle regional unemployment and rebuild cities and towns damaged by the war. But these attempts were constantly hampered by the planners' inability to confront market forces. The effects of the 1947 Town and Country Planning Act which attempted to nationalise development rights and their associated values (without nationalising land!) were neutralised when the Conservatives abolished betterment charges in 1951. Planners forced to act in collusion with property developers[24] found themselves in a situation not of control, but of having to manipulate market forces to achieve some pay-off to finance other needed public services.

Finally, the fourth current phase of social planning represents attempts to streamline, co-ordinate and make more efficient various aspects of the welfare services and planning. It is in this phase that demands for participation in planning are emerging at points of contact with rigid bureaucracies and in the face of the patent failure of the welfare state to reach those for whom it was designed.

Demands for participation in planning in Britain have stemmed from two main sources:[25] from local civic amenity societies linked to the Civic Trust, and from various experiences in Community Action. The former tend to view planning as a politically neutral activity and are concerned with aesthetic issues and conservation; the latter, although ideologically heterogeneous, are united in a concern for the have-nots in society and view planning very much as a political process. The civic amenity movement is predominantly the province of the professional practitioner and has had considerable influence on legislation.[26] This movement accepts statutory procedures and codes of behaviour which accentuate the imperfect competition between different interests in society. Community Action has a more credible base in social and political action.[27]

The statutory response to demands for participation was formulated in the 1968 Town and Country Planning Act and in the Skeffington Report. However, the stated intention[28] that

> People must be able to participate more fully in the planning
> process and their rights must be safeguarded . . . one of the
> government's main aims in the present review of planning

> legislation is to ensure that there are greater opportunities for
> the discussion of important changes while they are still in the
> formative stage and can be influenced by the people whose lives
> they will affect

has in reality done nothing significant to alter the underlying basis of
planning in relationship to participation. Although, on the face of it,
the public living under an assiduous local authority can be involved at
fixed stages in the planning process through various communication
and public relation exercises,[29] in effect, ultimate control lies with the
professional and the politician. Here one can see the machinery of
pluralism at work for, by keeping people absorbed in their daily lives
and by routine activities of superficial involvement, the real questions
of government and control are left to the aforementioned elites who
exert pressure both directly and indirectly on the government. In planning, this can be seen in the Skeffington Report's emphasis on the
activity of participation. By deflecting interest away from structural
changes in the planning system, people will feel satisfied by a feeling of
involvement within it. This, in turn, leaves the government, various
local authorities and elites free to exercise the 'second face of power'.

Experience of community involvement in planning

A degree of pessimism about the efficacy of T&CP and about institutional responses to demands for participation does not preclude an
important discussion on the actual experience of community involvement in planning issues. A closer look at strategies of involvement[30]
can open up the issue of wider politicisation and can pose alternative
roles for the disaffected professional planner. I do not intend to go into
the essential prerequisites for effective participation (such as a process
with intervention effectively built in, access to information and communication channels (Press, etc.) or community control over the outcome) but instead want to discuss ways in which certain groups have
operated.

When evaluating the action of a community group in terms of its
effectiveness, one needs to view it in the light of actual planning practice.
In order to evaluate, the following information would be required:

1 *Type of planning situation*
   plan preparation
   planning proposal
   development control

2 *Source of initiation of involvement*
  External to the interests affected: e.g. central government
                                              local government
                                              voluntary agency
                                              pressure group
                                              political party
                                              social/community worker
                                              professional advocates
  Internal from the people affected, but representing varying degrees
  of representativeness: e.g. all interest parties
                                coalition of interests
                                one dominant interest

3 *Stage of involvement in the planning process*
  pre-goal and policy formulation *or*
  post-goal and policy formulation.

The above factors by no means comprise a complete list, but the basic categories enable a wide variance of situations and people to be included. They enable one to view strategies of participation in the light of the whole planning process and also determine, to a large extent, the sorts of strategies employed by local and other groups.

Deliberately, this attempt to discuss British experience concentrates on the constraints of a planning system which has always viewed participation within a context of representative government. Responses are sought from the 'public' at strategic points in an idealised decision-making process.[31]

One can discern four ways in which community-based groups have been involved in planning issues:

1 pressure group methods
2 advocacy
3 community development
4 community action.

Very broadly, pressure group strategies are employed almost exclusively by groups in society whose perceived class situation is congruent with the prevailing social order. Such groups tend to campaign on their own behalf, and the emphasis is on preservation. All the other three strategies to some extent involve groups concerned with the disadvantaged (intentionally I do not say working class or proletariat, since there are dominant patterns of paternalism involved). These three categories are based on groups who view solutions to social inequalities in different ways, again according to their images of social order and ways of achieving change.

Pressure group methods include the formation of coalitions of interests which contain professional expertise as well as political influence and the use of formal statutory channels as a basis of rational questioning and argument. These groups often engage in fund-raising and publicity through the media and, for instance, in some cases[32] engage in the political arena. Such groups, based on the above membership criteria, are predominantly middle class in composition. Basically, their interest lies in improving the quality of decisions that are taken, operating within the accepted framework of decision-making. As such, and because their membership represents a degree of social homogeneity with their statutory opponents, they have been able to achieve a more satisfactory dialogue and effect change in some situations. Their concern is not with widespread community involvement, and is often biased in favour of particular class interests. One can, of course, point to pressure groups such as the Child Poverty Action Group who expressly campaign on behalf of an under-represented section of society, but this group illustrates an even greater lack of involvement of the people concerned.

Advocacy,[33] as a method of participation, is again concerned with challenging the technical competence of statutory planning authorities, but from the standpoint of the people who will be affected by the planning process. It is, therefore, as much concerned with a redefinition of the role of the professional planner as with local involvement. Advocacy is ultimately an indirect means of local involvement. It involves deliberate action on the part of professionals who have opted out of the 'bureaucractic' planning system to act for a particular group. The methods of the advocates imply their own involvement as specialists in lieu of the local people. This applies for example to the Sparkbrook Community Plan in Birmingham[34] and to the North Kensington Wheatsone Road Public Inquiry.[35] The latter two instances do illustrate a very close working relationship with local people, but it is ultimately the advocates who confront the Local Planning Authority (LPA). The means employed by advocates, therefore, mirror those employed by an LPA in terms of the expertise involved. The value of the advocacy approach lies in the personalisation of clients' needs and goals. However, inbuilt into the advocacy approach are difficulties of mobilising, maintaining and reconciling different local interests.

Community development strategies essentially imply the intervention of an agent of change, whose aim is to involve people with a recognised or unrecognised joint problem in solving this problem. Community development emphasises the therapy that ensues from the act of involvement and tends to view people as 'clients'. The goal of involvement and its formulation is sometimes less important than the activity itself. The Shelter Neighbourhood Action Project (SNAP)[36] project illustrates this approach to a certain extent. The use of formal channels of communication and co-operation with statutory authorities are stressed in order to help the people affected acquire the appropriate learning skills which will enable them to 'work the system'. The status quo is, therefore, accepted and adaptation to it is sought. The agent of change is central to the local group involvement and sets the tone of the whole exercise.

Community action, on the other hand, can be divided into types. One type of action, employed by the government in its Urban Programme in the community development projects, is a continuation of community development techniques with an emphasis on changing social work methods.[37] Thus, social workers are increasingly abandoning traditional one-to-one casework methods in favour of work with groups. The other type of community action strategies are employed by community workers and other interested people who are not necessarily sponsored by official agencies. These strategies are less likely to take notice of formal channels of communication and more emphasis is placed on populist methods of democratic control. However, this type of work also essentially involves a dialogue rather than a conflict with statutory authorities, in which the ultimate outcome is seen as co-operation.

When discussing more extreme forms of community action, the dividing line between it and groups characterised by direct action strategies becomes less distinct. Direct action becomes a strategy and a working method when conflict between the groups concerned and the authority structure is overt. This tends to occur with groups who have virtually nothing to lose by resorting to direct action methods such as squatting. Direct action starts from the premise that experience has shown that normal channels of communication fail, thus, in order to achieve stated ends, any methods are justified on the part of the people affected by the particular issue under discussion. This does not preclude the use of violence to counteract violence (the Redbridge squatters versus the local authority hired bailiffs). Direct action, therefore, implies a taking of the law into one's own hands, be it sitting in a council chamber so as to force a committee meeting to convene elsewhere,[38] taking over an empty site for use as a playground,[39] or men moving into the hostel for the homeless in protest against rules preventing them from living with their families.[40] Direct action methods also include publicity to gain widespread support and, as such, they are dependent on the media.[41] Direct action is also concerned with 'educating' the people concerned, so as to raise their consciousness, both of their situation in a wide sense, and of their ability to act for themselves. Alternative channels of communication, such as the community and underground Press and poster workshops, are part of the strategies of increasing self-sufficiency and awareness.[42] However, this method, as all the other methods discussed, does depend on the commitment of some agents of change. The important difference here is the level of politicisation of local issues achieved by such agents of change and their consequent emphasis on direct mobilisation and action on the part of those affected.

Despite the fact that many means of involvement in planning exist, they have been unequally utilised by all sections of society. Thus, the pluralist argument of equality of competition is patently untrue. In the instances where there has been direct mobilisation of under-represented sections of society by outside interveners, one comes up against the possibility of a conflict in goals between the agents of change, for example, community development and the interests of the groups they are trying to 'serve'.

Certain crucial factors will determine the type of involvement and the possibility of achieving success. The scale of the planning situation will influence the extent to which interests will be involved. This can work in two directions: for instance, in the case of the airport lobbies, nation-wide support was enlisted because of the types of vested interests that were threatened, whereas in the case of the Sparkbrook Plan, there was a fair degree of local involvement because the immediacy and relevance of the planning situation was readily perceived. The source of initiation of involvement will influence tactics employed and timing has crucial importance for the possible success of the outcome. Within this process the professional has been seen to play as important a role as the 'public' – this therefore has implications for his evolving a role within or outside the local authority.

The changing role of the professional planner

Traditionally the professional planner, a hybrid creature, has seen himself as politically neutral. This is in part a consequence of the technical domination of the profession by surveyors, engineers, architects, etc., and the current scientistic basis of systematic planning,[43] the myth of comprehensive planning,[44] and an emphasis on increased efficiency and qualitative techniques. Alongside this professional tendency, a move to radicalise (rather belatedly) the profession has been made by young planners and students. This has resulted in many planners opting out of 'straight' local authority or consultancy work in favour of working with 'community' groups. In addition, many professionals work in their spare time for local groups in an advocate capacity.

Involvement with local groups, however, is fraught with problems. An initial burst of enthusiasm often gives rise to temporary involvement (particularly in the case of students), and thus vital continuity and commitment are lacking. In addition, inexperience is a major obstacle. Political naivety or a desire to impose alien values on a group can create a situation in which the local group's articulated or implied goals are ignored. Thus, in some situations, the 'advocates' are doing no better a job than the local authority. However, this form of action does have an educative advantage for professionals and students by bringing them into real contact with people, and possibly the naivety and inexperience mentioned will be only temporary phenomena. For the planner, such part-time engagement may pose schizophrenic problems. How can such conflicts of interest be resolved? Within a local authority there are various types of work that a planner can undertake which are positive, bearing in mind that the system in reality is usually more flexible than envisaged. Here are only three possible ways in which a planner could work:

1 In the research area of plan preparation, in discussion and reports, the planner can consistently point out structural contradictions, e.g. commercial development dislocating local activities,[45] or redevelopment or general improvement areas pricing out working-class people. The often inevitable inefficacy of such action, in the light of the momentum of the planning process, is as much a result of a professional retreat as of political interest.

2 Planners can build up contracts with local groups and make themselves accessible – fighting red tape and confidentiality alongside local groups.

3 Data on social stress areas can be compiled systematically using simple methods, so as to amass a credible base for proposals aimed at redistribution of resources.

These are all explored, feasible roles a planner could adopt. Maybe they do little to alter structural factors, but they are examples of ways

Hcw

in which questions about structural inequalities can be raised within local authorities.

Conclusions

Participation in planning cannot be limited to a discussion of planning practice, but involves questioning the goals of the society one is discussing and the legitimation of power and control within it. One can view attempts to increase participation in two ways. One approach (accommodation) characterises the response of institutions and groups to increase opportunities for participation *within* the current system of government and the economic, political and social structure. The second approach (liberation) is adopted by groups within society who reject prevailing social values, goals and institutions and demand a greater degree of self-reliance.

Accommodation, and hence the current statutory responses to participation, fails to confront both the basic inequalities in Britain and the inadequacies of a pluralist mode of democracy. In the final count, control of planning (problem definition, solution and implementation) lies within the sphere of formal government – with people participating more as passive recipients than as the valid cue or base for action.

The experience of community action, on the other hand, has generated alternative modes of control over local government activity (neighbourhood councils) and alternative modes of communication (local Presses), but is very fragmented. The unintended consequences of this approach in terms of politicisation are immense. The problem of variegated and separate actions basically lies in the piecemeal assault that is made on various aspects of dissatisfaction with administrative or other procedures. Ultimately, this relates to the appropriateness of community action and direct action strategies of participation to different scales of planning situations. On a local level, community action directed towards specific aims may be very effective. However, this may only result in shifting the issue to another area. Certain aspects of maldistribution of resources may be remedied by a local service provision. But problems such as income inequality which give rise to poverty cannot be tackled at their source through discrete local community actions. Involvement of the working class in planning issues rarely happens, and community action is still in a weak competitive situation. Ultimately, as a political process, planning must come to grips with structural inequalities and participation can only become a reality as part of a political struggle.

Notes

1 Committee on Local Authority and Allied Personal Social Services, *Report* (Seebohm Report), Cmnd 3703, 1968; Committee on Public Participation in Planning, *People and Planning* (Skeffington Report), HMSO, 1969; DHSS, *The Future Structure of the National Health Service*, HMSO, 1970.

2 See John Westergaard, 'Sociology: the myth of classlessness', in Robin Blackburn (ed.), *Ideology in Social Science*, Fontana, 1972, pp. 122–9.

3 E.g. the need for a pool of cheap immigrant labour for service industries in the inner city, or skilled labour in New Towns.

4 'in a democracy it is difficult to reduce private affluence . . . all one can reasonably hope to do is to take a larger share of any increase from them . . . those who advocate that we should simply take more and more money, whatever is happening to the economy, aren't, on the whole, the people who have to win votes and stay in office and try to get things done. Large increases in expenditure on the social services are just not possible unless economic growth is going happily forward'; P. A. Walker quoted in *May Day Manifesto*, ed. Raymond Williams, Penguin Special, 1968, p. 28.

5 See Carole Pateman, *Participation and Democratic Theory*, Cambridge University Press, 1970, for a discussion of classical theories of democracy.

6 E.g. J. A. Schumpeter, *Capitalism, Socialism and Democracy*, Allen & Unwin, 1943.

7 R. A. Dahl, *Who Governs?*, Yale University Press, 1961.

8 Town and Country Planning Act, HMSO, 1968; Skeffington Report.

9 Pateman, op. cit., p. 24.

10 Gaetano Mosca, *The Ruling Class*, McGraw-Hill, 1939; cited in P. Bachrach, *A Theory of Democratic Elitism*, University of London Press, 1969, p. 11.

11 E.g. universal suffrage, free elections, etc.

12 Todd Gitlin, 'Local pluralism as theory and ideology', in H. P. Dreitzel (ed.), *Recent Sociology*, vol. 1, *The Social Basis of Politics*, Collier-Macmillan, 1969, p. 62.

13 Dahl, op. cit.

14 Nelson Polsby, *Community Power and Political Theory*, Yale University Press, 1963; Edward Banfield, *Political Influence*, Chicago, Free Press, 1961.

15 Skeffington Report, para. 60.

16 Ibid., para. 80.

17 Gitlin, op. cit., p. 77.

18 Skeffington Report, para. 70.

19 Ibid., para. 80.

20 P. Bachrach and M. Baratz, 'Two faces of power', *American Political Science Review*, 56, 1962, 947–52.

21 Leonardo Benevolo, *The Origins of Modern Town Planning*, Routledge & Kegan Paul, 1967, p. xiii.

22 John Palmer, Introduction to Robert Goodman, *After the Planners*, Penguin Books, 1972.

23 For a discussion of the rise of speculative housing, the growth of suburbia and the withdrawal of subsidies for public housing, see H. Richardson and D. H. Aldcroft, *Building in the British Economy between the Wars*, Allen & Unwin, 1968.

24 Oliver Marriott, *The Property Boom*, Pan Piper, 1967; Nigel Moore, 'The planner and the market', *Journal of the Town Planning Institute*, 56 (1), 1970, 9–12; *The Recurrent Crisis of London*, CIS Anti-Report on the Property Developers, Counter Information Services, 1973; Islington Housing Action and Research Group, 'A revitalised Angel', unpublished report, 1973.

25 John Ferris, *Participation in Planning: The Barnsbury Case*, LSE Occasional Paper no. 48, Bell, 1972.

26 Civic Amenities Act 1967; Town and Country Planning Act 1968.

27 See various articles on North Kensington, squatting, etc., in Anne Lapping (ed.), *Community Action*, Fabian Tract no. 400, 1970; or community newspapers such as *Grassroots* (Birmingham), *Street Research* (London), *Community Action* (London).

28 Ministry of Housing and Local Government, *Town and Country Planning*, Cmnd 3333, HMSO, 1967, para. 10, p. 2.

29 See self-congratulation of councillors and chief planning officers in the April 1971 issue of the *Journal of the Town Planning Institute*, and the criticisms of such exercises by the Coventry Community Workshop in *Public Participation in Structure Planning in Coventry*, November 1972.

30 Various typologies of participation have already been posed: J. Reynolds, 'Public participation in planning', *Town Planning Review*, July 1969, 130–47; L. Baric, 'The meaning of citizen participation', in *Urban Renewal*, University of Salford Symposium, 1968; S. Arnstein, 'A ladder of citizen participation', *Journal of the American Institute of Planners*, 1969, 216–24; E. Burke, 'Strategies of citizen participation', *Journal of the American Institute of Planners*, 34 (5), 1968, 287–93.

31 Unlike the situation in the USA, where participation, a concept which is a product of a tradition of decentralisation in government, has always placed value on grass-roots activity. It is often, therefore, viewed in an extra-governmental context in the light of community control. Continuums are constructed, which vary according to the ability of participants to employ strategies which result in their deciding on, and managing the outcome of, decisions taken.

32 The London Motorway Action Group, formed in 1965 to fight the Motorway Box proposals of the Greater London Council, ran candidates in one GLC election, the 'Homes before Roads' campaign.

33 Advocacy planning was first introduced in the USA by Paul Davidoff, 'Advocacy and pluralism in planning', *Journal of the American Institute of Planners*, 31 (4), 1965, 596–615.

34 The Sparkbrook Community Plan was produced by planning students at the Birmingham School of Planning, who worked directly to the Sparkbrook Association (1969).

35 The Wheatsone Road Public Inquiry was called in February 1971 by the Golborne Social Rights Committee, who were represented by professional planners working as advocates in their spare time. This inquiry successfully resulted in the local authority housing residents who would previously have been displaced because of the authority's unwillingness to explore fully their compulsory purchase and rehousing powers.

36 The SNAP project in Liverpool represented a coalition between Shelter and the local authority in trying to start work on an improvement area. In effect, all participation emanated from the SNAP workers, despite the use of neighbourhood councils and various communications exercises – see Roger Barnard, 'Community action in a twilight area', *RIBA Journal*, 1970, 445–53.

37 One definition of community work is provided by the first Gulbenkian Report (*Community Work and Social Change*, Longman, 1968, p. 3): 'it typically consists of work with groups of local people who have come into existence because they want to change something or do something that concerns them. Community work also embraces the attempts to relate the activities of social agencies more closely to the needs of the people they serve.'

38 A tactic employed in April 1971 by the Southwark Family Squatters' Association.

39 Play Space, a residents' group in Camden, took over an empty British Rail site in the north of the borough for a playground, with the support of candidates in the local election in April–May 1971.

40 King Hill Hostel, Kent, 1965.

41 'Whether in the courts or in the streets . . . we were able to conduct our continuous campaigns in which our most potent weapon was constant publicity', Jim Radford, from King Hill, to the Squatting Association (Anne Lapping (ed.), op. cit., p. 43).

42 Ken Warpole and Roger Hudson, 'Community Press', *New Society*, 24 October 1970.

43 B. McLoughlin, *Urban and Regional Planning: A Systems Approach*, Faber, 1969.

44 M. N. Webber, 'The new urban planning in America', *Journal of the Town Planning Institute*, 54 (1), 1967, 3–8.

45 Covent Garden is a case in point; various unpublished papers by Brian Anson, formerly employed by the GLC, make this clear.

Part III **Training**

David Jones

The Gulbenkian Foundation's *Community Work and Social Change* was subtitled 'A Report on Training', but most of the discussion it stimulated was concerned, probably quite rightly, with elucidating the nature and assumptions of community work and the role of the community worker and it is only recently that this debate has become systematically concerned with training. In the meantime, the amount of training has increased significantly.

Philip Bryers considers a number of the issues which have already been pinpointed and relates them to the present confused situation of training for community work. He concludes by suggesting that 'so long as debate, diversity and disagreement continue it is certain that community work is alive.' On this criterion, and at the level of discussion and aspiration, community work training is alive to the point of distraction, although suffering from indigestion. In terms of actual performance, the position is more obscure, although there is little doubt that significant advances have already been made.

Some comments seem to imply the prior question of whether training is needed at all. Training, it is suggested, is not the best use of resources, it is both unnecessary and ineffective. On the other hand, training is so potent that it conditions people into a permanently distorted perception of reality, a trained incapacity. At the extremes, neither version accords with common sense and common experience and closer examination reveals that the argument is not about whether training is required but about who should be trained, to what end and by whom, the assumptions, content and methods of training and so on.

If training is to be relevant and responsive to the developments and dilemmas indicated in this collection of essays, it faces a formidable task. The problem is not that of lack of relevant content. The so-called 'knowledge explosion' in the social sciences means that in terms of human capacity and the limited time available on courses, there is an excess of potentially useful material. The difficulties are those of

215

selection and emphasis and the relation of subject areas to each other and to the practice of community work.

Training for community work, in addition to providing background knowledge, must attempt to convey some general body of principles and methods relevant to community work practice. Ironically, this is possibly the least systematically developed subject area. The need is not only for the assimilation and development of theoretical content and conceptual frameworks relevant to practice but also for 'case studies' which go beyond narrative description to analysis and evaluation and explain the role and activities of the community worker in the situation.

While it is possible to study and discuss community work methods, assessments and predictions in a relatively value-free way, the practice of community work is inextricably interwoven with value-judgments both in terms of the ends it serves and the means it employs. Hence a need for workers to be aware of their own values and assumptions. In addition, workers need an understanding of the value systems of the individuals, groups, organisations and communities with which they work. Values in this sense are facts, part of the social reality the worker has to understand and work with. But beyond that, community work involves consideration of the values which justify undertaking it, at all, together with the ethical constraints which govern or should govern its practice.

One of the issues which Bryers touches on is that of 'imparting skills through direct experience'. However relevant and comprehensive the knowledge made available to students, skill in community work can only come through application. If students are to gain at least initial competence in practice they will need field training, that is to practice community work under supervision, and this sets one of the major problems in the development of training at the present time, for such opportunities are in limited supply.

In the second paper, Peter Baldock discusses some of his experiences in supervising casework students in community work. This may seem a somewhat oblique way into the subject, but it has the great virtue of reporting on actual experience while at the same time being much more broadly relevant in two major ways. First, an important task of training, and potentially a very fruitful one, is the development of the community work component of the training and work not only of caseworkers but of a wide range of professionals involved in human services. Peter Baldock demonstrates the contribution of appropriate field experience to this process. Second, casework has had substantial experience of field training and has subjected this experience to serious examination.

As Peter Baldock shows it would be highly irrational not to build on what is relevant from the casework field, despite differences of purpose and content in community work.

Despite some ambivalence, social work training is increasingly incorporating community work content and developing training for community work practice alongside other methods. This process seems likely to gather momentum although not quickly enough for some. Others, outside the social work field, regard this response to demands being made on social work courses with some suspicion.

Most of the issues of training are raised by these two contributions and it is evident that much more study and exchange of experience between trainers, students and practitioners is required. Both essays indicate the need for continuing experimentation, a variety of approaches and 'an openness to change'. Dogma is denial of basic assumptions in both education and community work practice.

Bryers also raises the much broader question of the role of education and community practice, rather than training, in making available 'practical information and insights to as wide a range of people as possible' and in facilitating 'local leaders'. A number of essays touch on this theme, explicitly or implicitly. Griffiths suggests that community groups 'need opportunities for training and education, they need consultant assistance from time to time, and also on occasions they need financial assistance. But over and above all else if they are going to support any new arrangements they need to feel they are a party to the enterprise.'

Dearlove and Kay in their contributions argue that such activities can be used for the 'control of change and the regulation of community action'. Ashcroft and Jackson on adult education and the Smiths on the community school see a much more positive role for education. Harry Liddell states: 'I don't think outsiders can come in and foist political views or attitudes towards political questions which the people may not be responding to.' Leissner and Joslin point to the potential reciprocity of the process and quote a worker's comment that residents provided 'much realistic help, advice and encouragement', although 'some were hard taskmasters, too'.

14 Community work training - drift, dogma and detente

Philip Bryers

The first report of the Calouste Gulbenkian Foundation working group entitled *Community Work and Social Change: A Report on Training* in 1968[1] had a catalytic effect on community work. It presented developments in a wide variety of fields – new communities, twilight areas, settlements and neighbourhood centres, further education, the youth service, schools, self-help organisations and voluntary agencies, the churches, civil service and local government – under one banner. The report sought to demonstrate through an examination of the values and objectives of workers and through a general problem-solving model that the generic term 'community work' can be applied to diverse activities at neighbourhood levels, at interorganisational levels and in the sphere of national and regional social planning. The second report of the working group, *Current Issues in Community Work*, published in 1973,[2] set itself a wider brief than merely that of reporting on training, though it did update our information about developments in the training field. It reiterated the dilemmas in developing curricula and re-emphasised the undesirability of too great concentration on neighbourhood work or social planning in separate courses unrelated to each other. The appendices demonstrate the considerable variety in teaching – in thirty-eight institutions running lectures or seminars in community work there were only four aspects of the subject out of more than twenty identified which were taught by more than half the institutions. Undoubtedly both reports have carried our thinking forward in several respects, but in order to embrace such a wide spectrum of activities they have produced broad, generalised definitions of community work.[3]

The fortunate aspect of the Gulbenkian Reports' broad framework for community work was their inclusion of many growth points which have produced an ever-increasing flow of community work appointments over the past few years. On the other hand, problems have resulted from the coming together of some very strange bedfellows and from the vigorous promotion of alternative interpretations of community work.

219

Some people have seen community work as identical with community action whilst others have defined it more in terms of community care and community service. In some quarters community work has become synonymous with troublemaking, whilst in other quarters community workers have been labelled 'servants of the status quo'. On the one hand a strong 'power to the people' lobby has opposed the development of professional practices amongst community workers, and on the other hand there have been demands for a tightening up of standards implying greater professionalism.

Whatever way can the trainer turn in the present situation? Can the Gulbenkian balancing act be sustained indefinitely or must we develop a clearer, more concise understanding of who is a community worker and what he should be doing? If we narrow down our concerns will our training programmes continue to adapt flexibly to changing circumstances or will they take on a strait-jacket of 'rigid formulas' and 'static patterns'?[4]

Few of these questions have been faced by training agencies. Rather, courses have drifted to their present positions, responding to changing fashions and adapting themselves from past patterns, but never clarifying where they are going. Some would like to see an open commitment in community work training to a particular interpretation of society and a particular strategy of intervention. This dogmatic solution to the dilemmas of training for community work is expressed alike by the 'revolutionary' school of thought and by the 'social engineering' school. Both extremes have in common a firm commitment to a certain value standpoint. By contrast the 'balancing act' solution, whilst pointing out the existence of alternative ways of viewing situations and the differing implications stemming from these for the person contemplating intervention, sees no need for community work training to take sides, arguing that a detente is possible in a training context between the competing orientations of academic/theoretical and practical/pragmatic.

Drift

How has the present, confused training situation come about? Partly it results from the vague, amorphous nature of community work itself, but partly also it is the outcome of differing starting points, five of which are set out here:

1   The traditional origin of many approaches to community work is community development thinking, with its emphases on non-directive

styles of operation, on a process rather than a task orientation and on community self-determination.[5]

2   A more recent influence has been the model of social work comprising casework, group work and community work. According to this view, community work shares the values and objectives of other forms of social work and requires similar skills and a similar knowledge base.

3   A third perspective sees community work as a radicalising element having relevance in social work, education and planning, and in a variety of other settings. Hence community work may be used as a safety valve on training courses permitting the expression of unorthodox views, and efforts to alter the status quo in practice settings may be labelled community work. This is possibly a valid function for community work, though some research has thrown doubt upon the radical credentials of many community workers.[6]

4   On a conceptual level, some community work training finds the literature of political science more valuable than that of fields more closely associated with social work and community development. Theories concerning the nature and dynamics of power and analyses of pressure group achievements, for example, are central to this view of community work training.

5   A final starting point is provided by a vague concern with instilling a community perspective and promoting 'holistic approaches'. The word 'community' has taken on a peculiar significance despite our inability to agree upon a generally accepted definition. This influence has been most marked in instances where a community work component has been inserted in courses with a primary purpose other than the training of community workers. It would seem important to prevent the identification of community work training with a quick glance at the concept of community, driven home by reference to a few community studies.

These influences have all played a part in the emergence of the present hybrid community work training scene. A considerable influence has also been exerted by actual or potential trainees. One driving force behind a lot of applicants for courses is a dissatisfaction with the narrowness and the constrictions of such established activities as teaching, social work and planning. For these students the attraction of community work is its open-ended nature and the scope it offers for imaginative experiment. The rhetoric of community work is the main appeal for other groups of students, many of whom have had experience of working with community groups and see community work as a means, however inadequate, of challenging 'the system'. American experience suggested that there was a rush of radical students to community organisation programmes in the early, halcyon days of the 'War on Poverty', but that these groups discovered that community work could not offer an effective means of taking up the large political issues of society and therefore sought satisfaction elsewhere. It is conceivable that training could offer an opportunity for an expansion of horizons whatever the shortcomings of practice. How closely related should training and practice be? Should trainers aim to offer what many students want, and ask fundamental but unresolved questions, or should they work hard at producing curricula which prepare students to fill competently the niches created by society as part of the superstructure of social control?

Course content

The diverse origins of community work courses and the differing degrees of influence exerted upon their form by the practical requirements of employing agencies and the questioning attitudes of their students will inevitably be reflected in course content. Let me attempt to identify the main strands here:

1   The first strand examines community work in what can be described as a mechanistic way. It offers a factual guide to the structures and responsibilities, the stated objectives and the written terms of reference of departments and agencies community workers will come into contact with. The main emphasis here is upon imparting factual information, but in the same way that mastery of a phrase book does not imply mastery of a language, so this rather static approach cannot guarantee an ability to apply information effectively.

2   A second strand in training introduces a much greater element of analysis and can be characterised as diagnostic. Through the examination of community study material and the discussion of case studies in community work, a practical picture is drawn of community work, its setting, scope and methods.

3   A diagnostic approach, despite its practical orientation, may not satisfy the wishes of the practitioner who will stress the importance of imparting practice skills through direct experience. Problems arise for the trainer in teaching skills in any other way because of the paucity of literature on the subject and a lack of agreement about which skills it is necessary to teach, or possible to instil.[7]

4   Each of the other three strands has set out to be practical. A final strand might be called theoretical, as opposed to applied. This approach

attaches importance to the underlying assumptions and outlooks rather than to the day-to-day activity, and introduces into training an element of intellectual rigour which might otherwise not exist. It also brings into the open questions of value and choice, and may challenge the legitimacy of avoiding or ignoring the necessity of choice. Many courses have tended to select bits and pieces of theory and to fit them together into a patchwork pattern without permitting a full consideration of the theories within their own context. It is open to question whether such procedures result in superficial treatment of issues, and indeed whether the constraints of course planning can avoid such selection and editing.

It has been suggested[8] that professional training passes through three phases. In the first phase training is ad hoc and empirical, emphasising apprenticeship on the job and being determined largely by practitioners. It then passes through a phase when skills and theory are evenly balanced into the final phase characterised by control of the education process by teaching institutions and an emphasis on theory, principles and intellectual concepts. Elements of all three stages can be found in community work courses, and future trends depend upon whether community work is accepted as a legitimate area of study by higher education institutions and thus runs the risk of dominance by academics, or whether it fails to establish itself effectively and thus has little choice open to it than to remain practical. It is conceivable that some courses will develop in a conceptual direction whilst others continue to be practitioner dominated, particularly in view of the differing motivations and vested interests behind existing courses.

An alternative way forward, attempting to adhere to the second phase in the model quoted above, is to try to maintain an equilibrium, as applied courses in other subjects have done. This solution has many attractions in that the course can be described as comprehensive and academic, whilst retaining its practical relevance. It is the solution which is most likely to meet with the approval of validating bodies and grant-aiding institutions, and it follows the pattern suggested in the later chapters of the Gulbenkian Report and that set out by Arnold Gurin for the American Council on Social Work Education.[9] Against these attractions, this approach runs the risk of boiling down to a 'standard course' containing the same component parts in the same proportions to each other approached in a similar way on all courses. This development is not an inevitable one, though pressures of time on a relatively short course and increasing agreement on major areas of knowledge deemed to be relevant make it a likely one. I would argue that diversity of approach is essential and that 'core content' must not be expanded to the point where it occupies the whole course and excludes variety.

An indication that this undesirable tendency towards uniformity exists is to be found by a glance at what is left out of courses as well as at what is included. The trend towards seeking material only from social welfare contexts (in which I include the social effects of educational provision and planning developments) may be excluding valuable evidence from the history of the labour movement, for instance. Do we pay enough attention, in our consideration of community structure and dynamics, to such organisations as Working Men's Clubs and darts and dominoes leagues? Their long-term success is often in marked contrast to that of our pet community groups and the reasons for the difference might be instructive.

On a theoretical level the same selectivity is at work. Urban sociology, theories of social change and perspectives on the power structure are widely accepted as important. Perhaps it would be valuable to give more concentrated attention to philosophical views which investigate and question the authority of society to impose laws and sanctions, with a view to clarifying the ethical issues and the likely implications of strategies which contravene society's norms – strategies which are adopted by squatters, by rent strikers or by mothers holding a disruptive protest. I am not implying that such strategies are a necessary feature of community work but that the worker requires a firm view of what actions he accepts as legitimate in pursuit of effectiveness and why he places the dividing line between legitimacy and non-legitimacy at a particular point. Teaching should make clear the value orientations between which choices must be made, and it is arguable, since value assumptions are so fundamental, that courses should make explicit the commitments they and their tutors embrace. Once again, a failure to do this may result in a uniform, colourless presentation of material.

If we accept the combination of theoretical and practical content in a single course it becomes essential to develop linkages between foundation areas and practice areas (to adopt Gurin's terminology). Examples of attempts to achieve this can most easily be found in American literature. Jack Rothman has devised a model comparing the three approaches of locality development, social planning and social action on twelve different criteria including goals, assumptions concerning community structure and problem conditions, orientation towards the power structure and conception of the public interest.[10] Spergel has undertaken a similar exercise in conceptualising the alternative analyses and the corresponding patterns of action open to a change agent in the context of delinquent behaviour.[11] Comparable exercises in a British context are hard to find but must be undertaken soon.

Models are not without their own dangers, and two mistakes need noting here. The first is that of applying them uncritically. In a practice setting numerous factors modify them almost beyond recognition – personality factors, resources available, past experiences of groups and individuals involved, external constraints ruling out certain options and so on. Until we understand more about these influences we cannot hope to steer a direct course between the point at which aims are determined and their achievement. Even if we did possess a greater understanding of them the 'predictability' of situations would always be subject to the human factor! The second mistake is the elevation of models of this kind to the level of general theory. When this takes place the value component in theory is inclined to be squeezed out by a technology claiming to possess universal rules but in fact comprising only broad rationalisations and over-rigid assertions. The strength of community work training will not depend so much on the development of a community work theory as on the effective relation of the perspectives and insights of the social science disciplines to real life situations.

Choices

No doubt my own assumptions will have been evident in the comments above, and some may wish to challenge them. The idea that future developments must grow out of present patterns of training can be questioned, as can the suggestion that courses should respond to the wishes of potential students or to the needs expressed by employers. Further, the fundamental proposition that community work should become a separate, specialist field of training and study can be challenged.

One body of opinion at present views the growth of community work courses with concern. Tom Woolley, in Scotland, has written a number of papers which stress the danger of outside intervention implicit in community work. He sees well-intentioned outsiders as part of the system which imposes middle class 'solutions' on working class communities and detects a tendency for those intervening to identify much more closely with the authorities than with ordinary people. Some useful contributions are made by such intervention, he agrees, but in the majority of cases more harm than good is done.[12] In Woolley's view, community work constitutes one more way in which the system absorbs 'progressive developments' without allowing them to present a serious threat. Gerald Popplestone is equally dubious about 'orthodox' community work thinking. He asserts, 'from an unashamedly conflict view of social relations', that 'the more clearly conflictual process of local groups opposing council decision-making bodies and thereby making explicit the clashes of interest between bureaucracies and local neighbourhoods is . . . unlikely to happen in an emerging profession'.[13] While this view is very relevant as comment on some of the areas of involvement of community workers, it runs the danger of becoming a plea for an army of correctly motivated interventionists who will protect communities from less enlightened intervention. But assuming there are some valuable lessons to be learnt from the 'power to the people' lobby, the implication for training might be that instead of turning out an elite group of community workers, it should be offering facilities to local leaders. Rather than continuing to offer 'balanced' courses, it should be concentrating on imparting practical information and insights to as wide a range of people as possible, focusing perhaps on the techniques of 'community defence against bureaucratic aggression'![14] The main growth points, according to this view, should be short courses of a non-academic nature and adult education activities. Study of community work in higher education contexts could still be seen as important but would not be regarded as training, and the roles currently adopted by the community worker should be redefined more modestly.

Another, very different, viewpoint which expresses concern with current developments is that which asserts that community work in Britain has become too engrossed in neighbourhood activity to the relative exclusion of 'change agent functions' at other levels within and between agencies. Some who feel this way suggest that community work training in its present form is missing the mark. Rather than preparing specialist community workers, it should be offering more in-service training for a variety of people designed to increase their awareness of the community work dimension of their own work.[15] Courses on community work in some professional training programmes and in-service courses for senior staff are tackling this aspect of work, but it is doubtful whether, now and in the future, they can deal with the issues sufficiently deeply to have more than a marginal influence on practice.

The lesson to be learnt from these two critical viewpoints is that community work training should not get carried away by its own momentum and thereby lose contact with the purposes it should be fulfilling. To some extent training exercises a formative influence on general thinking and its growth may be seen partly as a cause of the increase in community work appointments as well as a result of it. Bearing this in mind it should be at least as concerned with emphasising the roles of local people on the one hand and existing agency personnel on the other as with providing opportunities for students to study to become full-time, specialist community workers.

Conclusions

Will developments in training take any dramatic moves in the future? It seems certain that considerable diversity will remain a characteristic of community work courses despite the requirements of grant-aiding bodies, financing agencies and validation and recognition procedures. General thinking about change is always inclined to drift, whilst voices will always be found to champion dogmatic approaches, and certain people were born to try to be all things to all men, and will continue the attempt to please both employers and students by some kind of detente. Prescription for the future might take the same form as descriptions of the present state of affairs – flexibility must remain, there must be an openness to change, there is a role for a wide variety of approaches and dialogue between adherents of alternative views must be maintained. For those who regard such statements as escapist rationalisations there is a challenge to clarify the position without placing trainers and practitioners in a strait-jacket. So long as debate, diversity and disagreement continue it is certain that community work training is alive. If logic, tidiness and formulas take over, that fact will be less evident!

Notes

1 Calouste Gulbenkian Foundation, *Community Work and Social Change*, Longman, 1968.
2 Lord Boyle of Handsworth, E. A. O. G. Wedell and Dame Eileen Younghusband, *Current Issues in Community Work*, Routledge & Kegan Paul, 1973.
3 For example: 'Community work is essentially concerned with affecting the course of social change through the two processes of analysing social situations and forming relationships with different groups to bring about some desirable change' (p. 4) or 'the essential purpose of all community work is to enable people to play a more effective part in social affairs' (p. 143).

4 This criticism is levelled at orthodox American community organisation courses in the fact sheet on Saul Alinsky's Chicago-based Industrial Areas Foundation Training Institute.

5 For literature on this approach see Murray G. Ross and Ben W. Lappin, *Community Organisation – Theory and Principles*, Harper & Row, 1967; the writings of T. R. Batten, D. Brokensha and P. Hodge, *Community Development: An Interpretation*, San Francisco, Chandler Pub. Co., 1969.

6 Irwin Epstein, 'Specialization, professionalization and social worker radicalism', *Applied Social Studies*, 2, 1970, pp. 155–63, and 'Professional role orientations and conflict strategies', *Social Work* (USA), 15 (4), 1970, pp. 87–92.

7 A valuable categorisation of skills is provided in 'A Report to the Curriculum Committee Regarding the Class and Field Teaching of Community Organizers', Columbia University (undated). This lists five areas of skill: (a) relationship or engagement skills, (b) organisational or group management skills, (c) analytic skills, (d) strategic or political skills, (e) administrative skills.

8 J. Rothman and W. Jones, *A New Look at Field Instruction*, New York, Association Press, 1971, p. 46.

9 A. Gurin, *Community Organization Curriculum in Graduate Social Work Education: Report and Recommendations*, New York, Council on Social Work Education, 1970. Gurin outlines foundation areas and practice areas to be included in courses.

10 J. Rothman, 'Three models of community organization practice', in F. M. Cox *et al.* (eds), *Strategies of Community Organization: A Book of Readings*, Itasca, Ill., F. E. Peacock, 1970, pp. 24–5.

11 I. Spergel, *Community Problem Solving – The Delinquency Example*, University of Chicago Press, 1969, chapter 2.

12 T. Woolley, 'The politics of community action' (duplicated notes of a paper presented in Edinburgh on 5 December 1970). He has developed his views in a further paper entitled 'The politics of intervention' dated 5 March 1972.

13 G. Popplestone, 'The ideology of professional community workers', *British Journal of Social Work*, 1 (1), April 1971, pp. 85–104.

14 A recent publication arising from a series of articles in the *Sunday Times* Magazine by Antony Jay is entitled *The Householder's Guide to Community Defence Against Bureaucratic Aggression*, Cape, 1972.

15 The first Gulbenkian Report considered and rejected this view on the grounds that only if community work is a function exercised in its own right will it manifest its potential value (pp. 27–8).

15 Community work experience in social work training

Peter Baldock

While there has been a welcome expansion in specialised training in community work since the publication of the first Gulbenkian Report, a good deal of the initiative still rests with two relatively well established professions with a subsidiary interest in community work – the youth service and social work. In particular, social work has access to financial resources for field-work training in community work which, while limited, might still be looked upon with some envy by tutors on Community Development and Youth and Community Work Courses. One example of this is that the Central Council for Education and Training in Social Work is at present using money provided by the DHSS to support half a dozen Student Units in Settlements and Councils of Social Service which provide field-work experience wholly or partly in community work for students from local professional social work courses. Besides this sort of resource, social work also has a background of serious consideration given to the problems of supervision of students in a field-work situation. Because a number of issues are raised concerning the relationship of community work to social casework and appropriate forms of training for community work, current experience in community work placements in social work training should be a matter of concern to many community workers and especially those operating from what are essentially social work agencies.

The comments in this article are based on the first year's experience of the Student Unit at the Manchester and Salford Council of Social Service, one of the two such Units providing experience purely in community work. As supervisor I have worked mainly in three local authority wards forming the north-eastern sector of Manchester's inner city which is at the moment in process of redevelopment. Most of my students have also worked in that area though some have worked elsewhere. Each student has usually been given one major piece of work to do on placement (sometimes in co-operation with another student or worker) and altogether fifteen 'projects' were carried out or initiated in

229

the first year of the Unit. While it is difficult to categorise the work simply, one project was principally concerned with a neighbourhood care scheme, two were mainly concerned with establishing new services, six with 'social activities' and six with neighbourhood organisations seeking redress of grievances from the local authority and others. Relations with the courses have been close and useful within the limits sometimes set by distance; students come too from Sheffield and Liverpool. In particular, I have been involved in a small amount of teaching and the planning of community work content with the Certificate of Qualification in Social Work courses at Manchester Polytechnic from which more than half the students came.

As most of the students come from casework-oriented social work courses and intended to return to local authority casework after training, the whole issue of the place of community work in social work has been raised. It is beyond the point of this article to discuss this general issue, but I feel that some light can be shed on it by discussing the possible functions of community work placements for social work students.

Some would say there is none. At the Day Study Consultation on Supervision in Community Work Placements held in London in March 1972 Gerry Williams strongly questioned whether it was worth while sending social work students on community work placements in terms of the usefulness of such an experience to casework and the usefulness of developing community work in Social Services Departments. I accept many of the points he made on confused thinking in the social work profession about the place of community work in training and practice. But I believe that, given adequate planning and supervision, community work placements can be more useful for social work students than the alternatives Gerry Williams suggested (with tongue in cheek presumably) – working in Woolworths or a factory for six months.[1]

That any experience of relationships is potentially valuable to a social worker goes without saying. Where a well-organised community work placement differs from other sustained contact with 'ordinary people' is, first, in supervision (an issue to which I shall return), and, second, in its relatedness to the normal activity of the local authority caseworker. Stated in the most general terms, the functions of casework and community work are similar. But the work situation is different. Students on community work placements who have started courses after serving for some time in highly structured settings often find it very unsettling to be in an informally conducted office and to be dealing with both 'clients' and officials without the protection of a clearly defined professional role and status. Exposure to this situation can reveal a number of things to the students about themselves – to the more conservative the extent to which they are dependent on this protection in ways that could hinder their attempts to help, to the more radical the fact that the absence of authority structure and 'labelling' does not remove all problems from the relationship with 'clients'. For both it offers a new type of relationship with those who might be casework 'clients'.

One aspect of this is the emergence of 'cases' from community work situations in which students are involved. It is a fairly common experience for community workers to be approached for help with individual problems. This may be to 'try them out'. Alternatively, the 'client' may be ignorant of the available agencies, or not trust them, or he may wish to involve a second 'official' as 'insurance' that something will be done, or may not want to admit a problem 'officially' by self-referral to, say, Marriage Guidance (since it is not only radical sociologists who are concerned about labelling). Several of my students have had 'cases' arising from their work. Most of these were relatively simple ones of isolated old people or of people not receiving benefits or services to which they were entitled. Some were more complex. These were usually referred on because of the time problem. But sometimes they were too intricately related to the community work project for that to be viable. One student who had had a fair amount of experience in child care worked with a semi-organised group of young teenagers on a council estate. The leaders of this group were approaching a double climax. On the one hand they were expecting a local authority decision about the provision of premises for their group and, on the other, they were awaiting a court hearing that could have led to sentences to Borstal training for them. The student worked with them on both these problems and had some contact with their families also. The project might equally well have been labelled community work, casework, or detached youth work. Another example arose from work by a student in a depressed tenement block where play-space was an issue. After the student had put in a lot of groundwork this issue blew up with the death of a child on the near-by railway line, the playground for most children. The bereaved mother became the focal point of a protest and to a large extent was helped in her grief by neighbourhood support and the focus of aggression against the local authority and British Rail. Support given by the student in this situation was obviously of a very different nature from that provided by, say, a Medical Social Worker for a similar problem in a hospital setting.

Students have found it useful to consider how social workers help people with individual problems in the light of this experience of dealing with people who have not been referred in one of the usual ways. It can assist them to examine their attitudes to the ethics and techniques of casework intervention and their use of authority in the casework relationship. This can be one of the major functions of community fieldwork experience for trainee social workers.

A second lies in the possibility of increasing their skills in dealing with groups. The study of group processes should provide a major focus for a well-organised placement. Caseworkers are being urged to make more use of group resources, if only in family casework, but many of them have had only limited opportunities to develop group work skills. Of course, many of the groups with which community workers are concerned, such as committees of tenants' associations, are rather different from those with which caseworkers normally deal. But many community groups, such as mothers' groups built around their children's play activities, may have a latent function similar to that of an institutionalised therapeutic group even if their problems are less glaring than those of prisoners or psychiatric patients. And in some aspects of work subsidiary to casework, such as liaising with self-directed volunteers' groups, social workers may use skills closely related to those of the community worker.

A third function is to introduce the student to further resources available to clients, including informal and formal neighbourhood groups as well as smaller voluntary agencies providing various specialist services. In the example of the bereaved mother cited above, useful neighbourhood support was spontaneously forthcoming. In other cases it might be slower or more problematic in some way and this would create difficulties if the social worker was not certain of what he was doing in such a situation in relation to general principles or that particular neighbourhood. By and large, skill in dealing with such situations is more likely to be developed on placement in community work rather than in casework agencies. Formal neighbourhood groups also tend to be underrated by social workers. Work on placement with neighbourhood care schemes can break down the notion that volunteers must be people recruited by a social work agency and operating within its setting. And, while caseworkers may be more aware of actual agencies, their use of them may be inhibited by ignorance compounded by prejudiced views of voluntary organisations. It is fairly common, for example, for caseworkers to refer Asians when there are language difficulties to Community Relations Officers. This relationship might be much more fruitful if the caseworker had had substantial contact with Community Relations on placement beforehand and greater knowledge of and sympathy with their functions and objectives.

Finally, the placement can serve as an introduction to community work and one that will probably be more thorough and effective than that which most professional social work courses are able to offer their own students. Social Services Departments, and to a lesser extent other social work agencies, are becoming a major growth point for the employment of community workers and, in the absence of any other potential large-scale employers (apart from local education authorities), this trend seems likely to continue. In this case, it is of value for social workers in their training to become acquainted with the community work scene and learn something of the objectives, skills and strategies open to specialists in the field.

In the longer term it may be that social workers in the Social Services Departments particularly, will turn to community work methods to deal with certain situations originally brought to their attention through case referrals. There are already several instances of this. At the present moment, with the additional referrals brought about by the Children and Young Persons Act and the Chronically Sick and Disabled Persons Act, and with the reorganisation into Social Services Departments and impending reorganisation with local government reform, the administrative structure of most Departments is hardly geared to enabling their social workers to undertake this sort of initiative. But the decentralisation recommended in Seebohm would facilitate such intervention and many Departments hope to move in this direction.

The last few sentences apart, the functions of community field-work experience for social workers that I have outlined all presume that one is not training them for community work. It is all very well to define the functions of the placements in this way, but this does make them rather different from the standard casework placement. This becomes clear when one attempts to define criteria for assessment, for one is judging the students strictly speaking neither as caseworkers nor as community workers.

Ideally, either all students should have community work placements or the principles on which it is decided who should have them or not should be clearly laid down. If one were to opt for community placements to be universal in social work training then one would presumably have to extend the courses in time and resources to allow adequate treatment of both the community work and casework approaches. The logical extension of the alternative would be to build a designed community work option in to at least some of the courses or to have post-training courses in community work, in much the same way as there are opportunities for social workers to take additional training for work with the deaf.

In the meantime the problem remains that social work students are doing main placements (two or three days a week for three to six months usually) in community work which are not always fully integrated with the rest of their training. There are difficulties in this situation, but there are ways of coping with these difficulties in a constructive manner.

In the first place the placement has to be organised and the work selected for the student chosen with careful regard to the time he can bring to his placement and to his needs as a student. Both these problems exist also for those organising casework placements and, while the situations do differ in some respects, the experience of social workers in supervision can offer some useful guidelines here.

The issue of time is problematic as a student can only offer a few specified days a week for a period that has a defined end date. Except when they have been very lucky, most students have found that they have had time on their hands at the beginning of a placement, which has led to boredom and an apprehension that they might not be working well, and a period of hectic activity at the end. Some have had the demoralising experience of finishing just as a crisis has started to break out (though this may, of course, suggest a failure on the student's part). There are limits to the extent to which one can foresee such eventualities. But there are lines of approach to the problem of organising manpower. The field-work supervisor may need to extend his area of work to provide opportunities for students. The students need to have projects with fairly clear provisional objectives even if these are later dropped as other needs in the area emerge as important to the residents. In undertaking projects, students may have to force the pace in ways that one might not if one person were working in a neighbourhood over a long period. I do not mean that the student should be directive or inflexible, but that agitational devices, such as conducting surveys whose function is as much to impel people to action as to obtain information, may be employed. Another pace-forcing device might be to have students or students and workers operating in teams. This would complicate the process of supervision and assessment as it is normally understood, but possibly to the good. The worker must be able to assure continuity of support where necessary even where the need is not anticipated. Finally it should be possible to reach a situation in a couple of years in which the leaders of the groups with which the agency is working are sufficiently sophisticated to appreciate the needs and potential helpfulness of students and play a full part in deciding which students should work in their areas and with what roles. This might be one of the disturbing aspects of the placement for students used to operating with a degree of authority. It should help them examine the notion of 'professionalism' in social work as the client/ practitioner relationship is nearer in such a case to that in, say, medicine or law in so far as the 'client' is requesting services whose general nature he understands.

Relating the project to the student's needs is a more complex matter, as the student has to begin work early before a full assessment of his needs is possible and it is often difficult to anticipate how a project will develop. If only for reasons of morale, the student should have as much choice as possible and, where possible, should work with the sorts of people he is likely to deal with later as casework clients. The point made earlier about team work can also be raised in relation to students' needs. The social work literature on supervision lays great stress on 'sitting with Nellie' as a method of field-work learning because it provides the student with a 'professional model'. Without commenting on that suggestion, I feel that it is useful for an anxious student to work in close co-operation with workers or more confident students to persuade him of the feasibility of some of the methods of making contact that have been put to him and give him a sense of security in attempting them himself.

If a placement must be organised it must also be seen to be by the student. It is easy for the supervisor who is familiar with his field to underestimate the possible uncertainties of the student. Agency administration, objectives and techniques all need to be explained clearly. To provide some students with self-assurance it may be necessary to be more directive in the initial stages than some community workers may find comfortable. This may be the only way of ensuring that they will begin to make their own decisions. It is also necessary to explore the assumptions the student is bringing to the work on the objectives of community work or social behaviour of people in the type of area in which he is working, as these may be so inaccurate that it may not otherwise occur to the worker that anyone could hold them.

Exploring some of the student's assumptions should bring home to the supervisor how ignorant the student is in certain areas. This may come as a surprise. The student may well be a mature person of evident ability with some years' experience as an untrained social worker. The supervisor may have received little or no training directly for the work he is doing as a community worker. He may, therefore, overrate the student's knowledge and underrate the extent to which he himself has a systematic knowledge of the field that can be formally taught.

Social work students, especially those in the early stages of their course, tend to be ignorant of three general areas which are relevant to community fieldwork – community work itself (including not only principles, but also such basic information as the types of employing agencies), group dynamics, and certain areas of social administration (in particular planning) and sociology (in particular urban sociology and race relations). Courses and individual students will vary, but these are the areas where, generally speaking, difficulties arise. In order that the student can do his work properly and learn from the placement, the supervisor must teach many of the skills that he has at his disposal from the sheer mechanics of such things as public meetings, through an understanding of groups and personalities, through social and political analysis, to the consideration of ethics and fundamental objectives. It is the day-to-day matters which may require a greater and more conscious effort for the teaching. Students can be surprisingly uncertain about the forms that meetings can take and the sort of problems likely to arise at them. It is always useful to go over the possibilities in detail before any event in which a student is to play a major part. Quite apart from any information he may gain from such a session, it should also leave the student with greater confidence that he knows what he is doing. Group processes may also be something the experienced worker takes for granted, not appreciating how much he knows and the student does not about, for example, the nature of intra-group tensions and the ways in which they can derive from the group members' uncertainty about the group's function and identity as well as from personality clashes.

A good deal of teaching can be done through recording and the discussion of records. Here again is a difficult area for some community workers. Neighbourhood workers in particular are likely to be dealing with a limited number of people (and thus not need records as memoranda) and to be working with them on very friendly terms (and therefore find it difficult to write about them analytically). Given this sort of situation, a community worker may be inclined to dismiss record-keeping as a bureaucratic encumbrance. Whatever the validity of such a viewpoint for the worker, the fact remains that record-keeping has considerable educational value for the students as a discipline enabling them to clarify their ideas.

Besides day-to-day records there are three types it is useful for the student to make and discuss with others in the agency. It is helpful if at an early stage of his placement the student writes up a description of the area in which and the groups with which he is working. The basic format used for such reports in the Social Administration Department at Swansea,[2] which is outlined in Professor Leaper's book on community work, can be adapted for particular circumstances.[3] Occasionally a student may find it useful to analyse an event, such as a demonstration, playgroup session or committee meeting, in which he took part. Such a detailed 'process' recording should offer, not only a narrative account, but also information on the extent to which the session achieved its purpose, the feeling in the group, the contributions made to success or failure by individuals participating, including the student, and the lines of action that suggest themselves for the immediate future. A third and most important form of record is the final report by the student evaluating the project in which he has been involved. Evaluation is still at a fairly primitive level in community work and of necessity it will always be highly subjective. Recognising this, one can still be systematic. Such a report should start with an analysis of the objectives. It should then describe what happened, laying stress on the student's own role and defining as precisely as possible who was helped or not helped and in what ways. Those who were helped might include those who originally requested the intervention, local leaders who acquired new skills, local people who received new services and people helped with individual problems. Any conflicts of interest should be analysed. Failures and limitations should be described as carefully as achievements. And the report should conclude with suggestions on future needs and agency action.

A major issue as far as supervision itself is concerned is the nature of the student/supervisor relationship. Anyone with any acquaintance with professional casework knows a couple of more or less true horror stories about supervisors who have endeavoured to discover the nature of their students' relationships with their mothers or ascribed any difference of opinion to 'blocking' on the students' part. One sometimes hears it suggested that it is natural in a casework agency for the student's feelings to be explored, because the aim of the placement is to give him insight into himself, but that in a community work setting it is more natural to concentrate on social and political relationships and decision-making processes in the local authority. This is dangerous stereotyping. On the one hand, the casework student needs to understand as far as possible the problems and opportunities with which his client is faced, including, say, local housing policy, and, if the student does have emotional difficulties in coping with a case, it may be best to focus his attention on the problem in the situation rather than the problem in himself. On the other hand, in a community work situation a student may find it difficult to cope because of psychological disturbance and, while the best way of dealing with them may be to focus his attention on possible solutions rather than his own psycho-dynamics, it is as well for the supervisor to be aware of and sensitive to the student's feelings.

One such problem has already been mentioned – that of the student with local authority casework experience who finds the relatively un-structured nature of much community work disturbing. Exploration of the student's feelings may be forced on the supervisor here because they are strong enough to prevent the student doing anything. Other prob-lematic feelings which may arise are those of depression and frustration at 'not getting anywhere' in an early part of the placement or at having to leave a situation in mid-air at the end. Both of these can be dealt with to some extent by analysing with the student the necessary rhythm of his project. The student may also have feelings that relate to his ideological commitment. He may be impatient with a tenants' association he feels to be insufficiently militant. Alternatively, if he is on second-ment from a local authority, he may be disturbed to find himself associated with a group that is in conflict with his employers. Such problems can be reduced to intellectual terms to make discussion easier. Others may relate to the student's feelings of incompetence and here straight teaching techniques can help. Or the student may be required to cope with situations of intensive feelings. This may not happen as often as in some casework settings where the clients are facing such crises as death, imprisonment or family breakdown. But there are moments of emotional heat in the life of an association or when a student is rejected, scapegoated, deified or asked to take sides in an internal squabble or is asked for help with individual problems. This is as much the stuff of community work as local power structures.

The last issue facing a supervisor is that of student assessment. Most social work courses provide guidelines for final reports on their students. These usually ask for information on what the student has done and comments on his ability in administration, making relationships, plan-ning his work, relating theory to practice and other such matters. The difficulty with using these is that, as was said before, strictly speaking one is judging the student neither as a caseworker nor as a community worker. Formats supplied by courses can be used and may provide a good starting point, but the community worker needs to be more free with them than the casework supervisor. The important thing to remember is that in the present situation one can assume a degree of ignorance on the part of the examiners without insulting them. Comments should be detailed and self-explanatory to an outsider.

Community workers may be suspicious of the idea of making reports on people. But the report is only partly for the purpose of assessment. It should also be used as a device for helping the course tutors, the student and the supervisor to understand the experience. It is vital that the student should play a full part in the writing of the report and be allowed to submit objections if necessary. He needs this protection against a form of assessment that cannot easily be checked by outsiders. But the student's participation also creates an opportunity to discuss with him what he has been doing and it is often easier to discuss critical areas if one starts with a written document than if there is simply an unstructured conversation.

The objectives of community work placements for social work students and some of the methods for achieving them which have been suggested all imply a good deal of work on the part of the responsible community worker. Not all will feel able or willing to take this on, though in that case it is vital that they do not allow themselves to be bullied into accepting students from course tutors desperate to find placements and subject the students to the frustrations of unplanned field-work. I believe that this is more than a chore. The best students are a useful addition to manpower. There is also an important pay-off in that thinking through problems in order to help a student to learn can save the worker himself from drifting from situation to situation. And it is arguable that community workers as a group have a part to play in helping in the development of social work, though this does not imply any responsibility on the part of any one community worker. It is true that community work could have the same function in relation to other professions. But, with its approach to field-work training, social work offers particularly good opportunities. One would hope that by now the message that community work is not simply 'the third method of social work' would have got through and that community workers, no longer needing to get uptight about that particular issue, could work with social workers on a new basis.

It is not only community workers who can make a contribution. Casework agencies taking students could consider more carefully the opportunities their own work offers for students on placement with them to employ community work methods in dealing with, for example, groups of volunteers or the less pleasant local authority housing estates used for 'difficult tenants'. Courses could not only re-examine the content of their teaching but also their approach to field-work organisation. One way in which they might incorporate community field-work experience and give students time to establish themselves in neighbourhoods would be to organise the students into teams that could work on projects throughout the length of their course. There are problems here of increasing the manpower in what is already an area of boom employment and of securing adequate supervision. But the Youth and Community Work course at Manchester Polytechnic has used this form of field-work organisation with a good deal of success and it would be one way of ensuring that all students had some experience in community work.

But the brunt of the work will have to be borne for some time by community workers, many of whom do not themselves have a social work background. I hope that this article will indicate both the problems and the opportunities involved in taking on social work students for field-work training.

References

1 Aberdeen Association of Social Service, 'Supervision in community work placements', report on the Day Study Consultation sponsored by the Joint University Council for Social and Public Administration (Consultative Group on Community Work), 1972.
2 Developed for 'Experimental Training Course in Community Work' run by the National Council of Social Service.
3 R. A. B. Leaper, *Community Work*, National Council of Social Service, 1971.

Part IV Strategies for Change – Two Critiques

Marjorie Mayo

This section marks the break between community development in the traditional sense, as it was developed in predominantly rural, colonised societies, and community development in its predominantly urban context, in industrial societies. Traditionally, community development has been associated with highly generalised and loosely defined goals, such as 'social development', and 'education for citizenship'; in other words, with creating the economic, political and particularly the social and cultural context, within which underdeveloped countries could adopt the model of supposedly 'developed' Western social democratic societies. The contemporary, Western version of community development has arisen, in part at least, out of the critiques of that very model, in the USA and now, also, in Britain, in terms of the rediscovery of poverty and inequality, by liberal academics, and, more dramatically, from the anger and frustration which exploded in the US ghettos in the sixties. Community development, in the War on Poverty, has lost some of its previous appearance of universal acceptability and disengagement, in any but the broadest of social goals; instead, it has become increasingly identified with attempts to meet the needs and aspirations of the more deprived.

Community workers, those employed on government and local authority projects, but others too, are increasingly being driven to recognise and adjust to this shift, to realise that for better or worse, they are part of a process of social change, which is, by definition, also political, in the broadest sense, since it concerns disadvantaged people's claims for a redistribution of resources, rights and power, in their favour. The community worker is thus compelled to abandon his innocence, and to see that he has failed, if he has not assisted and supported his client community in thinking and acting strategically, to move nearer towards meeting that community's needs and aspirations. Hence, the key place of strategies for change, in this volume.

Community development projects are not normally organised for middle-class suburbs. For instance, the Government Project discussed in several chapters is based upon the assumption that the twelve project areas provide examples of communities suffering from multi-deprivation; i.e. that the dice is loaded against them on at least more than one count, whether that be job opportunities, housing, physical environment, health provision, education opportunities or transport and leisure facilities. It is in such an area that the community worker comes under very strong pressures to abandon the stance of supposed neutrality and actual support of the status quo in favour of that of communuity support and, where necessary, advocate.

To do this successfully involves, then, assisting the client community in understanding the sources of its problems and the most appropriate and feasible points for intervention in these. It also involves assisting the community to define itself in such a way that it can build up its own power base, to work constructively with other organisations which wield at least some power, locally and eventually nationally but without being taken over by them, in the process (the tenants' association which becomes no more than an auxiliary of the local trade unions, or voting fodder for a political party). Some of these themes recur, elsewhere in this book, particularly in the final section on conflict and the grass roots.

This section concentrates upon the critique of the institutional response to the present economic, political and social situation, 'the Urban Crisis' in the transatlantic terminology. Both these contributions analyse the recuperative element in official community development experiments; the way in which a fashionable terminology has been applied on a limited and relatively inexpensive, localised basis, whereas the major problems themselves, arising from conflicts of interest which derive from the social structure itself, must remain of necessity beyond their range.

In this situation, then, pilot programmes become ineffective gestures, significant only in as far as they neutralise or deflect the expression of popular aspirations. The consequent frustrations have been bitterly expressed, for instance, by Michael Dummett, who has described in this case, the government community relations structure as 'a confidence trick' relevant only 'as a means of deceiving the general public and as a means of camouflaging the actual voice of the black people in this country.'[1]

As Peter Marris points out, the initial value orientation of the official, sponsoring agency is crucial, in this sense, and, to a considerable degree, sets the limits to the experiment itself and probably to the degree of resistance to its findings.

On the other hand, even community development projects which begin as attempts to rationalise and economise on welfare spending or to provide some form of therapy or control for intransigent 'problem' families or problem areas can have unintended consequences and unplanned room for manœuvre as Peter Marris also suggests. John Benington's chapter concentrates on the hitherto limited manœuvrability at the level of the local authority. Elsewhere in the book, Bob Ashcroft and Keith Jackson demonstrate that the Home Office has been able, whatever their original expectations of CDP, to support the Liverpool Project in its identification with the client community in a struggle against both the local authority and, more significantly still, the government of the day. What is more, the Home Office has tolerated the identification by that community of the particular issue, the Housing Finance Act, in class rather than simply geographical terms; and this has helped the tenants to find support elsewhere in the working-class movement, thereby increasing their strength, rather than limiting it within the geographical terms; and this has helped the tenants to find support elsewhere in the working class movement, thereby increasing their strength, rather than limiting it within the geographical bounds of one depressed ward.

In this sense, the Liverpool Project has broken out of a locality-based definition of community which can be, for deprived areas, as Ray Pahl has commented, 'simply a constraint on the less privileged'.[2] Even the contributions which are most critical of the use of community development techniques and participation as means of neutralising or subverting popular goals (e.g. the chapter by Adah Kay) have also considered areas of manœuvrability where the professional can assist and support the client community. Ultimately, the very fact that it has been possible to popularise the notion of participation and community development is a source of strength as well as of weakness and liability to incorporation. There has been such a widespread and popular reaction against the unequal distribution of resources, power and life-chances, and against the bureaucratisation of official and political institutions which has helped to maintain this state of affairs; and this reaction has, within it, the possibility of further development too, as well as of neutralisation. Although the section on conflict and the grass roots describes elements in this process, its elaboration, in terms of its place in wider strategies for change, must now await a future volume.

There is also a gap in this section on the role of research from the perspective of the community worker in the field. There is therefore insufficient discussion, in this volume, of the role of research in assisting a community in the diagnosis of the underlying causes of its problems (for instance, the flight of capital investment, which has contributed to the economic and social depression of certain key problem regions and sub-areas within regions amongst several of the CDP projects). Nor is there adequate discussion of the role of research in relation to strategic planning, once this initial process of problem identification and analysis has taken place: the point at which the role of research merges with that of the community workers themselves, as a research and development unit of the community in which they work.

References

1 M. Dummett, Background paper for a talk given at the Third Annual Race Relations Conference – Queen Elizabeth College, London, 19–20 September 1968; quoted in M. Hill and R. Issacharoff, *Community Action and Race Relations*, Oxford University Press, 1971 (for the Institute of Race Relations).
2 Ray Pahl, *Patterns of Urban Life*, Longman, 1970, p. 105.

16 Experimenting in social reform

Peter Marris

Twelve years ago, when the Ford Foundation and President Kennedy's Committee on Juvenile Delinquency pioneered their demonstration community projects, they launched a fashion for experimental reform. They believed that any worth-while approach to the problems of poverty and urban decay must depend on changes in schools, social services, employment opportunities, the administration of justice and the provision of housing; that such changes must be co-ordinated, responsive to the people they were designed to help and based on a rational plan of intervention. They framed their projects as experiments partly because they wanted to explore a variety of innovations in the handling of social problems, concentrated in a few specific neighbourhoods, without imposing too many preconceived ideas; but they were also constrained by their resources and their political standing. Neither could claim a mandate to engineer reform. Even with far larger funds than they commanded only a few cities were likely to respond to such a radical approach with much sincerity. The idea of an experiment not only justified selectivity, but legitimised innovation: who can object to finding out, or attack the endeavour before he knows the outcome? To call a reform an experiment postpones the hard questions of political interest while its principles have a chance to take root. Conversely, it allows government to entertain ideas of reform without commitment to them.

When President Johnson adopted community action as a leading strategy of his campaign against poverty, research and experiment were at first less emphasised. He had a large majority and a willing Congress: he was impatient for results. But as community action soured in controversy, political opposition mobilised and hope of generating a national consensus for innovative social reform dwindled away, the concern with experiment revived. The Model Cities programme largely duplicated the aims of community action, but with a renewed emphasis on planning, evaluation and selective grants. A series of dismal assessments of

245

Economic Opportunities Act were commissioned by Federal departments, each attempting to define its researchable achievements in education and vocational advancement. President Nixon sought to return an emasculated Officer of Economic opportunity to an experimental, innovative role. The less successful the attempts at reform were, the more experimentation appealed.

The fashion spread to more and more aspects of government, and it has crossed the Atlantic. The Educational Priority Areas, the Home Office Community Development Projects, the Department of the Environment's Inner City Projects all represent, more or less explicitly, American belief in the value of approaching reform through tentative, imaginative exploration of the possibilities. Like their American counterparts, the British experiments reflect an ambiguous political commitment. They have been promoted partly because government is not ready to spend the much larger amounts of money that would be needed to tackle, wholesale, the problems it knows to exist. And if the experiments can show how, with more imagination, co-operation, rationality and community involvement, present resources might be better used, perhaps the need for more money will not, after all, be so overwhelming. Yet, at the same time, there is little point in experiments unless we are prepared to implement what we can learn from them. They imply a willingness to commit resources later, once a viable approach has been demonstrated. But this commitment is not explicit, and may at any time be very difficult to make. Hence, if the experiments are not to be mere diversions, they must, I think, themselves help to generate that commitment. What they can teach us about the nature and urgency of the problems they explore is as crucial, politically, as their achievements. Conversely, if we misconceive these experiments and ask the wrong kinds of questions, they will be politically as well as intellectually abortive. Especially, I think we risk being misled by an analogy with applied science, which confuses the issues and produces unhelpful conclusions. In this essay, I want to explain first why I believe the analogy to be misleading, and then to suggest another approach.

All the projects I have mentioned share characteristics which distinguish them sharply from scientific experiments, as these are usually understood. They do not set out to test some preconceived hypothesis about the relationship of discrete variables. On the contrary, their only assumption is that most of the identifiable social, economic and political variables are likely to be relevant, and the experiments should take account of these relationships in all their complexity – 'a total approach to the urban problem', as Peter Walker defined the aims of the Inner

City Projects. A spokesman for the Department of the Environment explained their experimental slant in these terms:[1]

> An essential feature of the experiments will be to look at the needs of the areas as a whole from the point of view of the people living there. We naturally hope that they will benefit the areas worked. But the main objective is to provide lessons on the powers, resources and techniques which the Department and local authorities will need to deal with the problems of our inner city areas generally. The evaluation of the work that is to be done will therefore be a particularly important feature of these studies.

This statement, in itself, leaves the approach and method of the experiment very open. But if you put together the insistence on looking at the problems as a whole, on relating this complex pattern of interaction to people's needs, and then translating these insights into an experiment from which government can learn what techniques to apply, it seems to imply a procedure analogous to research and development in engineering. The projects are to derive designs from some theory of interaction; the designs are to be tested; and if they prove successful, they will be reproduced more widely. The design may not be a single prototype of intervention, but it will represent, at least, principles and models which are adaptable to a variety of circumstances.

Some of the American social experiments set out to follow this sequence explicitly – especially the President's Committee on Juvenile Delinquency programme in its early years. Each chosen city was awarded a preliminary planning grant, so that it could develop a design for intervention; and the design had to be justified as a rational application of social science theory. The fundamental causes of juvenile delinquency were to be identified, and the plan of action related to them. The cities which succeeded in this were then to be given a chance to implement their designs. Each design was expected to differ – not, I think, in its underlying theoretical assumptions – but in the way it applied them. The achievements of each were then to be measured and costed. In three or four years, the most successful prototypes of a plan for reducing delinquency could be discriminated and reproduced more widely. This rigorous strategy soon collapsed in compromise and none of the other experimental programmes ever spelled out so exacting a procedure, but they all looked for rational plans which derived from an understanding of the causes of problems, and all sought to promote a range of plans whose achievements could be evaluated against each other, and against more general criteria of efficiency. All assumed that the evaluations would lead to demonstrably useful proposals which could be widely implemented.

In these teims, none of the experiments came off. Few managed even to complete a plan with any coherent theoretical foundation. But it scarcely mattered in practice, because the particular projects undertaken seldom derived from any plan, but were negotiated piecemeal in response to some individual initiative, the available funds, political pressures or the prejudices of sponsors. They tended to be much the same everywhere, and did not exemplify any meaningful pattern of variance. Nor were they ever really tested, because project directors, to the despair of their research teams, altered their practice pragmatically as they went along, without specifying exactly either their aims or their methods. Research tended to withdraw from the confusion of action into more respectable academic pursuits. But, in any case, experiments like pre-school programmes – or indeed community action itself – were adopted as national policy without waiting for the results, and with little regard for refinement. When, later, these national programmes were evaluated, the findings were at once negative and inconclusive. Little seemed to have been achieved, but the measures were so crude, the relevant criteria so arguable, the quality and consistency of practice so uncertain, that the potential value of such innovations is still an open question.

All these disappointments were, I think, inevitable. If we are to learn from American experience, we need to understand why this attempt to treat the projects as experiments in applied social science was so frustrating. At first sight, applied science seems to represent a model of rationality, as appropriate to social as to physical designs. It has, besides, proved enormously productive in industry, where our capacity to innovate has outrun our skill in coping with the social consequences. Why should we not borrow from the techniques of engineering? All the reasons which have led manufacturers to undertake research apply with even more force to social provisions – the scale of necessary investment in the final product, the difficulty and cost of retrieving mistakes once production is launched, the need to co-ordinate projections of the social, economic, technological and political factors that will determine future demand. If it is rational to spend several years developing the design of a motor car, at a cost of millions of pounds, before it goes into production, then surely it is equally rational to test and refine new forms of education, of providing services or urban design before we implement them. Yet the success of research and development in industry depends on a set of assumptions about their context which scarcely ever apply to social planning.

Industrial research and development presupposes that improvement can be routinised within the present structure. If every plausible invention, every original notion of design or new material is explored, the organisation will be able to discriminate those few which are viable by a simple criterion of efficiency. There will be many subordinate criteria of performance, but in the final judgment they can all be assessed against their effect on the long-term profitability of the enterprise. If the level of investment in research is well calculated, no possibility of improvement crucial to the competitiveness of the organisation will escape notice, and the whole cost of research will be justified by the ultimate profits. All this assumes that the cost of testing every promising idea is manageable, that the organisation can readily discriminate and assimilate useful innovations in design without much strain, and that it must do so if it is to survive.

With these assumptions, research and development proceeds from theory to design, and from design to production prototype, until some crucial drawback becomes apparent. For the most part, the theory must be already worked out – otherwise the conceivable lines of enquiry are too many and too long. The endeavour is rather to translate theory into designs, varying and testing models until a workable combination of features evolves. The model must then be redesigned as a reproducible prototype, and costed as a viable product. Finally, it must be evaluated against competing potential uses of the firm's resources.

None of these conditions and assumptions, which make industrial research and development so effective, can generally be reproduced in the field of social policy. In the first place, social improvement cannot be routinised after the manner of a research and development laboratory.

The strategy works in industry, because the range of exploration needed to yield profitable new ideas can be estimated and shown to pay off. But the level of investment in research is crucial: if it is too low, the risk that nothing useful will result becomes serious; if it is too high, the cost undermines the competitiveness of the final product. How can we hope to make a similar calculation for any field of social policy? How great an investment in experimental treatments of delinquency or poverty should we expect to have to make, before we discover one useful approach? How wide is the range of possibilities we ought to explore, before we assess the 'best' policy? In practice, I think, such questions only become manageable once the range of choice has already been narrowed by idealism, prejudice, political constraints, budgets –

Kcw

whose assumptions are themselves more crucial and debatable than the issues they define. But even if we could somehow conceive the field of experimental enquiry, we have no frame of reference comparable to competitive advantage by which to judge whether the investment would be worth while. The governments of American cities did, perhaps, believe that their survival was threatened if they could not find better solutions to the problems of poverty and delinquency, but they did not necessarily have to find the most efficient solution. No one could argue with any assurance that a given investment in research and development would be repaid by fiscal relief later. A few experiments scattered through the country might only scratch the surface of the problem. But a clumsy, expensive, ill-thought-out policy, carried out with determination, might work: and if it worked somehow, how much did efficiency matter?

I do not mean to suggest that social experiments can never be justified, only that they cannot be justified as a matter of routine. There is no way of arguing on principle that if a government spends so much on health or education, it should devote a given proportion of that budget to research and experiment. I do not think you can even argue convincingly on general grounds that it should at least spend something on research: for a low level of research runs a high risk of being unproductive, since good ideas are scarce. So it is not self-evident that experimenting with, say, total approaches to urban problems will be worth while. It depends what questions you are trying to answer, from whose point of view: and these issues are themselves controversial. To justify the experiment, you have at the outset to take a stand on questions of value and belief, which commit you to more than the value of experimentation itself.

A social experimenter cannot assume, therefore, as the manufacturer does, that if his ideas are shown to work, they can be assimilated by the structure within which he operates. Social policy cannot avoid questions of power and interest. This surely is the most fundamental flaw in the metaphor of social engineering. There is no single, ultimate criterion of good design, no over-riding common interest comparable to profitability, specific enough to discriminate, to everyone's satisfaction, between plans which affect differently the personal interest of various groups. So even if the plan works, its advocacy is still partisan; its efficiency cannot be meaningfully argued without some ideological commitment. Conversely, the present order which the innovation seeks to change is also an expression of ideology and the balance of interest, and it is unlikely to yield without a struggle. Hence a social experiment must be an act of political persuasion, however rational its procedures: by proving that something will work, and undermining the arguments against its practicality, it is also generating support, publicising an ideal, mobilising and recruiting interests. So, although it seems at first sight as if a government implementing a policy and a firm marketing a product have very similar needs to test and develop prototypes before committing their resources, the context is radically different.

Even if a framework of evaluation could be conceived for experiments with such wide-ranging concerns as those we are discussing, the sequence of steps from theory to design, and design to evaluation and implementation, present intractable difficulties. In the first place, there are no theories of social interaction in society comparable to the theories of natural science; and I suspect that it would be futile to search for them. The factors which determine aggregate social behaviour are very complex, and it seems inherently improbable that any particular constellation of factors will remain stable for long. Hence any pattern of relationship that we can perceive and act upon, as a theoretical basis for intervention, is likely to be ephemeral. So, for instance, the relationship between levels of employment and rates of inflation seems only to hold, so long as many other features of the labour market remain constant. At best, I think, social science can point to probabilistic relationships which recur in particular kinds of society in a given historical context; or to more abstract relationships which hold for artificially simplified models of interaction; or to the nature of the relationships which have determined a particular event. But none of these insights provides a secure basis for inference about the performance of a social design, because their predictions have so wide a margin of indeterminacy. The value of theory is largely negative – to expose the fallacies in prevailing misconceptions of causal relationships.

If the community action projects were to proceed as experiments in applied science, they would have needed some theory of the way multiple causes of deprivation reacted upon each other, which was specific enough to determine a strategy of intervention. They did, in fact, try to find such theoretical grounding in the notion of a poverty cycle, and in the tendency of all bureaucratic institutions towards malfunctioning rigidity. But these were little more than restatements of the original assumptions, that poverty had many related causes, and that this relationship was not taken account of in the division of institutional functions. To get from this general sense of where the problems lay to specific interventions required a leap of entrepreneurial imagination. The design of a social experiment can never, I think, depend only on analytic skills, but on creativeness, compassion, wisdom, courage and faith. At the same time, because the design is partly intuitive, its aim and method cannot be very rigidly specified. This compounds the difficulty of assessing the outcome.

Even if you take their theoretical justification for granted, and postpone all the ideological issues, the achievements of a social intervention are still very difficult to prove. Suppose, for instance, that you are seeking to test the value of a pre-school project: the ultimate purpose is to rescue the children in the project from a future of poverty, by preparing them better for the early years of schooling. Since this outcome is too remote, you must necessarily devise some interim measure: but what the relevant measure is, and when you should make it, are not at all obvious. Is it the performance in first grade? The child's attitude towards school? The responsiveness of its teachers? The quality of structured or unstructured learning? If the experiment seems to fail on all such counts, can you be sure that it was ever carried out as the design intended, or that benefits will not appear later? If it seems to succeed, was it the experiment or the concern it expressed which made the difference – the idea or the money? And how do you determine how sensitive the outcome was to particular aspects of the design: would it have failed with a less exceptional teacher? Succeeded with a nine months' programme instead of six? None of these questions is unanswerable in principle. But to answer them in practice requires a strictness of control, a consistency of method, a sustained systematic variance of design, a willingness to admit failure and to impose on children activities which you expect to fail, an inventiveness in devising measures and commitment to sustained enquiry over many years which are almost impossible to provide. For the most part, the elements of any social experiment are too variable, the time required for each experimental test to mature too long, and the limits within which it is either ethical or politically tolerable to treat people as in a laboratory too narrow, to attempt a rigorous evaluation.

Thus neither of the first two steps in a sequence of applied engineering research – from theory to design, and from design to the testing of prototypes – has a realistic social counterpart. The final step, from prototype to production strategy, is even less comparable, for the reasons we have already discussed: there are no uncontroversial criteria of cost and benefit by which to determine the priority of social policies at large. Hence the engineering metaphor is altogether misleading. The assumptions and procedures of technological research and development are both inapplicable to issues of social policy. The promoters of experimental community planning might protest that they never held such illusions: but it seems to me that they often set up their experiments and justified them as if they did. In practice, at least, the tendency to apply a limited range of very similar projects – such as pre-school programmes, vocational training schemes, multi-service centres, legal aid services – which became adopted as national policy; and the emphasis of research on measuring their achievements, imply that the experiments were intended to develop prototypes of generally applicable policies from a theoretical base.

Not that reasonably rigorous social experiments, with measurable outcomes, are impossible. If a government is already committed to a policy, and wants to know which alternative design for its implementation would be best, the questions may be contained within a framework specific enough for systematic experimental testing. Or if the question is narrow enough, it may be amenable to conventional experimental procedures. The recent American experiment with negative income tax, for instance, was to provide a definite answer to a specific question. But the conditions which enabled it to succeed as well as it did are very different from the circumstances and aims of experimental social planning. It shows, I think, how costly a rigorous scientific methodology tends to be, and how little in the end may be learned from it, when the issues concern social policy.

The negative income tax experiment was designed to clarify a specific issue: 'given a guaranteed annual income, how much, if any, would recipients reduce their work effort?'[2] About 1,300 families of 'working poor' in five cities of New Jersey and Pennsylvania, all intact families with able-bodied males between the age of eighteen and fifty-eight who were either in the labour force or physically capable of entering it, were selected. The families were divided into an experimental and control group; and the experimental group assigned to one of eight negative tax plans. These plans varied systematically the guaranteed level of income, and the rate at which the supplement was reduced as earnings rose. Some families were guaranteed an income of $1,650 a year, some $2,475, others of $3,300 or $4,125; and the rate at which this guaranteed support was reduced as total income exceeded it might be 30, 50 or 70 per cent of the value of additional earnings. All the families were required to report their income regularly, and they were interviewed every three months, over three years, about 'participation in the labor force, financial status, medical and educational histories, family structure and political and social integration'. But the crucial measure was weekly earnings: did the experimental group (seduced into idleness, perhaps, by the benevolence of the state) earn less than the control group by their own efforts?

The experiment was deliberately conceived to replicate the procedures of science.

> A social experiment as we view it has the same general design as an experiment in the natural sciences. One undertakes to identify the experimental population, then to change one of the variables affecting its behavior and finally to compare its subsequent behavior with that of a control population in which the variable has not been changed. If the experiment is well designed, the investigator can attribute any difference in the behavior of the experimental population to the stimulus. The question we faced was whether or not this approach would work when the population consisted of human beings, when the laboratory was the community and when the stimulus was a complex new social program.

One crucial feature of this experiment, however, is very uncharacteristic of natural science. It was almost certainly designed to *disprove* an inherently implausible hypothesis. I do not think anyone who had read the sociological literature on the satisfactions of work would suppose that people worked only for money, or that they would lose interest in increasing their incomes because they were guaranteed a living above the poverty line. But in a country where moral prejudice against welfare handouts is still politically influential, it may be important to demonstrate that negative income tax does not sap the spirit of self-reliance. Hence, I think, the main value of the experiment was propagandist – to undermine the plausibility of traditional puritan arguments against helping the poor. And since its purpose was negative, it did not need to explain a relationship, or justify the explanation in terms of any theory: it had only to prove that the relationship did not exist. In this it succeeded, more or less: the figures showed only a small difference between the experiment and control groups and these were predominantly in the secondary sources of income of the family. But since New Jersey liberalised its welfare regulations in the course of the experiment and those who improved their incomes above the level of support tended to stop reporting their circumstances, the findings were, as so often, contaminated by the reluctance of life to conform to the rules of a laboratory. In any case, the experiment seems to add little to our understanding: it can only speculatively explain the difference it did find, and so cannot interpret its policy implications. To be fair, the complete data of the experiment may well provide many useful insights into the patterns of low-paid employment, the constraints under which people seek work and the effect of negative tax on their freedom to explore the labour market. But the policy implications of such findings cannot be inferred from the experimental design, which gains its precision from much narrower terms of reference.

Experiments like this might still be worth while whenever government has decided broadly on a policy, but wants to explore what combination of possible arrangements would best satisfy its specific aims, or best protect it from some undesirable consequence. But the experiments in community action and social planning we have been discussing are not like this at all: they are designed to develop policies with very broad aims. They were intended, essentially, to grasp the complexity of social interaction, concerting the variety of purposes and interests within a plan which integrates a wide range of interventions. In what sense, if any, is such an endeavour open to experiment? If it is not like natural science, seeking to confirm some hypothesis about discrete relationships; nor, like engineering, seeking to develop a profitable design; if it cannot assume either the theoretical context or the reductive utilitarianism which make research and development predictably valuable, what questions can an experimental approach usefully answer?

The desire to experiment in social planning arises, I think, from a genuine uncertainty. We know that any intervention in the social system is likely to have widespread repercussions, and we cannot avoid intervening if we want to control our future. But our political and administrative institutions are very ill adapted to integrated planning. The bureaucracy is characteristically compartmented, and trained in a tradition of departmental rivalry. Its functions are co-ordinated, if at all, only at a highly centralised political level, which jealously guards its policy prerogatives. Yet this political authority is only representative of people's interest in the arbitrary sense that a majority of voters prefer this leadership to another. Hence the channels for exchanging information and arbitrating interests are very poorly developed: and these are crucial to any democratic process of planning. The problem arises at every level of government, from the devising of a national policy towards inflation to the redevelopment of a neighbourhood. How can we bring into the debate all the interests affected by the decision, arbitrate between them fairly, recognise those conflicts which we cannot and perhaps should not attempt to resolve, and spell out the implications of the decisions so that one kind of intervention does not continually frustrate the aims of another? I do not believe any government, however partisan its prejudices, can evade this issue: for if it cannot find a way to institute such a process, its plans will be both incoherent and unenforceable in the long run. But we do not know how to evolve a process of this kind. In this sense, the Prime Minister's discussions with the CBI and the TUC on a prices and incomes policy, the introduction of structure planning into local government, the Seebohm Committee's restructuring of the social services are all experiments – a groping after co-ordination and responsiveness which we have never yet achieved.

The American community action and model cities programmes, the Home Office community development projects, the inner city projects are all essentially concerned with these issues. How can government be made more sensitive to people's needs? How can we disseminate an understanding of the complexity of social interaction and integrate our strategies? At the same time, these experimental projects characteristically lack any powers to change the established institutional structure, and they intervene at a local level, where much of the social and economic structure which determines the life of the community lies beyond their scope. Hence they can only explore the adaptability of our social institutions – the extent to which the established structure is open to new kinds of response, can incorporate new processes of representation and discussion, integrate its functions in more informal and sophisticated ways and tolerate new forms of political pressure. But until we know how open to innovation the present political and administrative system may be, we will not know where or how to reform it. I believe, then, that these experiments are important, because they explore the limits within which the processes of government are malleable. Thus they show not only what can be done, but where the rigidities of the structure are indomitable without more radical changes: and as they discover these obstacles, they generate an understanding of the need for reform and a constituency for it.

It does not matter much, I think, what these experiments try to do – whether to initiate a playgroup, a new school curriculum or a redevelopment plan – so long as whatever happens tests the responsiveness of the governmental structure to new ways of representing people's needs – as they themselves define them – and, at the same time, tests the ability of the structure to comprehend and act upon problems as a whole, irrespective of jurisdictional boundaries. Nor does the value of the experiment depend on achieving success.

For if you can show that however people may organise to articulate their interests, whether by confrontation or accommodation, however you channel new information and interpretation into the councils of government or try to draw its various functions together, the structure cannot assimilate these changes – then you will have shown more clearly what the crucial obstacles are. Such negative findings are not merely evidence for radical polemics. They begin to define more constructively the new rights, functions and institutions which would have to be created to meet these obstacles, and show how they might evolve. In practice, the findings are seldom altogether negative: the community action programmes in America did, in some cities, help to promote a degree of organisation and self-confidence in the ghetto which influenced the political process, and to develop a new recognition of legal right to representation in decisions about planning and welfare. Whether these changes can be sustained and built upon for the benefit of the poor is still very uncertain. Yet, for all the ambiguity of their achievements, and the endless frustrations which beset them, I believe these experiments were valuable, because we understand more now about strategies of change than we would have been likely to discover without them.

Thus the distinctive quality of these experiments in social planning is their attempt to explore the adaptability of the processes of government to two demands: first, that they should bring the people they serve into their councils, as a party to the discussion, negotiation and choice of policies, and second, that they should integrate the functions of government intelligently around problems as a whole. I have tried to show that this diffuse testing of the tolerance for innovative processes cannot be conceived in terms either of an experiment in natural science, or of technological research and development. Once we have seen this clearly, we can see too how to record and analyse the experience.

Research into community action is contemporary political history, interpreted for its relevance to future action. Students sometimes ask, anxiously, what the methodology of such research is. The answer, I think, is straightforward, if not very reassuring: to be everywhere, know everything that happened and how it happened, to record all this – and then, behind the mass of detail and the accidents of personality, to discern the general pattern of issues which determined these events. In many ways, it is more demanding than the interpretation of a scientific experiment, because so little can be taken for granted – neither the way the aims were defined, nor the methods, nor the perceptions of relationships which informed the actions, nor the meaning of the outcomes. And it cannot afford to be any less careful in recording its data. Yet the findings will not have the conclusiveness of a scientific experiment, because there is no single frame of reference by which they must be evaluated. Every indicator used to measure changes itself implies assumptions about relevance, whose political and ideological implications have to be articulated. The interpretation of a scientific experiment may be controversial, but the controversy concerns its validity in terms of the theory which is to prevail. In these social experiments, not only is the validity of the interpretation in question, but its relevance from the point of view of its critics. From the perspective of differing ideologies and interests, the same history reveals different patterns, which are all insights into its meaning, though their implications may be contradictory. Hence the researcher has to decide for whose interest he speaks, and whom he is seeking to influence, while still recognising that the force of his argument depends on the intellectual integrity of his analysis, not his commitment.

This conception of research does not require that the researcher control the experiment. It helps if he can persuade everyone to keep accurate records of their activities and achievements, but the value of the experience, as a source of understanding, does not depend upon adherence to any systematic experimental design. Nor does his own role in the experiment need to be strictly defined, so long as he has access to observe everything that goes on. In principle, he might be as much involved in the activities of the experiment as anyone else, though in practice, I think, no one can be at once a detached, reflective observer, as interests in failure as success, and an energetic schemer. Political memoirs are relentlessly self-justifying – records of consistent statesmanship unaccountably frustrated by the machinations of intriguers. They promise so much, and reveal so little.

So I think it is essential that these experiments recognise research as a distinct role, and unless they are open to close observation, we will not learn much from them. But since any interpretation can only be selective, however perceptive and well informed, no research should be treated as the exclusive account, pre-empting any other enquiry. If the experiments are really interesting, they ought to attract several studies, from varying points of view, more or less integrated with them. And for the same reason all the research must be publishable with the least possible discretion. Above all, I believe, these experiments are propaganda for the importance of the issues they explore, and their final justification, outside the communities where they work, is the quality of the debate they can provoke.

All this will perhaps seem obvious. Yet much effort, ingenuity and money has been wasted in an abortive attempt to impose scientific methodology on community action, and I think we are still confused by a technological metaphor which at once over-elaborates the structure of research, while it forces the findings into a clumsy and insensitive framework of analysis. I have argued for a conception of these experiments which seems to me to describe their nature more relevantly and practicably – though the style of research it implies is intellectually more exacting, and harder to prescribe.

Notes

1 Mr Speed, in an address to the Institute of Municipal Treasurers and Accountants, 9 June 1972.
2 This and the quotations which follow are taken from David N. Kershaw, 'A negative income tax experiment', *Scientific American*, October 1972.

17 Strategies for change at the local level: some reflections

John Benington

Sociologists in search of the meaning of 'community' have so far come up with ninety-four different definitions.[1] Their diffidence has not prevented politicians and professionals from using it as a kind of 'aerosol' word to be sprayed on to deteriorating institutions to deodorise and humanise them. Thus – at a stroke – schools are transformed into community schools, planners into community planners, doctors into community physicians, approved schools into community homes – and paper delivery boys into a communicorps.

When in July 1969 the Home Secretary announced a national Community Development Project (CDP), this too was in danger of being presented as an 'instant' political solution to the problems of local concentrations of multiple deprivation. The early Home Office documents suggested that 'more of the same' was not enough to solve such problems. The new additive to be tried, and monitored, was 'community development'. Which is where the sociologists' dilemmas about definition became more than of academic interest.

To Richard Crossman, then Secretary of State for Social Services (and no doubt to many others also), 'community development' appeared to mean helping lame ducks to stand on their own feet. In announcing the CDP in Coventry he defined the problems of areas like Hillfields in terms of people suffering 'multiple personal hardship or family malfunctioning'. The solutions were seen as lying in self-help and better co-ordination of services at the field level. Community development was here conceived as an alternative form of therapy for intransigent 'problem families': an extension of social work practice from casework to group work within the community.

We found this interpretation of community development inadequate to the situation on two counts. Although labelled as a 'problem area', Hillfields did not emerge as having abnormal concentrations of 'problem families'. Second, the main problems experienced by residents did not appear to arise from personal or family handicap so much as from external factors such as low income, poor housing and environmental stress.

Another current view of community development defined the problems of areas like Hillfields in terms of the fragmentation of local community relationships. The solutions were seen to lie in greater community involvement and public participation. The notion of community development as the regeneration of self-help may be an attractive proposition to governments which have committed less than £1 million to a poverty programme to find solutions to local concentrations of deprivation. But CDP staff have increasingly come to recognise that the word 'community' is often used 'almost as an incantation to conjure up feelings of loyalty to locality among the most geographically mobile people in the world and to bring forth a kind of ectoplasm of inter-generational continuity where actual history has been both brief and fitful. It may even represent a kind of wistful yearning for what we never were and can never be.'[2]

Any assessment of strategies for change via community development must be made in relation to declared objectives. It is important therefore to assert that we have not seen ourselves as concerned with therapeutic group work within the community; nor with the development of local community as an end in itself; nor indeed with the practice of community work as a new (and growingly lucrative) pseudo-professional art. We have taken our general objective from the early description of CDP as 'a concerted search for better solutions to the problems of deprivation than those we now possess . . . including the establishment of more valid and reliable criteria for the allocation of resources to the greatest social benefit'.

Strategies for change must also be assessed in relation to the characteristics of a particular situation. The following profile highlights some of the features we have come to see as important. The general context for the Coventry CDP is one of economic growth. A steady rate of increase in population and in employment up until the end of the century is forecast for the city and for the West Midlands region as a whole. Rates of unemployment in Coventry were among the lowest in the country from 1941 to 1971. Average earnings of men in manual jobs in the Coventry area were the highest in the country as at April 1973 – £58 gross per week compared with a national average of £38 gross.

The political history of the City Council since the war is one which has encouraged progressive management, and a concern to be first in the field with new initiatives. There has been only one break of five years (1967–72) in the Labour control of the Council since the war, and in a real sense the crucial political decision was taken in 1946. The decision to completely rebuild the bombed City Centre in many ways predetermined the priorities for expenditure for the next twenty years. This decision seems to have been taken with an all-party consensus; and once taken it gave the officers a far-reaching mandate to develop and implement a comprehensive plan within very broad parameters. Thus for the last twenty-five years Coventry has provided a unique setting for progressive, and often relatively young, professionals (particularly planners, architects, engineers, solicitors and accountants) to implement their visions with minimum constraints. This has not only contributed to Coventry's pace-setting image, but has often provided a rapid springboard to promotion elsewhere. This has resulted in a series of 'first-ever' achievements but they have sometimes remained as one-off monuments, rather than the foundation for high standards of provision across the board.

The dominant values within the local authority often seem to have been those of professional excellence rather than political choice. The City Council has in effect declared the end of ideology over many areas of decision-making and developed instead a set of managerial values. 'Planning' replaces 'politics' as the basis for major decisions about the long-term distribution of finance, land and manpower.

There is a sense in which the main political energy in the City has gone into the struggle at the work-place. The trade union movement within the motor industry is highly politicised. Coventry is seen not only as the norm for wage-claims throughout the country's engineering industry ('the Coventry tool-room rate') but as the battlefront of a basic ideological struggle. The motor industry in Coventry highlights the vulnerability of a labour force which is dependent upon the profit-seeking of multi-national capital investment.

The *Leitmotifs* for the City since the war have thus been those of economic growth, the affluent worker, embourgeoisement, municipal socialism and pace-making professionalism. I have implied that some of these have become established as civic myths which obscure a very different reality.

During the same period a complementary set of myths developed around Hillfields. Known before the war as a respectable working-class community, the area gradually became stigmatised as the City's black spot, a centre of vice and crime, an area in physical and moral decline. The solutions envisaged by the local authority seemed to be in terms of redevelopment of the physical environment, and community development in the social (and moral?) environment. Our own analysis suggested a quite opposite pattern of cause and effect. The 'decline' of the neighbourhood did not seem to have been precipitated by any significant change in the composition or behaviour of the local population, but by the change in official policy towards the neighbourhood when it was designated a Comprehensive Development Area immediately after the war. The giving of investment priority to reconstruction of the City Centre resulted in twenty years of protracted delay in implementing the redevelopment plan for Hillfields. This created a vicious circle whereby planning blight led to deterioration in the condition of both housing and the environment. Public labelling processes then helped to set in motion a self-fulfilling prophecy in which the area gradually came to be defined as a black spot. This kind of scapegoating focused attention on the locality as the source of inherent problems and shifted attention away from the city-wide processes which had caused those problems. This allowed a dangerous myth to develop that the rest of the city was part of a progressive upward trend – a Phoenix rising gloriously from the ashes of war-time destruction.

An alternative perspective

We saw Hillfields, and neighbourhoods like it, in terms of the competition between different interest-groups in the City (and in the wider economy) for shares of the scarce resources of land, houses, jobs, educational opportunity and the benefits of the welfare state. We argued that their distribution is not governed simply by the market for goods and services, nor even by the political process of resource allocation. Managerial and administrative processes (e.g. land-use planning, procedures for the letting of council houses, the style of delivery of welfare benefits, the form of organisation of schools, etc.) can combine with the wider forces of inequality to bring togther in certain geographical areas those who have been left with the worst share of all the basic resources.

In contrast, local government often seems to act in the belief that the public sector removes resources from the inequalities of the private market, and that its operations are uniform throughout the population. The working assumption often seems to be that 'the community' is homogeneous in its general needs within broad age-groups. At simplest, this tends to result in a degree of insensitivity to cultural and social diversity. To take some mundane examples – the Asian preference for living with the extended family might suggest the provision of eight- to ten-bedroomed houses, or the amalgamation of two or three adjoining terraced houses, rather than the strict application of overcrowding laws. Planning and public health standards suggest that an indoor toilet is a desirable amenity; many people in older property would prefer to keep the extra space inside, and to have a covered walkway to the outside toilet.

The management processes in local and central government are increasingly concerned with planning in the context of the macro-system (the metropolitan region, the sub-region) and of the long-term (ten-year forward plans, five-year rolling programmes). These are important developments but they inevitably tend to focus on the broad grain – on the generality rather than diversity. Furthermore, the process of aggregation tends to reflect the dominant values of ruling elites, rather than a highest common factor among conflicting interests.

However, the problem is not simply one of governmental failure to reflect or respond to a plurality of diverse and conflicting interests within the community. Government actively defines norms for the community, and defines certain categories of people as failing to meet those norms. The notion of 'deprived people' or 'deprived areas' seems to assume a common set of goals and values in society. The focus then turns on the disabilities which supposedly prevent people from consuming the goods and services offered by the welfare state (e.g. 'the problem of take-up of means-tested benefits'; 'the cycle of deprivation'). Questions are less frequently raised about the relevance of the welfare state's goods and services to the goals and values of different sections of the population. When discussion does focus on the delivery of services, it is frequently in terms of increasing the efficiency of administration so that people in need do not slip through the safety-net. The problem is seen as one of improving quality control of services, so that 'unfortunate mistakes' do not occur, rather than as a question about the values implicit in existing provision. There is a sense in which the notions of 'deprivation' and 'poverty' themselves set baselines for the consumer society, and offer support to people in meeting that baseline, without raising discussion about the nature of that consumer society. More relevant concepts are those of 'inequality' and 'disadvantage', which relate to some notion of goals and values.

Project strategy

Within this general perspective, the Coventry Project has fallen into two main phases so far. The first defined the problems in terms of, on the one hand, the powerlessness of disadvantaged people to bargain for the protection of their values and interests; and, on the other hand, the unresponsiveness of the governmental system to their needs and aspirations. This led us to adopt a 'dialogue' model of change: working within the neighbourhood to encourage groups in representing their views; and within the local authority to interpret the demands arising from the grass roots, and to encourage more sensitive and relevant responses. The aim was to gain greater influence for disadvantaged groups on policy-making, and to develop towards structures which would guarantee them a constitutional right at important decision-taking tables.

The second phase developed out of a gradual awareness that this approach represented an over-simple view of power. New perspectives and further data brought by the arrival of the research team led us to see that the problems experienced in Hillfields were not only symptoms of city-wide processes, but were not even peculiar to that neighbourhood. Although the problems had a particular burden for that population, they were the same in kind as those which affected people throughout other parts of Coventry, and indeed the country as a whole (i.e. problems associated with low incomes, poor housing, restricted educational opportunity, old age and so on). The more relevant communities of interest were those of a particular consumer group (e.g. claimants of social security; local authority tenants), and ultimately those of the working class. It was therefore misleading and unrealistic to try to intervene from a local neighbourhood base alone. Clearly a local CDP on its own is not in a position to tackle the ultimate sources of disadvantage in the wider economy or in national government policy. However, national policies are often mediated through local institutions, which sustain or even reinforce the inequalities of the wider economy. Our objective for Phase II thus came to be expressed in the following way: to analyse and attempt to modify the processes within key government agencies which sustain or reinforce disadvantage at the local level.

Within each of these two phases, with their differing emphases, a variety of means of achieving change have been attempted. It is difficult to assess them adequately while still in mid-course; and when we try to do so, both the strategy and the assessment somehow seem very simplistic. This partly reflects the sense of decreasing competence which one is apt to experience in trying to move from abstract analysis to planned strategy, and then to actual intervention in complex processes. But it also reflects the absurdity of the officially-sponsored illusion that small teams of progressive young professionals and social scientists put in positions of inflated status with a seductive budget but with limited executive powers can begin to tackle the problems of areas of multiple-deprivation. Perhaps for this reason it is important not to be over-defensive about the naivety which becomes apparent when the enterprise is assessed. It may be important to debunk the Quixotic illusion of managerial or technical solutions to urban problems, so that the problems can be put back into the context of fundamental inequalities in society; and so that community activists may resist being bemused by the illusion and begin to concentrate on the more limited but tangible contribution that may be possible.

Phase I

Our early work involved trying to mobilise external and internal pressures for change simultaneously. For our own clarity and (we assumed) for that of those we were working with, the internal and external roles were split between different members of the team. However, the neighbourhood worker found that he was regarded as ambiguous by many residents. Knowing that he was an employee of the local authority, with links in central government also, they looked to him to act as a 'fixer' to get things done for them within the bureaucracy. Our commitment to collective action leading to dialogue led him to decline the 'fixer' role, and to encourage them to take action into their own hands. Similarly the local authority sometimes looked to us to act as their 'fixers' within the community system. Both the local authority and the residents were concerned to know 'whose side' we were on. Sophisticated definitions of the role of the community worker as broker or go-between began to seem like professional casuistry. In Peter Marris's terms, we had to choose between acting as agents of established power or of community power.

Indeed, we came to feel that by the mere fact of existence as an agency working within both the neighbourhood and the local authority, we were in danger of acting in the role of a buffer between the two, cushioning the impact of some issues. It was very difficult not to get into the position of 'the interpreter' in the dialogue, and becoming the central channel of communication. This seemed likely to lead to the institutionalisation of a new profession of go-betweens rather than the new decision-making structures that we were after.

Dialogue defused

The whole notion of 'dialogue' came to have a bit of a hollow ring in Hillfields. The evidence began to suggest that dialogue actually deferred getting things done. For over twelve months local action groups negotiated about the problem of derelict houses. Letters were sent to all relevant departments, ward councillors were enlisted, public meetings held, a campaign in the local community newspaper, the Lord Mayor lobbied, the local MP taken on a walkabout in the area. At the other end, the CDP team documented the problem, convened an interdepartmental working-group, submitted reports to the Chief Officers' Board, had meetings with the Department of the Environment in Whitehall and at the regional office. But after more than a year, there was still no visible improvement in the situation. The local authority reported that its hands were tied by legal, financial and administrative constraints.

One night a child got stuck on the roof of a derelict house, and the following night a local adventure playground leader led an angry group of mothers and children down to the Council House and interrupted the council meeting from the public gallery. Although ejected from the Council Chamber, the subsequent publicity on television and in the Press produced an immediate response. The derelict houses in question were boarded up – in spite of legal, financial and administrative constraints. Although the gain was short term, the conclusion that residents drew – quite logically – from their experience was that dialogue does not deliver the goods, and that more blatant agitation is necessary to get results.

A similar disenchantment has been experienced even in those cases where the dialogue has been institutionalised 'as of right'. Following discussions with ourselves, the Education Committee agreed to experiment with a dialogue model for their new nursery centre and play centre. In the case of the nursery centre, the Director of Education invited the parents of all children under five within the catchment area to a public meeting before the Centre was opened. An advisory group of twelve parents was nominated by that meeting; they in turn sent representatives forward to a management committee in which consumers and Councillors each had 50 per cent of the places. This management committee is responsible for policy and so far has selected staff, and made decisions on opening hours, charges and so on.

This structure has given consumers a constitutional right to equal say at the decision-making table. But in practice the balance of power has shifted very little. The formal structure obscures the extent to which politicians and professionals retain control over important decisions. The resident representatives are less familiar with formal committee procedure and probably less adept verbally. The agendas for meetings are prepared in discussion between local authority officers and the Chairman (a councillor). The officers' advice in meetings is very influential. It is probably fair to say that the effect of all this has been to secure consumer consent to a number of decisions in the formal committee; but to some extent to pre-empt the possibility of parents engaging collectively in deeper debate. They have been more successful in influencing decisions in their terms when the Advisory Group has acted as an external pressure group.

The negotiations between the local authority and residents in a pilot General Improvement Area has revealed even more serious limitations in the dialogue model. An interdepartmental team has been formed by the local authority to liaise with the residents' association for the streets concerned. A proposal to close the street to traffic was challenged by a small near-by factory who said they needed turning space for their lorries. The firm is a subsidiary of Chrysler UK and the dialogue in their case was carried out not at the field level, but directly with the senior policy-makers in the authority. It seemed to residents that some interest-groups were able to by-pass the established negotiating structure, and to gain undue influence at another level of debate. A similar inter-pretation was put upon the speed with which a large hotel combine was able to get planning permission to build a staff hostel just next to the GIA. In contrast, the long delays in seeing any action within the GIA were seen by residents as evidence that the dialogue in which they were engaged was a dummy exercise with the real decisions still being influenced by dominant interests.

Community control

Gradual awareness of the risk of this kind of tokenism and co-optation within the dialogue model led us to think much more of community control. We began to explore this in terms of control over finance, man-power and decisions. Grants totalling over £13,000 per annum have been given to a local federation of community groups. This has allowed them to employ two adventure playground workers, an organiser of activities for the elderly and a full-time secretary to provide duplicating and other facilities to residents' associations. They act as sponsors for a shop-front Information and Opinion Centre which is now fully managed, controlled and staffed by local residents. They also sponsor a neighbourhood newspaper, and give 'seed money' to a variety of resident initiatives (playgroups, pensioners' luncheon clubs, and so on). These have all contributed marginally in meeting locally felt needs and in encouraging locally controlled responses. A worth-while side-effect has been the creation of a number of jobs for local residents.

But there have been a number of problems, too. The administration and distribution of a relatively large grant have resulted in a degree of bureaucratisation of the umbrella community association. What began as a federation of action groups has (inevitably perhaps) developed into a kind of holding and co-ordinating body. In order to arbitrate between competing bids for its resources, it has been concerned to be seen as a representative and efficient organisation. This has creamed off a kind of neo-elite of residents who see themselves as concerned with the community as a whole. They have naturally come into tension with those who are concerned with sectional interests, e.g. play needs of young people or social security claimants at the Information and Opinion Centre. In common with other studies, we have found that the universalistic orientation of the community association has attracted the more aspirant people, who are keen to improve the reputation of the neighbourhood and to establish 'responsible' relationships with civic leaders, etc. The Information and Opinion Centre has more particularist concerns in the welfare rights field, and its lower-working-class customers and helpers look for much shorter term solutions and are prepared to use semi-militant tactics to achieve their rights. It is not surprising that the latter has been more effective as an action group (recovering over £1,000 per year in extra payments from the SBC) than the federation of community groups who have had to divert a lot of energy into maintaining their internal consensus.[3]

One of the general features of Phase I was the way in which our notion of power slipped from political and sociological meanings into the softer area of psychology.[4] We began with an analysis of the powerlessness of the disadvantaged in terms of the barriers to the intrusion of their goals and values into decision-making and their lack of access to or control over scarce resources. In practice it was all too easy to settle for how powerful a group *felt* in a particular bargaining encounter. What was lacking at this stage was any analysis of powerlessness in terms of the position of the disadvantaged within the class structure.

Phase II: Social planning for institutional change

As already implied, we came to feel that in Phase I:

a. the dialogue model embodied an inadequate analysis of the distribution of power within the class structure;
b. it did not deliver the goods for residents;
c. our existence as a mediating agency actually served to obscure some of the issues and to cushion out some of the conflicts between residents and the authorities;
d. our engagement in this way at the neighbourhood level colluded with the notion that the problems were somehow peculiar to that geographical black spot;
e. there was pressure upon us to provide solutions from within our own resources, which could only result in small-scale compensatory provision – playgrounds, community newspapers, information centres, etc. – all good in themselves but marginal to the major problems of income and housing experienced by residents.

The alternative strategy we decided to attempt was to hive off neighbourhood work as an independent operation; and to use CDP's special resources to analyse (via theoretical analysis, data collection, participant observation) and attempt to modify (via financial incentives, access to senior policy-makers, and trading on central government and grass-roots pressures) the operations of key government institutions which mediate disadvantage at the local level.

Neighbourhood work has been 'hived off' by

a. grants, with no strings, to community groups;
b. handing over complete management and control of the Information and Opinion Centre to local residents;
c. acting as joint sponsors in the setting up of a Joint Community Work Committee and funding that body to appoint an independent community worker;
d. collaborating with other independent community workers;
e. the appointment of a salaried solicitor to work with residents' groups on community law issues, and the setting up of a Legal and Income Rights Trust.

The creation and support of autonomous counter-agencies of this kind seem to have given a number of opportunities for supporting external pressures for change. However, it is probably true to say that we have taken too little account so far of the existing community power structure. Certainly we have only recently begun to explore the possibilities for keying in to the trade unions and the wider labour movement, or other ways of relating neighbourhood issues to those of the class struggle.

Our attempts to mobilise internal pressures for change have been fairly diverse, and are very much related to the particular position which CDP occupies within central and local government and the leverage which we have found to be available. Strategies within this field are very hard to describe in terms more precise than general 'wheeling and dealing'. However, the following categories of work can be commented on:

Joint programmes: We have found certain agencies with which it is possible to negotiate on the basis of some shared goals. Within the fields of education and social services the current concepts of good practice, as defined by official reports like Plowden and Seebohm, can accommodate notions like disadvantage, positive discrimination and client control. On this basis it has been possible to use our (limited) financial incentives to open up questions about the relevance of existing policies and provision to the goals, values and culture of particular disadvantaged groups. In the case of both the Education and Social Services Departments the process began with groups of field-workers being invited to meet with us to examine the problems; their reports led to the formation of higher-level working parties to look at the policy implications; and eventually to joint programmes being established between ourselves and the department. The programmes are jointly financed, and managed by a joint steering committee, but staff involved form part of the establishment of the parent department.

It is perhaps not surprising that these two major people-processing agencies have responded to our definition of problems in their fields. In some ways they stand to gain from evidence about unmet need because in many cases this will provide ammunition for the appointment of more staff.[5] Our funds have been successful as incentives to redeploy or redirect staff in the field; but less successful in redirecting policy at the centre of the agency or institution. The result may be the acceptance and later institutionalisation of roving catalytic teams as appendages to such agencies, but only limited impact on the central structures or policies of the host agency.

Our financial and other incentives have not been sufficient to induce changes in resource-allocating agencies like Planning and Housing Departments. Because land and housing are much scarcer and higher valued resources, evidence of problems or unmet need is likely to demand some redistribution within existing priorities rather than resulting in increases in absolute resources. The responses required are not primarily in the field (where there is greater plasticity) but involve modifications in the central decision-making structures and have political and inter-organisational implications also.

Consultancies: An alternative strategy attempted where the problems have not yet been defined in terms which can accommodate our goals has been the introduction of outside consultants. The two fields involved so far have been the Youth Employment Service (the problems of transition from school-life to work-life) and Area Improvement Policies for the Inner City. The consultants in each case have been funded 100 per cent by CDP out of a research budget, and the client agency at the beginning was asked only for a commitment to the notion that the problem area we have defined is one worth exploring further.

Experience with these two examples suggests some success in gaining acceptance for a sharper definition of the problem area, and in placing particular new policy choices on the agendas of the authority. In the case of the Youth Employment Service the relationship with the consultants over a period of twelve months generated a fairly strong degree of commitment to the final proposals, although these were quite radical in terms of existing practice. The obvious limitation of commissioning outside consultants as a strategy for institutional change is that it depends upon developing a constituency to support and press for the proposals. In the case of the Area Improvement study, the consultancy relationship was established mainly at senior policy-making levels, which restricted the base for later influence.

Policy debate: The two general strategies mentioned so far have been mostly concerned with the operations of a single discrete agency. In broader fields of policy-making which concern the local authority as a whole, and sometimes involve central government departments also, we have used seminars and discussion papers as a means of introducing alternative perspectives on policy in relation to the disadvantaged. Over a period of time these have helped to extend the parameters of political and professional debate, and perhaps to introduce 'disadvantage' and 'redistribution' as legitimate policy themes. Once again, however, we have probably so far focused too narrowly at the apex of the formal power structure (councillors, chief officers, middle-management) and failed to develop the lateral networks of influence sufficiently (fieldworkers, voluntary agencies, MPs, trade unions).

Furthermore, some of these issues have not yet been established on the agendas of national political and professional debate, and this will often be a prerequisite to change in practice at the local level. We have recognised this in relation to problems in the area of income maintenance in particular. Here we have relied upon a much longer term strategy based upon a historical analysis of the Supplementary Benefits system as being on a knife-edge of political opinion, which would suggest that fundamental critical research could have a strategic influence on future policy in this field.

Not too little, not too much

This strategy points up one of the ironies of the CDP situation. Having a social action budget of £45,000 per annum dangles many tantalising opportunities in front of CDP teams, but may turn out to be one of the most dangerous of our many seductions. It allows us to flirt with – and sometimes to implement – the kind of whimsical scheme which almost justifies A. H. Halsey's description of CDP as 'licensed buffoonery'. More seriously, it arouses expectations within the study area that extra resources are now available. An array of imaginative and sometimes original enterprises have been funded, but they remain marginal to our analysis of the problems. It has been difficult to relate our expenditure to any coherent intervention strategy, because the budget has not been substantial enough to make inroads on any of the major problem areas. In an ironical way a middle-range budget of this kind may be almost more of a diversion than no budget at all.

Different hats in high places

Similarly, CDP's access to relatively heady policy-making situations in local government may turn out to be a neutralising factor rather than a significant point of leverage.[6] To take the professional system first, our acceptance at Chief Officer level, and access to the various processes of the senior management system, have been flattering; but this has sometimes subjected our proposals to screening and modification which have been accepted in order to retain the support we have felt to be necessary for a particular strategy. But these very alliances have some-times prevented issues being brought forward to politicians as sharply as we would have wanted. This was certainly the case with agenda items for the first few meetings of our Project Management Committee. As officers in the Town Clerk's Department we brought Project Committee papers first to the Chief Officers' meeting. Our perspectives were sometimes seen as controversial or threatening, and on a number of occasions it was suggested that we would have to modulate particular recommendations to gain officer backing at the Committee. However, this kind of absorption into the professional consensus tended to alienate us from the political processes of the City.

The pressure has been to define us as either inside or outside the professional arena. If inside, access, information and consultation are offered in exchange for our acceptance of the officer conventions, i.e. ritualised relationships with elected members and the public, in which conventions of 'neutrality' and 'confidentiality' have to be maintained. Too close a relationship or too committeed a discussion with elected members is often seen as questionable or even illegitimate.

Elected members, on the other hand, have been keen for us to have a much more direct and less ritualised relationship with them. But some have also been interested in tapping our inside knowledge of the officer system, and imply that officers are depriving them of necessary information. The underlying impression is that politicians and professionals feel themselves to be rivals in the policy-making process. They appear to accept a convention in which officers predetermine many policies, but go through the ritual of deferring to elected members as their lords and masters.

Central government – therapist or client?

The formula for CDP suggests that the collaboration of central and local government, voluntary agencies and the universities in an unprecedented 'concerted search' will produce 'better solutions to the problems of disadvantage than those we now possess'. Originally this was seen as a corporate enterprise, with a central steering group bringing together central and local government representatives, and local steering groups bringing together local government, officers and councillors, the university, the voluntary agencies and local residents. It is significant that these unconventional structures lapsed very quickly and more traditional relationships have been restored. The programme is administered nationally by Home Office civil servants without any structured reference to other government departments or the local authorities. At the local level the traditional division of roles between officers as councillors operates in the Project's management structures, and no Project Committee includes resident representatives.

These divisions may be appropriate managerially, but it is significant that each constituent agency sees itself as the change-agent and the others as the problem.[7] Perhaps because each agency absorbs so much energy in maintaining a definition of itself as therapist rather than client, its attempts at changing the others look rather like token gestures. Home Office civil servants still talk about 'leaning' on local government or other central departments, but this is conceived almost entirely in terms of diplomatic contacts with opposite numbers. There have been six changes in the triad of civil servants responsible for CDP in the first three years of the experiment.

In the main the Home Office has taken up a role neither as change-agent nor as client, but as funding agency. Its interests are perhaps reminiscent of Gouldner's 'overdogs' in the master institutions who need and seek information about 'underdogs' in order to plan public programmes. Although such programmes have to be administered at the local level, central government seeks to maximise its control by discrediting the effectiveness of local government in meeting need.[8]

Some conclusions

1   An exclusive focus on 'small neighbourhoods of concentrated multiple deprivation' may prove to be misleading. Many of the critical problems identified in the Project study area are not inherent in or specific to that neighbourhood, but are manifestations of wider processes in society. To isolate a small geographical area for study or action can isolate that population from the wider class structure within which 'deprivation' has to be examined.

2   Because their causes do not operate at the local level alone, many of these problems are not susceptible to solution at the local level alone. Self-help and community action within the neighbourhood may help to gain marginal improvements and some compensatory provision. But the crucial determinants of the residents' quality of life remain unaltered. 'Participation' can pre-empt real debate of issues, and co-opt possible conflicting interests.

3   Although the fundamental causes of inequality often lie ultimately within the national economy, they are sustained and reinforced by the operations of particular local social institutions, many of which have a direct face-to-face contact with disadvantaged groups. Many of these institutions are subject to government control, directly or indirectly.

4   Some of these institutions and services appear to have the un-intended effect of confirming and reinforcing the social problems which they were originally set up to tackle.

5 Government planning and policy-making take place on a larger and larger geographical scale and longer and longer time-scale; this means that decisions are increasingly based on a macro-view of the community which generalises issues up to a level where conflicts and diversities are 'reconciled'. 'The community' is treated as uniform and homogeneous in its needs. Issues which in fact involve fundamental conflicts of interest are now often processed technically before they reach the arenas of political debate. Techniques like cost-benefit analysis, in their attempts to quantify intangible factors, introduce important value-judgments and biases.

6 The concept of 'deprivation' is in some ways related to this assumption of a homogeneous community with a consensus about basic goals and values. The notion implies a common baseline of consumption to which all in society aspire and below which some unfortunately fall. In accepting this notion, CDP in some ways serves as one of the 'midwives to a meritocracy'.[9]

7 The focus of study for CDP and the locus for change need to be shifted, therefore, from 'deprived people or areas' to the institutions and organisations of local and central government. The Project should be concerned with identifying and analysing the crucial points at which government provision appears to be failing to meet relevantly the needs of the most disadvantaged.

8 To date, CDP appears to have had only limited effectiveness as an instrument of social change. It has proved to be a labour-intensive operation, having greater success in introducing extra innovatory and entrepreneurial workers at the field level, than in achieving organisational or policy change at the centre.

9 CDP needs to locate its strategies within a longer time-perspective, and a historical view of change. This should lead to the identification of plastic areas within the movement of political ideas, and strategies for injecting our small-scale commentary into arteries of the wider debate.

10 At the local level this is likely to imply working more directly within local political processes rather than simply being part of the bureaucratic apparatus. Our position allows us to chart the differential distribution of resources, showing who gains and who loses from particular public programmes. Within this kind of analysis, action may take the following forms:

a. trying to service interest groups of the 'worst off' sections of the working class in Coventry with information, analysis and hard skills, in order to develop greater consciousness of the nature and sources of inequality and to encourage collective struggle against oppression;

b. trying to develop connections and alliances between the Project, 'worst off' groups and the organised sections of the labour movement (the Labour Party, the ward parties, shop stewards' committees and the trade unions) on issues of inequality and their eradication;

c. trying to use whatever opportunities the CDP framework provides to lodge propositions about the needs of people living in disadvantaged urban areas, and to contribute to wider movements of political debate and action demanding:

i. major increases and redistributions in public and private invest-ment, and

ii. increased levels of and new forms of control over such investment.

References

1 G. A. Hillery, 'Definitions of community: areas of agreement', *Rural Sociology*, 20 (2), 1955, 111–23.

2 Warner Bloomberg, jun., 'Community organization', in R. M. Kramer and H. Specht (eds), *Readings in Community Organization Practice*, Prentice-Hall, 1969, pp. 91–127.

3 Martin Rein and Robert Morris, 'Goals, structures and strategies for community change', in *Social Work Practice*, Columbia University Press, 1962, pp. 127–45.

4 C. Wright Mills, 'The professional ideology of social pathologists', *American Journal of Sociology*, 49, 1944, 165–80.

5 Howard Aldrich, 'Organisational boundaries and inter-organisational con-flict', *Human Relations*, 24 (4), 1971, 279–93.

6 Irwin Epstein, 'Organisational careers, professionalism and social worker radicalism', *Social Service Review*, 44 (2), 1970, 123–31.

7 Elisabeth Herzog, 'Who should be studied?', *American Journal of Ortho-psychiatry*, 41 (1), 1971, 4–12.

8 Albin Gouldner, 'The sociologist as partisan', *American Sociologist*, no. 3, 1968, 103–16.

9 S. M. Miller, 'Poverty research in the seventies', *Journal of Social Issues*, 26 (2), 1970, 169–73.